THE FATHER OF MODERN SPORT

The Life and Times of Charles W. Alcock

Keith Booth

WITH A FOREWORD BY RT. HON. JOHN MAJOR C.H.

The Parrs Wood Press
<u>Manchester</u>

First Published 2002

THE PARRS WOOD PRESS
St Wilfrid's Enterprise Centre
Royce Road, Manchester, M15 5BJ
www.parrswoodpress.com

© Keith Booth 2002

ISBN: 1 903158 34 6

This book was produced by The Parrs Wood Press
and Printed in Great Britain by:

Fretwell Print & Design
Healey Works
Goulbourne Street
Keighley
West Yorkshire

To Bryon Butler, who first aroused my interest in Charles Alcock, but did not live long enough to produce the biography which was always his ambition.

CONTENTS

ACKNOWLEDGEMENTS

I am grateful to staff of the following Libraries and Archives for their unfailing help in making their facilities available and for directing my often obtuse enquiries into the correct channels.

Brighton Local Studies Library
British Library
British Newspaper Library
Family Records Centre
Football Association Library
Harrow School
London Metropolitan Archive
Minet Library, Lambeth
Richmond Local Studies Library
Rugby Football Union Library
Sunderland Local Studies Department
Surrey County Cricket Club Library
Surrey History Centre
Sutton Libraries
Waltham Forest Archives and Local History Library

The following have been particularly helpful and my special thanks go to them: Several Alcocks in the Wearside telephone directory, for their interest and gallant, but ultimately unsuccessful attempts to establish a family link between Charles Alcock and the present generation; David Barber, Librarian of the Football Association, for allowing me access to the Association's extensive library facilities in Soho Square; Jane Baxter, Local Studies Librarian at Richmond, with her uncanny ability to locate a Census of Population entry within seconds; Barbara Butler for letting me have Bryon's papers and correspondence on Alcock; Rita Gibbs, Archivist of Harrow School, for two educational days in the School Archive and unearthing admissions registers, trials results and scorebooks which had not seen the light of day for several generations; Jeff Hancock, Librarian at Surrey County Cricket Club, for his enthusiastic support and allowing the use of rare magazines and photographs; Chris Harte, Secretary of the Association of Sports Historians, for the use of his extensive collection of books and publications; Adrienne Reynolds, local researcher and former teacher at Forest School, for very useful specialised information on the School, the early history of the FA Cup and the history and geography of Chingford and Woodford; Andrew Searle, my publisher, for his support throughout the project and the loan of a number of reference books, which have proved invaluable secondary sources; finally, my wife, Jennifer, for sparing her limited free time to help with deciphering semi-legible handwriting, interpreting less than perfect microfilm reproduction, crawling round graveyards, "improving" the manuscript and maintaining her enthusiasm for the project as a whole.

FOREWORD

THE FATHER OF MODERN SPORT

AMONGST THE GIANTS of sport, the name of C W Alcock may seem out of place: it is not. His lifelong love of sport created a legacy that millions enjoy to this day, without any acknowledgement.

C W Alcock was sportsman, administrator and writer. As a sportsman, he captained the Wanderers in the first ever FA Cup Final at the Oval, led the England National Team to victory in an unofficial game against Scotland and played cricket for the Gentlemen of Essex. But it was as an administrator that he stands out.

It was Alcock who dreamed up the idea of the FA Cup and subsequently refereed two of the Finals; it was Alcock who helped found County Cricket; Alcock who promoted international football and instigated the first Test Match between England and Australia. He also championed the birth of professionalism in sport, whilst being Secretary of the Football Association for 25 years and Secretary of Surrey County Cricket Club for 35 years.

Keith Booth charts the astonishing sporting life of this remarkable man from his earliest days in all its varied guises. We owe C W Alcock more than we know and this book places him on the pinnacle he deserves: as one of the founders of modern sport.

John Major
April 2002

PREFACE

THE TITLE OF THIS BOOK is an amalgam of the late Bryon Butler's "the father of English sport", Dr Eric Midwinter's "the inventor of modern sport" and J A H Catton's "the father of international association football". Charles Alcock's influence on sport spread beyond his own historical and geographical limitations and is still apparent today. His management style and breadth of vision would certainly not be out of place in a twenty-first century boardroom.

Alcock has been the subject of a certain amount of hagiography by writers on football, but, occasional references apart, remained largely neglected by the cricket establishment until Basil Easterbrook's feature in the 1980 edition of *Wisden* to mark the centenary of the first Test Match in England 2002 marks the centenary of Alcock's own book *Surrey Cricket: Its History and Associations* and a time between the Football World Cup in Japan and South Korea and the Cricket World Cup in South Africa seems an appropriate time to recognise the occasion with a biography of the man whose foresight was a contributory factor to both competitions.

Biography can be treated chronologically or thematically, but Alcock's life was so multi-faceted, that neither would be entirely appropriate. Straight chronological treatment would lead to some fragmentation as he would simultaneously be involved with journalism, football, cricket and civic duties and thematic treatment finds him playing, organising and writing about football and cricket over a long period of time. As Bryon Butler rightly said, he made history and then recorded it. I have therefore compromised and dealt with themes within four broad chronological bands; first, his childhood in Sunderland; then, his school-days and their immediate aftermath; next, his virtually simultaneous three full time-jobs (impossible for most, but very much Alcock's bread and butter) and finally, the broadening vision as the competitive, professional and international sport which he has pioneered begin their journey to globalism. Even then there has to be overlap. His writing and journalism, for instance, were life-long and have therefore been retained in one chapter rather than spread piecemeal throughout the book. It is a tribute to the man that he cannot be contained in neat, watertight compartments and there has to be a certain amount of intermingling of times and themes.

When Alcock's grave in West Norwood Cemetery was rededicated in 1999, Bryon Butler regretted that no full scale biography of Charles Alcock had ever been produced. It is a sentiment shared by other correspondents. This effort is intended to rectify that omission.

Keith Booth
Sutton
August 2002

CHAPTER 1

HOME AND FAMILY

Sunderland

A MAN WHO WAS to change the face of world sport and the Sunderland Women's Centre may seem an unlikely coupling, but they are linked by 10 Norfolk Street, a double-storey end-of-terrace premises where, a hundred and sixty years ago, Charles Alcock first saw the grey light of what is now the City of Sunderland, but was in 1842 the Township of Bishopwearmouth. The house, until recently the headquarters of the aforementioned organisation, lies a few hundred yards east of the commercial district and the same distance south of the river that in the mid-nineteenth century was at the centre of one of the world's largest shipbuilding areas.

Sunderland's initial development was as a port for the Durham coalfields, but by the time of Alcock's birth its commercial strength derived from a freestanding and flourishing shipbuilding industry which flanked the mouth of the River Wear. The origins of shipbuilding on Wearside can be traced to the fourteenth century, the first recorded shipbuilder being Thomas Menville at Hendon in 1346. In 1790, nineteen ships per annum were being produced and by the 1830s Sunderland was among the most important shipbuilding centres in the country. At the end of the decade, there were 65 shipyards and ten years later 150 wooden vessels were built in Sunderland. 2,025 shipwrights worked in the town with a further 2,000 employed in related industries. The first iron ships were built in 1852 and wooden shipbuilding ceased in 1876.[1]

Just as the handloom of the Pennines had been overtaken by the spinning jenny, the water frame and the mule, so the medieval craft of Wearside had been subsumed into an industrial revolution that brought with it social, human and sporting consequences. Shipbuilding, supported by coal-mining, was the heartblood of the industrial north-east and was to remain so until the post-industrial society of the mid and late twentieth century saw their decline and eventual demise. Sunderland's last shipyard closed in the

1960s: for several years the area lay bare and derelict, disused cranes pointing to the sky, recalling an earlier, more industrially dynamic era. In recent times the area has been attractively landscaped and used for other purposes.

At the time of Alcock's birth, the local newspaper, the *Sunderland and Durham County Herald*, was reporting on plans for converting Sunderland harbour into a floating dock and on an Anti-Corn Law League meeting, a movement capturing the moral indignation of the middle classes which saw the legislation as a relic of the pre-industrial era resulting in the price of the basic commodity of bread being kept artificially high. Alongside, there were detailed time-tables of a number of local private railways and a company of London consulting surgeons was advertising an elixir, sent in a sealed envelope and guaranteed to restore manhood, the premature decline of which might have been caused by excessive indulgence, solitary habits or infection. Manufacturers' belief in consumer gullibility has evidently changed little over a century and a half.

On a more serious note, the newspaper was, perhaps, somewhat ahead of its time, an advocate of social reform and, some 25 years before the 1870 Education Act, a strong supporter of the education of the working classes. A hard-hitting editorial of 11 April 1845 reads:

> Our legislators are deeply criminal for their past neglect. It has ever been the blind prejudice of the ruling classes that to improve and advance the intellectual culture of artisans would render them too independent and unfit them for the discharge of their duties as members of civil society.

In this world of industrial progress and social conflict, Charles Alcock (the William was added later) spent his early years. He had been born to a privileged life in what is now considered to be a disadvantaged area, though the shipowners, shipbuilders, marine insurance brokers, skilled, semi-skilled and unskilled workers, some of whom lived in what would today be regarded as slum conditions, would not have seen it that way. They regarded themselves as a constituent part of a thriving industrial community, albeit one stratified into a rigid class system that was to remain in force, certainly challenged, but hardly changed until after the First World War. The combination of a moneyed family with its roots in business and commerce and the experience of northern industrialism was one that was to serve

Alcock well in later life. His father was heavily involved in shipbuilding and the entries in local trade directories relating to his and other branches of the family leave no doubt that in the class structure of the time, the Alcock family was certainly 'above stairs', part of the newly emerging middle class of industrialists and entrepreneurs.

Charles' mother, born Elizabeth Forster, daughter of John Forster, a shipowner,[2] had married Charles senior at Bishopwearmouth Parish Church on 19 December 1839 and was to give birth to nine children of whom Charles was the second. Other writers on Alcock,[3] doubtless basing their findings on the 1851 Census of Population and on each other, refer to five sons, but the International Genealogical Index, the 1861 Census and a file on the family in the local library reveal that there was also a sixth, who died in infancy, and three later daughters. The dates of birth of the nine children span a twenty-one year period from 1841 to 1862. So, Charles' childhood was perhaps typical of one of his class, one of a large family with a paterfamilias and a mother giving birth every two years or so, the essence of Victorian respectability.

The Norfolk Street where he was born is today showing traces of inner city blight. Part of the now disused Edwardian Central Post Office building opposite, having previously been the Customs House, adjacent to the local Christadelphian Headquarters, is now used as a 'day centre' by the Lazarus Foundation, an organisation devoted to the rehabilitation of alcohol and drug addicts. No 11 next door houses the community addiction team and there is a motley collection of picture framers, hairdressers, solicitors and financial and printing services. The boarded-up birthplace has attracted the stickers of the animal rights lobby. A picture of a couple of bears has the slogan *Keep Bears Wild: Gardez-les au Naturel*. The Norfolk Clinic at no 7 has closed.

In the 1840s, Norfolk Street, until the 1830s known as Sunniside (the opposite side of the road on the other side of what on 19th century Ordnance Survey maps is called The Shrubbery is still West Sunniside), was a thriving community comprising a timber merchants' clerk, master mariner, chemists and druggist, accountant, schoolteacher, bookseller, physician, an ironmonger, Surveyor of Works and sundry merchants, mostly with housekeepers and servants.[4] Along the road, at no 24, was the home of Uncle Samuel, who now fronted the family upholstery business, established by his father in the early part of the century.

3

The Family

The Alcock surname derives from Old English and means son of Al, a diminutive of several forenames - Alan, Allen, Athel, Alfred etc - and has its roots in Staffordshire and Nottinghamshire.[5] There are eighteen entries under 'Alcock' in the Wearside telephone directory and correspondence with some of them has unearthed a Potteries background in some cases and a movement to work in the Durham coalfields in the early years of the nineteenth century, but no connection with Charles' family has come to light. Nor does there seem to be such a geographical connection in Charles' ancestry. Although his great-grandfather, Samuel, lived in Newcastle it was not "under-Lyme" but "upon-Tyne".

He was an Innkeeper and Hackney Horse keeper of the Cannon Inn, situated first in the Fleshmarket, then at 63 The Close.[6] In 1770, he had married Barbara Hopper, Charles' great-grandmother at St Nicholas Cathedral Church. It is possible that he was a relative of Giles Alcock who was Custom House Keeper and Collector of the Duke of Newcastle's dues. The Cannon Inn was demolished in the 1850s and Samuel had died in 1791, more than fifty years before Charles was born.[7]

A file on Alcock family history held in Sunderland's Local Studies Department contains extracts from an indenture dated 1777, which refers to the Cannon Inn as being in use as a Public House "with a brewhouse, stable and other appurtenances". The notes are an extension of earlier manuscript ones by the Sunderland historian, James Corder, which relate to "a modern family starting with John, Samuel's son, who married in 1797 and moved from Newcastle to Sunderland where his family was born. Sons, Samuel, Henry carried on the business in Nile Street, but John Thomas and Charles went in for shipbuilding in Low Street, the site now part of the Scotia Engine Works, built many boats 1835 to 1865, many being large barques, sailing ships to 840 tons gross. Charles went out by 1842 and started as a shipbroker...John twice married with many children." It is the Charles referred to here who is the father of Charles William and who in the year of the latter's birth had already extended his interests beyond shipbuilding to shipowning and broking. He is described as a shipowner on his son's birth certificate.

John, Samuel's son and Charles' grandfather, had been born in 1773, the second of seven children and baptised where his parents had been married, the Cathedral Church of St Nicholas. He moved to Sunderland shortly after his marriage to Elizabeth Preston at St George's in Hanover Square, London, on 4 March 1797, and established the family upholstery business in Nile Street, which runs parallel to Norfolk Street.[8] By 1828 the business had become John Alcock and Son and moved to High Street,[9] which runs at right angles across the northern end of Norfolk Street and Nile Street. Three years later, the business had expanded and was described as "Upholsterers and Cabinet Makers".[10] He lived in Norfolk Street (at the time Sunniside) and later moved to Charles Street on the other side of High Street to a copyhold property which, along with his freehold property in High Street, gave him a dual qualification for appearance on the electoral roll. His younger brothers remained in Newcastle: one was a brush manufacturer, another a grocer.

Elizabeth, Charles' grandmother, died in 1810, having borne seven children, and John remarried the following year. His bride was Hannah Crawhall, aged 34, of St Nicholas, Newcastle, the wedding taking place at St Nicholas Cathedral Church. Hannah was to bear him four more children. John died on 8 January 1838, Hannah on 25 April 1845 and in between, John's distinguished grandson (Hannah's step-grandson) was born on 2 December 1842

Not that other members of the family were without distinction. John's eldest son, Samuel, Charles' uncle, assumed control of the upholstery business on his father's death in 1838.[11] It had been Alcock and Son for some ten years before that and Samuel is additionally recorded as having his own upholstery business in Frederick Street.[12] He continued and expanded the family business and became sufficient of a local dignitary to be a Councillor for Bishopwearmouth, Alderman, Magistrate and River Wear Commissioner. He was three times Mayor of Sunderland in 1853, 1859 and 1860. The 1861 Census of Population records him as living with his wife, Elizabeth, the daughter of a naval officer, his son Samuel, Solicitor and Attorney, and daughter Margaret. Resident staff included a cook, housemaid, serving maid, coachman and gardener and his home, Ashmore House, on Stockton Road, stood in six acres of paddocks, lawns and formal gardens, all reflecting a family affluence that was an integral part of Charles' upbringing and development. Samuel's entry in the 1847 White's Directory for Sunderland, while doubtless an advertising opportunity and mini-ego-trip, does give an indication of the way the business had grown. Alcock and Son are now described as "cabinet makers, upholsterers, carvers and gilders, carpet, floor cloth, drugget and damask ware rooms."

There are six Alcock entries in that directory; in Ward's Directory for 1857 there were ten. The previous year the Register of Electors, qualification for which depended on a property franchise, had six, Charles' father, three uncles, a cousin (John Wright Alcock, Samuel's eldest son who took over the family business now his father styled himself a 'gentleman') and Thomas Crawhall Alcock, uncle by his grandfather's second marriage, who had pursued neither upholstery nor shipbuilding to earn himself a living, but had entered the legal profession. Samuel Alcock, junior, Samuel's second son and Charles' cousin was to follow a similar route after early career ventures as a merchant and insurance agent, later becoming a solicitor, operating from 4 Norfolk Street, a few doors away from Charles' birthplace. He also followed his father on to the Town Council. A note on the file, quoting Tyndall Green, the Sunderland historian as the source, provides the information that he helped build the New Arcade whose tenants included Maynard's, the confectioners, Marks and Spencer's Penny Bazaar and the National Telephone Company which he started in London He does, however, seem to have been the black sheep of the family. Green suggests that he might have followed his wife's uncle, William Snowball, as Town Clerk, but he "would not stick to his job". He became bankrupt, was involved in embezzlement and fled the country, though apparently not to South America, as suggested by Green, but to the somewhat nearer Isle of Wight where he was supported by his son, William. So, the indications are that whether the objective was furniture and upholstery, shipbuilding and insurance or telephones and embezzlement, there was no shortage of initiative, entrepreneurship and vision in the Alcock family genes.

Charles' father was the sixth of John's sons, two of whom died in infancy. With his elder brother, John Thomas, the second son after Samuel, he diverted from the family furniture and upholstery business into shipping, first as a shipbuilder from 1835 to 1842, then as a shipowner, before finally expanding into the lucrative marine insurance business. Described as a shipbroker and ship and insurance broker,[13] his office or 'counting house' as it was styled at the time, was at 54 Sans Street, now absorbed into the A1018 trunk road to South Shields. In the 1860s the business expanded to take offices in London where it continued in various forms beyond the end of the century.

At the beginning of the nineteenth century, trade for Britain was a convenience; by the end of the century it was a necessity. As late as the 1820s, the coastal coal trade had exceeded all overseas trade in value. By the end of the century, industry, agriculture and finance were all oriented around overseas trade, and Britain's population, nearly four times what it had been at the time of the first census [1801], was dependent for its livelihood on its ability to sell abroad, and for its daily bread on its ability to import from abroad.[14]

Nevertheless, as much as one third of Britain's shipping was involved in the coal trade between Newcastle and London and the East Coast ports as, despite the rapid development of roads and railways, coastal shipping remained an integral part of the internal transport system.[15] Adam Smith estimated that what six men and one ship could take from Leith to London in a few days would require 50 wagons, 100 men and 400 horses and take six weeks to haul overland. Shipping, shipbuilding and related activities were, therefore, an integral part of this booming economy.

The Alcock shipyard of which Charles' uncles, Samuel and Henry, were joint owners was at 1 Low Street, Sunderland and was in family ownership from 1830 to 1865. The previous owner was Matthew Russell, and in 1855 John Thomas expanded the yard by conveyance from M M Chaytor and others (Joint Stock Banking Company), plus the grant of an escheat from the Bishop of Durham. In 1870, it was sold to Collin Smart of Sunderland, John T Alcock being described as "late shipbuilder of Sunderland and now of the City of Potsdam in Prussia".[16] Nor was this the only family connection with the East. A younger sister, Elizabeth, had married Samuel Dunn, an inventor and engineer of Pogmoor in Barnsley, among whose contributions to society was a form of tunnelling equipment. He later became engineer to Emperor Nicholas, whose certificate and seal were still in the family's possession in the 1950s.

The yard was opposite the end of Russell Street and the Glass Works.[17] By 1895 what were previously the Alcock and Potts shipyards at no 1 and no 2 Low Street had disappeared under the Scotia Engine Works buildings.

Each yard had a patent slipway, engine house, cranes and ancillary buildings. The boundary between the Alcock shipyard and Hutchinson's Docks to the west was until the 1980s still marked by a pathway from Low Street to the river. Since the demise of shipbuilding in Sunderland in the 1960s the area has been modernised and now forms the base for the development of attractive student residences by the University of Sunderland.

During the 35-year period of family ownership, more than fifty ships were built, varying from schooners of under 200 tons to a sailing ship of over 840.[18] The yard was one of a number on both sides of the river and followed the common practice of building on speculation rather than by commission. Only wooden ships were built. Steam propulsion, metal hulls and the skill of the naval architect were to change the face of the industry after the Alcocks left it to concentrate on brokering and insurance

Before young Charles was nine years of age, the demands of a growing family occasioned two moves of house and the increasing affluence from the shipyard provided the means to make it possible. The first move was to 10 Fawcett Street.[19] The house no longer exists, having been demolished to make way for Sunderland's main shopping area. Then, about 1851, the family moved to 17 John Street where the 1851 Census finds them with a nurse, cook and general maid. There had been no live-in servants at Norfolk Street where the neighbours had included a physician, an ironmonger and a merchant. John Street - or at least the side of it on which the Alcock family resided - was obviously more up-market. The neighbours were now a notary and solicitor, shipowner and shipbuilder, while across the road the residents were more artisan and included a blacksmith, chain-maker and shoemaker. The 1851 Census of Population records Charles and Elizabeth with their five sons John, Charles, Edward, William and Arthur aged ten, eight, six, four and two. The sixth, Horatio Robert, had died in infancy aged six months in November 1850 and the three younger sisters Anne Elizabeth, Ada Mary Eugenie and Edith Maria were born in 1853, 1856 and 1862.[20]

The remainder of the Alcock family continued to thrive in Sunderland long after Charles senior had moved his family to the London area where Charles junior and his elder brother John were educated at Harrow School. Both initially were engaged in their father's marine insurance business, which was subsequently continued by John; Charles, after a brief flirtation with commerce, branched out into journalism, publishing and sports administration. His business experience had added a useful professional dimension he could bring to jobs which had hitherto been the province of the gentleman-amateur.

Charles senior, however, was strengthening his southern connections before John and Charles junior left Harrow. While his warehouse and shipyard continue to be recorded in the Sunderland directories[21] and electoral rolls for 1858 and 1859, he was resident in Chingford, Essex in 1858 and is the informant on the death certificate of his son William, Charles' younger brother, who died, aged eleven, of heart failure in April of that year.

While the family's move south had the dual purpose of establishing his business in London and his eldest two sons at Harrow School, the reason for the choice of Chingford is not entirely clear. At the time it was a small rural community with fishermen's cottages along the River Lea and agricultural labourers' homes around The Green. There were only a few professional families and there was no railway before 1873. It does not seem the obvious choice for a family bent on upward social mobility. Charles Alcock, senior, is described on William's death certificate as a "gentleman" and in the 1861 Census of Population, both he and his wife understate their ages. Charles was 54 and gave his age as 48 and his birthplace, not as Sunderland, but London; his wife Elizabeth, only half as mendacious, claimed to be 36 (she was 39) and her place of birth remains Sunderland. The substitution of London for Sunderland was perhaps a mishearing by the enumerator or perhaps sprang from an innate class-consciousness, a perception that London produced more "gentlemen" per square mile than did Sunderland. The household was completed by a servant and kitchen maid, both recruited locally rather than brought with them from the north-east.

The north-east London link and some misinformation in N L (Pa) Jackson's *Association Football* in 1900[22] has led to a myth that the Alcock brothers attended Forest School before going on to Harrow. The error has been perpetuated in reference books and continued by Dr Eric Midwinter and the late Bryon Butler. The school, established in 1834 and now co-educational, has conscientiously kept its School Register since the 1840s and John and Charles do not feature. There are, however, accounts in the School Magazines of Charles playing football against the School for the

Forest Club. The evidence is therefore strongly against their attendance at Forest School as pupils.[23]

His younger brothers, Edward and Arthur, however, were at Forest: Edward in 1857 and Arthur from 1856 to 1862. Adrienne Reynolds, who has undertaken research into football at Forest School, points out in a letter to Bryon Butler that it was quite common for the eldest boy to be sent away as a boarder at one of the major public schools while the younger ones were educated locally at Forest and this seems to have been the case with the Alcocks.[24] Edward had previously been at Bramham College in Yorkshire and it may be more than coincidence that this was a school which was among the ten listed in the early members of the Football Association. It is at least possible that there may have been an Alcock family influence. Charles clearly retained a strong connection with the area in the few years after leaving school, basing his Forest Football Club there and playing cricket for the Gentlemen of Essex of which cricketing county Epping Forest is still a part, though for administrative purposes, it is now part of the London Borough of Waltham Forest.

By 1861 Charles senior had established his business, Charles Alcock and Co, Ship and Insurance Brokers at Colonial House, 155 Fenchurch Street.[25] The business is listed under "Supplemental Names: Persons who have commenced business since the compilation of the Post Office London Directory for 1861", which makes it possible to pinpoint the date of its foundation with a reasonable degree of accuracy. The business moved several times and underwent several changes of name and location, and control gradually passed from the father to his eldest son. In 1865, Charles William is listed separately as an insurance broker and by 1869, as having moved to pastures new; Charles Alcock and Co, Shipbrokers had moved to Ethelburga House at 70/71 Bishopsgate Street Within. By 1879, the business had passed to John and was at 7 Union Court, 41 Old Broad Street and a further move in 1881 took it back to Bishopsgate, though to no 98. All were addresses in the heart of the City of London and premises were shared with wine and spirit merchants, land agents, iron merchants and stockbrokers. The final move was in 1889, when the organisation, now John F Alcock and Co, relocated to 21 Great St Helen's where it remained until the proprietor's death in 1910. In 1895, however, John Forster Alcock and Co, Shipbrokers, had a change in size and direction and became John

Forster Alcock, Ice Merchant. It was the last change. John died on 13 March 1910 at Northchurch in Hertfordshire from where he had commuted to London for some time. His widow continued to live there until the First World War.

Although their ninth and last child and third daughter was born in Bishopwearmouth in February 1862, Charles and Elizabeth returned to Chingford where they lived at 'Sunnyside'[26], adjoining Chingford Green and King's Head Hill. There is no record of any 'Sunnyside' in the 1851 Census of Population, where the only named house in King's Head Hill is Rose Cottage, so it looks highly likely that the Alcock family decided to call their home after the street in which the family lived in Sunderland. Today, a rather more modern house called 'Sunnyside Lodge' stands at the junction of King's Head Hill and Woodberry Way and a short distance away is a small cul-de-sac named Sunnyside Drive, so it appears that, probably unbeknown to its contemporary residents, a small piece of early nineteenth century County Durham has been transplanted in a corner of a foreign field that is suburban Essex.

By 1876 Charles had retired from business, but took some part in the public life of Chingford after that, being a J.P. for Essex, Merchant, Overseer and Guardian.[27] He died on 23 February 1881 and was buried alongside William. Elizabeth continued to live in Chingford until her death in 1890.[28] The family grave is in a sheltered corner of what used to be Chingford Parish Church[29], its inscriptions still legible. It was first used for William in 1858 and subsequently for his parents; it also serves as a memorial to the infant Horatio. From The Ridgeway where the church is situated, the towering structures of modern London can be clearly seen some ten miles to the south, Canary Wharf particularly prominent. It is perhaps appropriate that the final resting place of Charles and Elizabeth should overlook the area where Charles distinguished himself in the city and his sons did likewise in the initially different, but soon to be connected, areas of commerce and sport.

Arthur continued in the family shipping business and local registers suggest that he continued to live in Chingford, though he is not in the family grave. In 1871, he is recorded as the owner of three cottages[30] and in 1894 as a shipbroker.[31] He died unmarried in 1902. Meanwhile, Charles junior had left the family business and turned his attention to other matters.

Victorian Values

Charles Alcock was born at the beginning of a period which historians have called "the Great Victorian boom". The Queen who was to restore some respectability to the monarchy and give her name to an era had been on the throne for five years. Recovery from the devastation of the Napoleonic Wars continued as Britain became "the workshop of the world", its industrial supremacy epitomised in the Great Exhibition of 1851. Sunderland with its shipping industry and the hinterland of the Durham coalfield was very much part of this boom. So were the railways, which during Alcock's lifetime developed from carrying a handful of passengers to well over a billion per annum.[32] Without them, modern sport would not have developed in the same way, nor would the socially advancing Alcock family.

The discovery of gold in Australia brought awareness of that far continent as something other than a convict colony. In his own way, Alcock too was to discover gold in Australia. There was a downside to all this prosperity, however. In the first half of the nineteenth century, the population of London had doubled. So, inevitably, had the amount of slum housing - in the capital and elsewhere. It was a society of ambiguity and double standards. Beneath the affluence was poverty; beneath the respectability was hypocrisy and the much-lauded Victorian values hid an unhealthy prurience.

For its proponents, Victorian Values stood for cleanliness, hard work, strict self-discipline and economy, and a code of morality centred on 'normal' heterosexual family life - all values supposedly paramount during the Victorian era, but demolished by the sexual permissiveness and general liberalism that took hold in the post-war era. For its opponents, Victorian Values stood instead for social and sexual oppression, exploitation and abuse, and belonged to a different era, an era best left behind.[33]

The Alcocks were part of the emerging middle classes, self-made entrepreneurs, in social terms below the landed gentry whose income was not dependent on their working, but above the labouring classes whose toil, in Marxist terms, contributed to their wealth. The term "middle-classes", however, is misleading. Certainly they bridged the gap between rich and poor but they were not in the middle. They comprised about 11% of the population. In terms of both income and social standing, 2% were above them, 87% below. In the starkest of terms, it was Disraeli's "two nations". It was a discrepancy that the young Charles Alcock would absorb into his social awareness and would be valuable to him later in life in conflicts between those who needed to work for a living and those who did not.[34]

The social structure did not go unchallenged and the mid to late nineteenth century was an era of the great reform movements. The parliamentary system was itself in a state of change as a result of the Reform Acts of 1832 and 1867. Trade Unionism, Chartism, the Co-operative movement, temperance societies, the Anti-Corn Law League all have their roots in this period. The 1870 Education Act introduced compulsory primary education and would in the medium term improve levels of literacy. In 1871 Bank Holidays became public holidays. Half day holidays, early closing legislation, the Ten Hours Movement and a series of Factory Acts and later Shop Hours Act would restrict working time and change the work-leisure balance, while the Sunday School movement, Mechanics Institutes and sporting organisations provided opportunities for the working class to fill the resultant free time by reading "improving literature" and/or playing and watching organised sport.

In short, the certainties of upper and middle-class England were being challenged:

> The working-class which, raw and half developed, has long lain half-hidden amidst its poverty and squalor, and is now issuing from its hiding place to assert an Englishman's heaven born privilege of doing as he likes, and is beginning to perplex us by marching where it likes, bawling what it likes, breaking what it likes. [35]

Eric Midwinter sees it as no coincidence that the Salvation Army and the Football Association came into being in the same decade. Charles Alcock was no zealous reformer in the John Cobden, Richard Bright, Robert Owen, John Ruskin, Earl of Shaftesbury mould. Indeed, although socially conscious, he would not have seen social reform as part of his remit. He could not, however, remain unaffected by the great nineteenth century ideologies of liberalism and nationalism, embracing both with enthusiasm and extending the nationalism to an international dimension. He was certainly aware of reformist currents and in his own area of journalism and sports administration was able to harness them for the benefit of sport and, consequently, of society.

Professional sport was a developing part of this society and needed to be addressed by administrative bodies which were essentially amateur. There was no "one size fits all" remedy and the solutions of cricket, association football and rugby football were different. Directly or indirectly, Charles Alcock was part of each of them.

In the mid-nineteenth century the age profile of the population was almost the reverse of what it has become at the beginning of the twenty-first when earlier retirement and increased longevity have resulted in actuarial strain on pension schemes. At the beginning of the twenty-first century, 7% of the population are over 75. There were no such problems 150 years ago: there were few pension schemes anyway and only 25% of the population was over 45; just 1% over 65. High birth rates of six to eight per family more than nullified an infant mortality rate of around 13.5% and resulted in 50% of the population being under twenty years of age. Consequently, boys were thrown into working life at an earlier age, the working class in the mines, the mills and the shipyards, the middle class into positions of responsibility in management and commerce. Lower class girls were expected to work; middle class girls were expected not to, or at least to do so in sheltered employments such as those Clerkships in the Post Office, previously reserved for the daughters of clergymen, lawyers and literary men, which a letter to *The Times* wished to protect from open competition on the grounds that it would provide unjustifiable opportunities of self-improvement to those for whom it would be inappropriate.

Now, Sir, it is proposed to throw these clerkships open to public competition. When we consider how many more employments are open to those of other classes, is this quite fair to the ladies of the class that I have mentioned?
ONE DEEPLY INTERESTED IN THE FEMALE POST OFFICE CLERKSHIPS [36]

The Alcock family fits the general demographic pattern almost exactly: Charles was one of nine children, one of whom died in infancy; he himself had eight and again one died in infancy. He and his brother occupied positions of responsibility in their early twenties. John was to continue in business for half a century and Charles was to devote a similar period to changing the face of sport. We are all products of heredity and environment, but few use those twin influences to the same extent as Charles William Alcock.

REFERENCES

1. Simpson *The Millennium History of North-East England*
2. Charles and Elizabeth's Marriage Certificate
3. Appleton *Sunderland Echo* 30 April 1984
   Midwinter *Cricket Lore* May 1992
   Butler *Daily Telegraph* 24 August 1999
4. 1841 Census of Population
5. Cottle *The Penguin Dictionary of Surnames*
   Bardsley *A Dictionary of English and Welsh Surnames*
6. *Newcastle Directory* 1778
7. P W Alcock *The Alcock Family of Sunderland*
8. *Sunderland Commercial Directory* 1820/23
9. *Pigott's Directory* 1828
10. *Burnett's Directory* 1831
11. *Sunderland Echo* January 1838
12. *Burnett's Directory* 1831
13. *William's Directory* 1844
14. Tames *Economy and Society in Nineteenth Century Britain* pp 86-87
15. Tames *Economy and Society in Nineteenth Century Britain* p 72
16. Durham County Record Office - Deeds relating to Panns abutting on the dog-leap dividing Sunderland from Bishopwearmouth on the east, King's Street (later Queen's Street) or Low Street on the north
17. *Ordnance Survey* 1855
18. The *Lobelia*, built in 1855
19. Electoral Roll and *Ward's Directory* 1849/50
20. *International Genealogical Index* and *The Alcock Family of Sunderland*

21. *Ward's*

22. p 143 ...*After receiving some preliminary tuition at Forest School, Walthamstow, he proceeded to Harrow.*

23. Letter from Gerald Wright, Archivist of Forest School, 5 June 2001

24. 16 January 1997 in Bryon Butler's private collection

25. Post Office *London Directory* 1861

26. sometimes spelled 'Sunniside' in local records

27. *Epping Forest Register of Commerce*

28. Chingford Parish Registers and *The Alcock Family of Sunderland*

29. 'The Old Church', on The Ridgeway, suffered serious structural damage in 1904 and as a result, the New Church (of SS Peter and Paul) on the Green became the Parish Church and remains so today. The Old Church, on which site a building has stood since the twelfth century, was rededicated in 1930 and became All Saints.

30. Rate Book - Highways

31. *Epping Forest Register of Commerce*

32. Tames *Economy and Society in Nineteenth Century Britain* p 75

33. Martin Myrone in *Exposed: The Victorian Nude* p 23

34. Tames *Economy and Society in Nineteenth Century Britain* p 144

35. Matthew Arnold in 1869: quoted by Tony Collins in *Rugby's Road to 1895* in *Sporting Heritage*

36. *The Times* 7 September 1880

CHAPTER 2

HARROW AND BEYOND

"The prominence of public schools in English social and political history
may not be admired or even admirable but it is inescapable"
Christopher Tyerman: *A History of Harrow School* [37]

The Academic and Social Ethos

HARROW IS AMONG THE BEST KNOWN public schools in the
English speaking-world, in the unofficial pecking-order second only to
Eton which has a tradition for educating the sons of royalty, while its
slightly less illustrious rival on its famous Hill has tended to concentrate on
the landed gentry. In the early nineteenth century the School's fortunes had
been at a low ebb. When Christopher Wordsworth was invited by the
Governors to resign the Headmastership in 1844, the number of pupils was
as low as 69 [38] and Arthur Haygarth was to recall forty years later that "grass
grew in the streets of Harrow".[39] The financial crash of 1825 and the
agricultural depression which followed the Napoleonic Wars had not
helped and the public schools as a whole received a bad press from Liberal
and Radical reformers who were critical of "the intellectual and academic
conservatism of the classical curriculum, as well as the uncontrolled
barbarism of schoolboy life and the negligence of the teachers."[40] The
destinations of most Harrow school leavers remained the Church, the
Army and the Law. Business barely featured either among parents or
Harrovian careers. Wordsworth's alleged intention was to produce boys
who were Christians, gentlemen and scholars, in that order of importance:
but the reality failed to match the rhetoric and it was left to his successor
Dr Charles Vaughan to translate into practice the educational theories he
had absorbed as a pupil of Dr Thomas Arnold at Rugby.[41]

Vaughan was one of Harrow's more forward-thinking Headmasters
whose liberal politics and reversal of previous trends encouraged the more
socially-ambitious of the emerging middle-classes and entrepreneurs to
have their sons educated there. Among these were the offspring of

Isambard Kingdom Brunel and George Hudson, 'the Railway King', and the not quite so well-known Charles Alcock of Sunderland whose eldest son, John Forster Alcock, arrived there in January 1855, followed a term later by Charles William Alcock. In the School's Admissions Register, John's name is pencilled in at the foot of the page, almost as an afterthought, indicating perhaps that he was a late arrival. The brothers were in Druries' House and both began in the Fourth Form, John in the Head Remove, Charles in the First Remove.

Dr Vaughan had taken up his appointment in 1845 at the age of 28 and the school's fortunes were on an upward spiral when the Alcock brothers joined. John was to stay for two years, Charles for just over four, leaving coincidentally at the same time as his Headmaster. The new boy had been registered on his birth certificate as simply Charles, but as two or more initials at public schools are, if not absolutely *de rigeur*, then certainly the norm, he arrived as Charles William Alcock, having acquired his second name either as a baptismal name or as an additional name at his prep school, Walter Todd in Woodford, one of seven private boarding schools and two day schools that are recorded as existing in the town in 1848.[42] The fictional Tom Brown, albeit at Rugby a quarter of a century earlier, was the exception in having a single Christian name, but the objects of his education were not dissimilar - not to be crammed with Latin and Greek, but to be a good English boy, a good future citizen, ready to take his place in the Empire.

The reasons for Dr Vaughan's departure remained something of a mystery until references to John Addington Symonds' *Memoirs* as recently as 1964[43] suggested that it might have been as a result of blackmail because of a homosexual affair he was apparently having with one of his monitors, a boy named Alfred Pretor. The evidence is not conclusive, but Christopher Tyerman in his history of the School finds it convincing enough and no other reasons have been advanced for his sudden departure. If the story is true, then it is not far from a perfect example of Victorian values underlaid by Victorian hypocrisy, for while Dr Vaughan, a clergyman, was preaching and teaching Christian morality, he was engaging in practices which at the time carried the death penalty and even in more enlightened times would scarcely have met with general approval.

It can be said with some certainty, however, that Charles Alcock, who left the school about the same time, would not have been aware of his

Headmaster's extra-curricular activities and his departure from the School in the same year must be seen as pure coincidence. Charles had doubtless benefited from the less unsavoury side of Dr Vaughan's time at Harrow. A more liberal curriculum had been introduced and, as well as the compulsory Latin and Greek, the adolescent Alcock was able to try his hand at French and German.[44]

Academic achievements were not the main objectives of public school education, but what would today be perhaps seen as a distortion of emphasis cannot conceal the fact that there were examples of academic excellence. Witness for example *The Triumvirate*, precursor of *The Harrovian*, edited by three boys at the school which, as well as Greek and Latin prose and poetry, contains political and sociological comment.

> The labourer who can read, and write too, is now the general rule, not the exception; and there are but few in this generation who depend upon the help of their neighbours in this respect. All this is due to the interest taken by the higher classes in the education of the lower; and to the excellent system of National Schools which few parishes are without.[45]

Class-conscious and complacent, certainly, but nonetheless demonstrating an awareness that there was life outside the ivory tower.

Viewed from the twenty-first century, the curriculum looks unreasonably biased towards the classics. True, there were Mathematics and Modern Languages, but a glance at a mid-nineteenth century time-table demonstrates an emphasis on Horace, Pindar, Juvenal and the Septuagint, even translation from Greek into Latin and a hundred years later, the 'streaming' device of placement in Shell or the Fourth Form still was, guided primarily by competence in Latin.[46]

The Games Ethos

In his *Jubilee Book of Cricket*, Ranjitsinhji is complimentary about Harrow's health aspect, but less complimentary about the conditions of the playing fields which provide the training ground for the nation's future social élite:

19

The school buildings are most healthily perched on a hill, and at the foot thereof are its playing fields which form a natural reservoir to receive the drainage of the hill aforesaid. When to this natural humidity is added the misfortune of a clayey, clinging soil...[47]

He goes on to say that batting averages have little meaning at Harrow and that an average of 20 on the 'Upper Ground' may be regarded as equivalent to 50 elsewhere.

Vaughan, influenced by Arnold's emphasis on Christian morality, was not noted principally for his encouragement of sports and games, but sanctioned the establishment of the Philathletic Club in 1852-53, thus formalising what had previously been an informal practice of allowing the boys the right to run school sport. While games played a significant part in the life of the public schools, the concept of muscular Christianity, and games as a disciplinary and moral force, Tyerman suggests, came later, after 1860, when Montagu Butler was Headmaster and Alcock's Wanderers teammate E E Bowen an Assistant Master.[48]

That may be so. "His Christianity was of the muscular kind," says Disraeli in *Endymion*. That was 1880, but the phrase was used in the *Sportsman* in 1865[49] and had appeared in the lesser-known *Tom Brown at Oxford* (1861), although it was probably around earlier and the concept certainly was. *Tom Brown's Schooldays*, dealing with life at Rugby School around 1830, was published in 1856 and there are passages which suggest a link between sport and the Christian ethic, with playing games in general and cricket in particular raised to a quasi-mystical level.

"...What a noble game it is too!"

"Isn't it? But it's more than a game. It's an institution," said Tom.

"Yes," said Arthur, "the birthright of British boys, old and young, as habeas corpus and trial by jury are of British men."

"The discipline and reliance on one another which it teaches is so valuable, I think," went on the master, "it ought to be such an unselfish game. It merges the individual in the eleven; he doesn't play that he may win but that his side may."

"That's very true," said Tom, "and that's why football and cricket, now one comes to think of it, are such much better games than fives or hares-and-hounds, or any others where the object is to come in first or to win for oneself and not that the side may win."

"And then the captain of the eleven!" said the master, "what a post is his in our school world!..."

Certainly, Bowen was among those who followed that credo being, according to Tyerman, "archpriest of the adoration of games as a serious activity for adults and boys alike".[50]

Football and cricket had been compulsory at Harrow since the early part of the century. The first cricket professional was appointed in the 1820s and regular fixtures with Eton and other schools began.[51] There had been a match with Eton in 1805 when Lord Byron had played for Harrow, but this seems to have been a one-off, scratch affair. There was another in 1818, but it was not until 1822 that Eton v Harrow proper was launched and, wartime and the occasional missed year apart, it has been an annual fixture at Lord's ever since. Though now diluted to a one-day match and entering the twenty-first century as a limited overs affair, it was one of the highlights of not only the cricket season but the London season until well into the twentieth century. In 1871 the match attracted 20,000 spectators on the first day and 18,000 on the second, more than twice the paying attendance for some county clubs for a whole season nowadays

Sporting rivalries developed not only between schools but within the school and the finals of inter-house competitions were seen as only marginally less significant in the school calendar than Speech Day, Founder's Day and the Lord's match.

One of the great features of Harrow cricket are the house matches. The first ties are played before "Lord's" and, after "Lord's", until the last week of the term, they are in full swing, the enthusiasm of the spectators being apparent to the onlookers, and audible at the Metropolitan Railway. The house which wins Cock House Match is entitled to keep the Challenge Cup presented by Lord Bessborough. "Cock House Match" is played, as a rule, on the last Saturday of the term.[52]

Football matches were organised on a similar basis. The whole house took part in the initial stages of the competition, but in the later stages teams were reduced to eleven and there were subsidiary and friendly matches at levels called "seconders", "thirders", "fourthers", etc. The rules of Harrow football were among those which contributed to the unified

Laws established by the Football Association, but nevertheless the game survives to the present day as a separate and distinct entity.[53] It was a requirement that:

> The above Rules should be put up conspicuously in every House at the beginning of every Football Quarter, and new Boys should be required to make themselves thoroughly acquainted with them.[54]

The ultimate sporting ambition for cricketers and footballers was, of course, to make the school eleven and, as Hughes implies, to captain it.

> Only boys in the School XI wear white flannels: to obtain a place in the XI is "to get your flannels".[55]

It was not, of course, an ethos that went unchallenged. Kipling wrote of "the flannelled fools at the wicket or the muddied oafs at the goals".[56] But that was for the future, in the light of post-school experience. For the moment, in the school hierarchy, closely behind the captaincy of the school eleven was the captaincy of one's house eleven with a quasi-obligation, if defeated in the Cock House Final, of addressing one's opposite number in the following terms:

> Congrats, old chap. Thanks awfully; it was a good game. How well your fellows played.[57]

The language may have changed, but the sentiments remain.

Games were played throughout school, lack of ability being no reason for exemption. At the pinnacle of the grading scheme was the Sixth Form Game, then the first 5th form game, second 5th form game (A), second 5th form game (B), third 5th form game, then down through the Remove game, Shell game, 4th form game, Founders' game, Nondescripts' game, Professors' game and Duffers' game. In addition, school scorebooks of the 1860s include a number of ad hoc encounters and alongside matches against Eton, MCC and Ground and Cambridge University are whimsical ad hoc team creations such as 'Those about to leave v The School', 'Left

Side of the Road v Right', 'Fast Bowlers v Slow Bowlers', 'Round Hand v Under Hand' and 'Dark Hair v Light'. Competition for trophies remained a significant aspect of Harrow life. Correspondence on the School's insurance policies in March 1982 listed 173 Cups for internal competition. There is no reason to believe that the number has diminished since or that the situation is different at other public schools. It would be futile to suggest that all the boys enjoyed games.

> I find it a dubious pleasure
> While the rain patters down,
> And the wind moans around,
> And youths thro' the town
> Shiver many a batch.
> 'Tis a biting-cold day,
> Yet but thinly-clad they
> Seek the slippery way
> That leads down to the match.

> And when you have got to the field with your shoes
> Full of water and heavy with clay,
> You're tormented with numerous fears lest you lose
> Your house match by some villanous play
> Either kick the ball skew
> Or some other thing do
> Which you'll bitterly rue,
> And get into disgrace;
> Or else get behind,[58]
> Through distraction of mind,
> Or horrified, find
> That you've kicked before base.[59, 60]

Nonetheless, the fact that games were not optional is a clue to the importance with which they were regarded. The whole public school emphasis was - and is - on conformity and on being a member of the group, of an exclusive community, and those whose inclinations were not towards games, however gifted they might be in academic or other areas, fell outside that community.

THE FATHER OF MODERN SPORT

The boy who shuns the river, the cricket-field and the fives court in play hours is always regarded with suspicion, if not with actual dislike.[61]

But for those who did enjoy games and/or were good at them, they created a bonhomie, a unity and fellowship that was to extend beyond school and strengthen the bonds created by the old school tie, providing Victorian moralists with over-simplistic analogies of sport - especially cricket - and life. From Henry Newbolt's "Play up! Play up! and play the game!" through offerings by less well-known poets to serious prose writers there is a naïve and unquestioning belief that the discipline of games will lead to discipline in life and to becoming a "good citizen".

It is by no means unusual to come across miniature homilies propounding such themes in the sports literature of the time, for instance in *Cricket*, Alcock was happy to give space to features such as "The Influence of Cricket on the Lives of Men" written under the pseudonym of "Mid-Off" expounding the *mens sana in corpore sano* ethic and suggesting that cricket taught endurance, modesty, self-confidence, abstinence, good-temper and thoroughness - Victorian values by the bucketful.

He who cannot control his temper on the cricket field will if he does not take care make only a poor show of his life, and an unhappy home for his wife and children; and as a control of temper is one of the greatest needs of daily life, let the boy begin early and the earlier the better, to learn the lesson in the best of all schools, the cricket field.

Let any one compare the chances missed in the field with the chances missed in life, they are in both cases attributable to bad judgement, carelessness, sloth or conceit...let men revisiting their old school be prouder of nothing than that their names were found in the School Eleven. [62]

It was an attitude fully endorsed by an established church which drew its ordained clergy from the public schools and universities.

The salt of good manners, good morals and every manly virtue is to be found in the cricket field and gives a tone to every good cricketer. [63]

Certainly, nostalgia, team spirit, the cult of eternal youth and the simplistic belief that life is an extension of the games field, all supervised by a benevolent English deity, infiltrate the popular school songs, not least in the Harrow equivalent of the *Eton Boating Song*, E E Bowen's *Forty Years On*. This remains the School Anthem and its attitudes continued into the following century.

> Routs and discomfitures, rushes and rallies,
> Bases attempted and rescued and won,
> Strife without anger, and art without malice -
> How will it seem to you forty years on?
>
> O the great days, in the distance enchanted,
> Days of fresh air, in the rain and the sun,
> How we rejoiced as we struggled and panted -
> Hardly believable, forty years on!
>
> God give us bases to guard or beleaguer,
> Games to play out whether earnest or fun,
> Fights for the fearless, and goals for the eager,
> Twenty, and thirty and forty years on.

All were bound together by the old school tie, a garment whose trans-generational symbolic significance is completely disproportionate to its sartorial use as part of a schoolboy's and gentleman's daywear.

Men may meet in after life who never met at school - men of different years - yet the fact that they were there, members, perhaps of the same house, at once lays the foundation for friendship, and the superstructure is raised.

Cricket and athletics do much to foster this spirit of comradeship and, in the writer's opinion, ought to do still more. Sport has a wonderful levelling influence, and has done much to soften class distinctions. Personally, the writer will hail with pleasure the day when "Mr" and "Esq" ceases to find a place upon the cricket score cards. [64]

It was a wish which was to remain unfulfilled for more than half a century and when in 1963, cricket became something of a classless society, the abolition of amateur status in the game had far more to do with changed social patterns than the reforming zeal occasioned by the fellowship of ex-public school boys.

THE FATHER OF MODERN SPORT

The elevation of the significance of sport to the quasi-mystical and pseudo-religious can be interpreted as another example of Victorian hypocrisy and of public school influence being, as Tyerman says, neither admired nor admirable, but inescapable. Harrow songs, he says, still played regularly at Harrovians' weddings and funerals, represent the school's grip at its tightest[65] and the sporting cult is not far behind.

In July 1934, the final report of a future Permanent Secretary included the following: "Although he has not fulfilled his early promise at games, he did become twelfth man to the School Cricket XI. He also won a scholarship to Trinity College, Cambridge."

The games obsession was not Quixotic. It provided important cohesion within the School. Inability to converse at length and in detail about school and other sport placed boys at a considerable disadvantage. Until paper rationing during the Second World War, the Harrovian carried full reports of all house as well as school matches including, for cricket, complete scorecards. Games inspired approval from parents as well as old boys. In the words of one inter-war housemaster, 'to many parents, a good bowling action wipes out blots on their sons' reports'. The governors' concern at the poor standard of cricket in 1945 was based on more than sentiment or passion. They believed the school's prestige was at stake, no doubt recalling how the unexpected victory over Eton at Lord's in 1939 concealed from many the true state of the school. Even though greater academic competitiveness and educational utilitarianism in the later twentieth century promoted the importance of form work, sport retained an institutional primacy in the attitudes of the school and its structures. If sport's moral dimension was emphasised less overtly, it survived in the minds of many teachers as a general justification. As the range and nature of the games being played diversified from the 1960s, the rhetoric shifted to concentrate on the physical benefits of exercise, in Beer's words[66] 'so that [Harrovians] may enter society as fit adults'. None the less, assumptions equating sporting skill and success with positive and personal qualities persisted not least in Head Masters' Speech Day addresses. Many masters continued to take for granted that lessons as important as those received in formrooms could be learnt on the gamesfield, even if they were more shy in articulating what they were.[67]

Cardus was later to suggest that the propensity of the Victorian public school to endow games with moral virtue was nothing but cant. It was part of the veneer of respectability that concealed hypocrisy and subterfuge.

26

The Victorians so endowed the game with their own moral grandeur that to this day the president of Little Puddleton cricket club cannot take the chair at the annual meeting without telling his audience that cricket is 'synonomous' with straight conduct, honour bright, and all the other recognised Christian virtues...

The joke of the matter is that while Victorians dipped cricket in moral unction, Grace and Hornby were giving to the game all that was in them of skill and wit, art and craftiness. [68]

Tyerman points out that academic pursuits receive only a cursory one-word mention in *Forty Years On*, a song that is essentially about Harrow Football.[69] That should be no great cause for surprise, as it is a fact of life that, whatever may happen in continental Europe and the rest of the world, certainly in Britain, from schooldays onwards, those who excel at sports and games are more likely to be the subject of hero worship than those who pursue academic and intellectual excellence.

Charles Alcock at Work and Play

Like that of Byron before him and Churchill after him, Charles Alcock's academic record is not among the most distinguished and like those fellow Harrovians, he too is best remembered for his achievements after he left Harrow. He did not reach the Sixth Form and early examination results have not survived. The Trials (Examinations) Broadsheets for the "Fifth Form - Head Remove" of December 1858, the year of the death of his younger brother, show Alcock in the "Third Class" in seventeenth place out of eighteen in the order of aggregate marks. He was 17th in Classics, 15th in Mathematics, but a more respectable fifth in Modern Languages. Perhaps William's death was a factor, and so possibly was the ill health that hampered his school career, or maybe he chose to put the emphasis on football, rather than on his academic work.

By Easter 1859, when he left Harrow, there was a distinct improvement. Form numbers had now increased to 33 and he was placed in the "First Class", fourth overall, still languishing at 28th in Mathematics, but fourth in Modern Languages and now first in Classics with the additional distinction of a 'copy'. In the three sets of Trials Results for the 1858/59 academic year, in the "Monitors and Sixth Form" section, Alfred Pretor was generally in first or second place with an abundance of prizes and "copies", but whether his excellent academic results were a cause or consequence of Dr Vaughan's alleged affection is a matter for speculation.

Charles Alcock never reached such heights of scholastic success, but his Harrow experience was sufficient to make of him an obviously educated man whose writings in later life are literate and erudite with Greek and Latin quotations and numerous allusions to classic and modern literature.

His sporting achievements are even less marked. He came nowhere near "the Eleven" at either cricket or football. An interview with W A Bettesworth, which appeared in *The Cricket Field* on 29 April 1893 and was subsequently reproduced in *Chats on the Cricket Field*, refers to his being "delicate", a notion confirmed by his Obituary in *The Harrovian*,[70] but medical records do not survive and there is no sure way of confirming it. Reports describing his later footballing style suggest that if there were any delicacy, he had left it behind by his late teens and early twenties.

He did, however, claim to play for his House XI at cricket. Compulsory sport meant that unless his health were exceptionally bad, he would be obliged to do so at some level and in his interview with Bettesworth he refers to playing for his house "at the same time as Mr Lang, the fast bowler and Mr Maitland, the slow bowler".[71] That is probably true, but the only extant Match Books (scorebooks) from the Alcocks' time at Harrow are Sixth Form ones and although "Alcock sen" and "Alcock jun" are listed under "Fourth Form (1)" in 1855, Shell (3) in 1856 and "Fifth Form" in 1857 and "Alcock" under "Upper V Form (2)" in 1858, there is no record of their participating in any matches.

Lang and Maitland were not in Druries' House, but in the Headmaster's, and it is possible that Alcock played against them or simply played for his house at the same time as Lang and Maitland played for theirs, and that "forty years on" (or almost - the "Chat" with Bettesworth was in 1893) his memory may have dimmed a little. Both went on to have distinguished careers. Lang was captain of the Harrow Eleven in 1858 and 1859 and played for Cambridge University from 1860 to 1862 before becoming a clergyman in Bedfordshire and involving himself with the Church Missionary Society. William Maitland (also known as Fuller-Maitland) arrived at Harrow in January 1858, so the summer of that year was the only season that he, Lang and Alcock were at Harrow together. He subsequently obtained a Blue in all the four years he was at Oxford, distinguished himself at rackets, long and high-jumping and the quarter-mile and was later MP for Breconshire for twenty years.

The most distinguished of the Alcocks' contemporaries and near-contemporaries, in cricketing terms, however, were four of the Walkers of Southgate. All were members of Mr Oxenham's House, now known as Moretons. A H and V E had already left before the Alcocks' arrival, but R D started in September of the same year, 1855, and I D and Charles overlapped by a year, Charles' final year being I D's first. But, while Charles's contemporaries, the Walkers especially, were preparing for Oxford and Cambridge, he was preparing for the world of business.

Charles played football for Druries' House at Harrow and says in his interview with Bettesworth that he "was fortunate enough to get the goal which made us the cock house".[72] According to W G Grace with whom Alcock was to develop a close friendship in later years, Alcock played no games at Harrow until his final year, when he took to football.[73]

While many thousands of people play football for their school without ever representing their country, he represents the much rarer, reverse phenomenon of playing international football without having obtained a place in his school team.

Nevertheless, despite the relative lack of sporting and academic achievement, Charles Alcock emerged from Harrow a literate and educated young man, having absorbed the public school virtues of self-rule, fortitude and public spirit, doubtless with a personality allegedly rounded by doses of fagging, beating and bullying, but above all having absorbed the atmosphere and made the contacts that qualified him for membership of that great public school freemasonry and provided him with the social skills and influence that were to contribute to a successful professional career.

In the following century, popular cynicism had it that a grammar school education provided ability without confidence and a public school education confidence without ability. Like all sweeping generalisations, there are many exceptions, some doubtless emerging from either of the systems with neither or both. Charles William Alcock was in the latter category. He left Harrow for the "real world", a world on which Harrow and other public schools had a perhaps disproportionate influence, a world of the rich man in his castle and the poor man at his gate, a world in which every one knew his place, but nevertheless had the capacity for self-improvement.

After Harrow, "Something in the City"

It is no surprise that on leaving Harrow, Charles chose not to return to his native north-east, but joined his father and elder brother in establishing the London branch of the family business, moving in the sporting circles that he was later to expand to global dimensions and the social circles that were to lead to his meeting and marrying Eliza Caroline Ovenden, daughter of Francis Webb Ovenden, a water colourist and marine artist, and senior to Charles by two years. It was on Eliza's twenty-fourth birthday, and his parents' Silver Wedding Anniversary, 19 December 1864, that the couple were married at the church of St Philip the Evangelist in Islington. On the marriage certificate, he is described as a shipbroker residing at 33 Sherbourne Street, Islington. Eliza became pregnant almost immediately and their first child William Edward Forster (the latter his grandmother's maiden name) was born on 26 October 1865. Their second child, a daughter, Elizabeth Maud followed on 21 September 1869. It was about this time that Charles left the family business to concentrate on his journalism, but not without absorbing something of the resource awareness and business technique that was to be one of the foundations of his subsequent tripartite career.

By 1871, Charles and Eliza and the first two of their eight children had moved to Grassendale House, Rosendale Road, Norwood, where a third child, Florence Caroline had been born on 20 October 1870. The entry under 'Occupation of Father' on the children's birth certificates is enlightening. On his marriage certificate in 1864, both Charles and his father are described as ship brokers. The following year on William's birth certificate, this has been modified to 'Insurance broker', but by the time Elizabeth is born, he is a 'Reporter' and on Florence's, little over twelve months later, he is a 'Journalist', a switch of career and then upward progression. Interestingly, he continued to describe himself as a journalist on subsequent birth certificates, though by the time of the birth of his last child in 1878, he was well established in two parallel posts, Secretary to Surrey County Cricket Club and the Football Association. So, it seems clear that notwithstanding his contribution to the administration of the country's major sports, he saw himself primarily as a writer and his other positions as second and third strings to his bow.

The 1871 Census of Population finds Charles, Eliza and the three children, plus a couple of Irish servants at Grassendale House. Eliza, though 30, gives her age as 29, a habit to be repeated on subsequent Censuses. To maintain the differential, Charles, 28, also understates his age by a year. The children are aged five, one and six months. Neighbours at Clifton Villa include a police constable, his wife and infant son and, at Rutland Villa, a 37 year old Professor of Greek and Italian, Abraham Harris. The occupation of his co-resident, Elizabeth Pink, aged 22, is given as 'Doubtful'. Clearly the Enumerator had his suspicions. Bakers, clerks and gardeners make up the population of what was and remains a respectable suburb within easy commuting distance of the Kennington Oval, which was to be the base for Charles Alcock's multifarious activities for more than half of his time on the planet.

REFERENCES

37. p 1
38. Tyerman *A History of Harrow School* p 240
39. Tyerman *A History of Harrow School* p 167
40. Tyerman *A History of Harrow School* p 168
41. Tyerman *A History of Harrow School* p 171
42. *Victoria County History for Essex*. Kelly's Directory of Essex for 1855 records a Woodford Academy run by William R Todd, the 1851 Census of Population lists William Todd and a nephew, Walter Todd, at a school in Woodford Street (now Woodford Road) and a later article (1910, reproduced in 1986 in the Transactions of the Woodford Historical Society) mentions Truby House "a boys' school kept by Dr Todd".
43. Tyerman *A History of Harrow School* p 246
44. Tyerman *A History of Harrow School* p 256
45. *The Triumvirate* 1860 p 234
46. Manuscript note in E D Laborde *Harrow School: Yesterday and Today*

47. *The Jubilee Book of Cricket* p 291
48. Tyerman *A History of Harrow School* p 250
49. 12 August 1865
50. Tyerman *A History of Harrow School* p 261
51. Tyerman *A History of Harrow School* p 174
52. Howson & Warner *Harrow School*
53. Steven *Unique Styles of Football at Three English Public Schools*
54. Football Rules - Harrow Game - 1858
55. *Ayres Cricket Companion* 1908 p 21
56. *The Islanders* 1903
57. Lyttelton, Page and Noel *Fifty Years of Public School Sport: Eton, Harrow and Winchester*
58. offside
59. A "base" is a goal in Harrow Football
60. *The Triumvirate* 1861 - p 94
61. *Harrow School - Something of Its Cricket History* in *Ayres' Cricket Companion* 1908 p 7
62. *Cricket* 25 November 1886
63. Church Congress of 1869- quoted in *The Journal of the Cricket Society* Autumn 1987
64. *Harrow School - Something of its Cricket History* pp 8-9
65. Tyerman *A History of Harrow School* p 345
66. Dr Ian Beer, Headmaster of Harrow 1981-91
67. Tyerman *A History of Harrow School* pp 467-468
68. Cardus *Cricket* p 58
69. Tyerman *A History of Harrow School* p 348
70. Vol XX no 2 23 March 1907
71. Bettesworth *Chats on the Cricket Field* p 19
72. Bettesworth *Chats on the Cricket Field* p 27
73. Grace *'W G' Cricketing Reminiscences and Personal Recollections p 320*

CHAPTER 3

THE SPORTSMAN

WHILE CHARLES ALCOCK will be primarily remembered for his substantial contribution to the administration and promotion of sport through his journalism and influential appointments at the Football Association and at the Kennington Oval, his performances on the field of play were by no means insignificant. Many people who have stepped on a cricket or football field will perhaps have dreamed of playing for MCC at Lord's, being the winning captain in an FA Cup Final, scoring a goal for their country or - for the more sadistic - refereeing a Cup Final. Yet Alcock did all of these and more besides.

Alcock, the Cricketer

His health had seemingly restricted his sporting opportunities at Harrow, but once he had left school, he was from his late teens to his early thirties an enthusiastic cricketer and footballer. Unlike those on the football field, Alcock's cricketing performances were relatively modest. His Obituary in *Cricket* says that he made many hundreds in club matches[74] but there is no evidence of this. While he was an important catalyst in the organisation of first-class and international cricket, his own appearances were restricted to what we would now call the wandering "fancy hat" sides. I Zingari had provided the template in 1845 and others had followed suit. Although the best clubs attracted players of quality, the emphasis was on social cricket and standards were variable. Alcock's entry in *Who Was Who* suggests that he played for Essex, but it was in fact the non-first-class Gentlemen of Essex. It was in the winter of 1864-65 that a County Club for Essex was formed in Colchester; the present Club was formed in 1876 and first-class status achieved in 1894.

On 17 and 18 May 1865, he played in what was to become the regular annual fixture for the Gentlemen of Essex against the Gentlemen of

Norfolk at Dereham[75] (one of the best grounds in East Anglia, according to *Scores and Biographies*); he batted at seven, made four (c T E Bagge b R S Bagge) and took two catches in a victory by an innings and 46 runs. In the same team, batting at eight was the eighteen year old C A Absolom, later to distinguish himself with Cambridge University, Kent and England and to die in tragic circumstances at the age of 43 when, employed as a purser on a ship, a crane loading sugar cane in Port-of-Spain collapsed and crushed him to death.

In his *Scores and Biographies*, Arthur Haygarth says of Alcock:

> His name will but seldom be found in these pages; but he is a great lover of the noble game, being also a steady bat, a fair change fast bowler, and an excellent long stop or long field.[76]

There is evidence of these attributes in Arthur Wilson's description of a game played in France in which Alcock took part. Basil Easterbrook in his appreciation in *Wisden* 1980, commemorating the centenary of the first Test match in England in the organisation of which Alcock played a significant role, mentions that he "once had the curious experience of captaining France in a match against Germany in Hamburg, although the writer of his obituary, noted in the Wisden of 1908, does not say how this came about".[77] Easterbrook was clearly unaware, as the obituary writer before him may have been equally unaware, of Alcock's own description of events in his 'chat' with W A Bettesworth. There is no reference to Alcock's being captain, but his recollection of events is clear enough:

> "...In Germany I had the honour of playing for France against Germany."
> "How did that happen?"
> " Well, I was one of the eleven 'Gentlemen of England' who went over to play 'Eighteen of Europe' at Homburg. [sic] J J Pattison and S C Voules were in our team. Afterwards a match was arranged between France and Germany, and under the name of 'A L Gallus' I became a Frenchman for the time being. By the way, the papers on the next morning raised me to the rank of an earl, and the nearest approach they could get to it was Earl Gaz. The match took place in the Kursaal grounds, and on a most atrocious wicket between clumps of trees. As I was lucky enough to make the top score, I was presented with a bat..."[78]

On another occasion, when Alcock was visiting Paris with the Butterflies in 1865, the team got themselves involved in the political controversies of the time.

"I once played for the Butterflies in Paris...It was during the Empire, at a time when strangers were viewed with the greatest suspicion. We were dogged about by detectives wherever we went and one of our team - now a well-known stockbroker - was so persecuted by a gendarme that at last he couldn't put up with it any longer and knocked the man down. Of course, he was at once locked up. We could not understand what had become of him, and it was not until the last morning, after making enquiries everywhere, that we discovered his whereabouts and obtained his release..."[79]

This was the trip on which Arthur Wilson, later honorary secretary of the Derbyshire County Club, who had founded the Butterflies three years earlier, says that 'C W Alcock distinguished himself as longstop on one of the very worst grounds ever seen."[80]

Despite Alcock's internationalist instincts, the game of cricket, although spreading rapidly through Britain's former Empire has not, until very recently, begun to take off in continental Europe. An attempted cricketing visit to France was planned for 1789 by the 3rd Duke of Dorset, who was Ambassador to that country at the time. The trip was rapidly aborted, however, when the team met His Grace at Dover fleeing in the opposite direction from political events which the French considered to be of rather more significance than a cricket tour.[81] In 1867, Napoleon III, who apparently showed a warm interest in the Paris Club, granted permission to level and enclose the ground in the Bois de Boulogne,[82] but three years later was in no position to grant permission for anything.

The Butterflies, still in existence, had been established to provide a club for ex-Rugbeians who had not made the school eleven. Membership of the only other ex-Rugbeians Club, the Pantaloons, was restricted to those who had represented Rugby School, but that folded within a couple of years and the members joined the Butterflies. A G Guillemard, later Honorary Secretary and President of the Rugby Football Union but then, like Wilson, seventeen years of age, was a fellow founder-member, and the Club was shortly thrown open to old boys of five other schools - Eton, Harrow,

Winchester, Westminster and Charterhouse. That extension of membership allowed Alcock to be included. A regular player was fellow Harrovian, A N Hornby (he of Francis Thompson's 'my Hornby and my Barlow long ago') and his elder brother, C L Hornby.

Their fixture list was of modest proportions; by 1873 it was no more than ten matches. Elections to membership were in the early days relaxed and informal:

> "Guillemard and I did it all in a casual sort of way for the first few months. Someone would come into our study and say, 'I say, you fellows, can I be a Butterfly?' Whereupon, if he was a good fellow, we used to say, 'My dear fellow, you are one'; the election being instantaneous."[83]

The qualifications and procedures for election to membership of another Club of which Alcock was a member were a little more formal and restricted. It was, however, not a Club for which he played regularly. His one appearance for MCC was at Lord's against Middlesex on 28 and 29 July 1862. It is difficult to resist the conclusion that he was qualified to play by availability, a last minute selection making up the numbers, especially as the *Field* reported that arrangements for the match were done 'on the quiet', "as none of the heralds of fame had given tongue towards making it a match of great importance."[84]

His Harrow contemporary, R D Walker, was in a Middlesex side that was beaten narrowly by two wickets, having scored 121 and 153 against MCC's 142 and 133 for 8.

Alcock batted at no 11 in the first innings and was bowled by the professional, Thomas Hearne for 0 - no disgrace in that: Hearne took almost 300 first-class wickets in a career which included 59 matches with Middlesex spread over seventeen seasons. Eventually he became manager of the ground bowlers at Lord's, a post he held until after his seventieth birthday.[85] Alcock did not bowl, nor take any catches and was denied a chance of glory in the second innings. The *Field* in its quaint, mid-nineteenth century style, has it that "When the eighth man retired, 121 runs were placarded" and he sat with his pads on to watch the ninth wicket pair of E G Hartnell and E Ekard add the required twelve runs to win the match. Ekard's 63 not out brought him the equivalent of the man-of-the match award in the form of a bat presented by Mr Dark. Nonetheless, an appearance in a match at Lord's, however modest the fixture or the individual's achievement, is the qualification for a biography in *Scores and Biographies*. It is brief and not overflattering of his abilities as a cricketer, but at least it is there, a recognition not achieved by the vast majority of club and school cricketers.

Bettesworth mentions[86] and Eric Midwinter repeats[87] that Alcock played for the Incogniti and Harrow Wanderers, but there is scant evidence of such involvement in *Scores and Biographies* or contemporary press accounts. As an Old Harrovian, he was no doubt connected with the Harrow Wanderers and was sufficiently friendly with A N Hornby to be visited by the latter when ill in bed.[88] His cricket journalism carries a number of contributions by 'Incog': so there was a clear connection with both clubs, but it is debatable whether he actually played for either of them

The Incogniti - established in 1861 - were among the stronger wandering sides, numbering the Walker brothers among their membership and playing regularly against Southgate when the Walker family were at their peak. They played 20 matches in 1865, 26 in 1866 and their fixture list included a regular tour of the Midlands.[89] By 1869 they were playing 28 matches and the following season 34. Haygarth, for reasons of space, includes only a few in *Scores and Biographies*, so it is at least conceivable that Alcock may have played in one or more of the unrecorded ones. Some would also have gone unrecorded in the press. While newspapers covered the "great" matches and county matches, some of which might have been less than great, coverage of club games was dependent on secretaries submitting the details and then, as now, there were inevitably deficiencies.

There were a number of Harrow Old Boys teams, most notably the Old Harrovians, the Harrow Wanderers and the Harrow Blues, the latter including non-Harrovians in their ranks and thus qualified for downgrading in the chronicles of Arthur Haygarth who excluded their results from *Scores and Biographies*. At one stage, Haygarth regrets that the Harrow Wanderers did not style themselves Old Harrovians (although a team under that name existed in parallel) in the same way as he laments the nomenclature of Eton Ramblers rather than Old Etonians.[90] Playing membership of Old Harrovians and Harrow Wanderers seems to have been virtually interchangeable, the Hornby brothers and various Walkers playing regularly for both. For a number of years the Harrow Wanderers had a tour of Yorkshire, playing against York, Leeds Clarence, Lascelles Hall etc.

The "fancy hat" ethos comes through in Haygarth's report of the Leeds Clarence v Harrow Wanderers match on 1 and 2 August 1873.

A word of praise must be given to the Leeds Eleven, which, in true cricket-like spirit, played ten minutes beyond the stipulated time, to allow the match to be finished. Let this example be copied by others.

The report goes on to comment that the Harrow Wanderers played eight matches in their fortnight, winning six and having the better of two draws, and were now a very powerful gentlemen's club, adding that the Leeds Clarence were also strong with two county players in their ranks. But we have here a clear example of a form of the game that was less regulated, more flexible, more carefree, where the result was less important than the occasion. Charles Alcock's own public school roots were planted firmly in this ethos and it was perhaps thanks to his influence that by 1874 the Harrow Wanderers were playing the Surrey Club at Kennington Oval.

It was in 1857, while Alcock was still at Harrow, that Thomas Hughes had famously put into the mouth of one of his characters in *Tom Brown's Schooldays* that cricket was more than a game, it was an institution. It was a distinctive, perhaps unique, feature of the 19th century English social scene that institutions such as cricket, rugby and association football were to be extended beyond schooldays and into adult life. They reflect the *puer aeternus*, Peter Pan complex, at its best an extension of childhood innocence, living out the lessons of the 'holy game', learned in 'God's classroom' of the cricket field[91] and at its worst a misinterpretation of the significance of sport, an escape from reality, a reluctance to grow up. Whichever interpretation is chosen, it was a phenomenon beyond the comprehension of foreigners. Organised sports in other countries, with the exception of the United States, tended to develop later, in the 20th century. Yet it was a phenomenon that was to play an important part in shaping Charles Alcock's career.

Alcock the Footballer

...He must always be remembered, as the right arm of the Association, a player who was second to none in every department of the game; and to whose exertions the Wanderers chiefly owe their victory in the Challenge Cup competition.[92]

The game played in the 1860s was almost unrecognisable from the one which graces our television screens umpteen times a week a century and a half later. The playing formation was not 4-4-2, 4-3-3, 5-3-2 or anything which remotely resembled any of the numerous modern variations. Rather it was 1-1-8 with an emphasis on dribbling, charging and 'following up' - ie closely pursuing the man with the ball and being prepared to take over from him when he was tackled. The 'passing on game', influenced by styles of play in Scotland and the north of England, was gradually to eclipse the dribbling game over the next decade as the press continued to debate at length the question of hacking and the use of shin pads. Ground markings in the present style were unknown, as were goal nets; what was to become the crossbar was a tape running between the posts. Ends were changed when a goal was scored; the throw in was one-handed and heading unknown.

To be a good dribbler was the Alpha and Omega of the forward's creed in the early days of Association football. At the same time it must not be understood that he was unprovided with support in case of any obstruction in the course of a run. There was the provision, of course, of backing-up, i.e. of a player who followed the ball ready either to receive the ball if it were passed to him, or to hustle or ward off any interference by the opposing forwards or backs.[93]

Alcock himself was clearly in the dribbling camp and although after his retirement from playing the game, he was to acknowledge the merits of 'passing on', he concludes that the most effective tactic is the combination of the two styles of play:

At one time in the early history of Association Football dribbling was everything; but the frequent changes in the game of late have placed dribblers a little in the shade, and players advancing with the times have had to go in for the more effective and less showy practice of passing on..."Passing on" is different to "backing up" and it was only the conversion to pass on at the proper time that suggested the necessity of more general passing on, and placed dribblers comparatively at a discount. It has been the combination of dribbling and passing that has made the Queens Park and Vale of Leven elevens such splendid teams.[94]

In the 1860s, however, matches were still dominated by the skill of dribbling:

'To see some players guide and steer a ball through a circle of opposing legs, twisting and turning as occasion requires, is a sight not to be forgotten.'

Charging and physical contact were key features of the game and tackles which would nowadays attract a red card were considered an integral part of a "manly", character-building pastime which had spilled over from schooldays, introduced by former public schoolboys to a wider society:

'...goalkeepers could be charged for the fun of it regardless of where the ball was. Indeed one of the earliest tactical ploys was for one forward to fell the goalkeeper while another was shooting.'[95]

Fixtures were ad hoc, starting times erratic, playing conditions variable, organisation frequently very casual and it was not unusual for the press to react with surprise on those seemingly infrequent occasions when both teams turned up with full sides. Games were started when reasonable numbers were present, were generally about an hour and a half, but were sometimes curtailed because of the closing time of the park gates. When the Civil Service played Wanderers on Tuesday 20 November 1866 (Time off in mid-week seemed to present no problem for government workers and ex-public schoolboys), the match began at 3.15, but as the park gates were due to close at 4.15, little time was left for play.

Much the same occurred twelve months later and the generally disorganised and casual nature of 1860s football can be inferred from the following match report from the *Field*:

The game was to have commenced at half-past two, but the Civil Servants, true to their principles of circumlocution, did not arrive until long after that hour...

the ball…provided by the Civil Servants was of a very pulpy nature in consequence of the non-arrival of various blown balls which were expected from the stores of the fickle Wisden.

4.15, and a remonstrance from those obnoxious park officials put an untimely end to the game just as the play was commencing to assume a lively aspect…

Both teams were afflicted with the too prevalent mania for absenteeism.[96]

Again, a month later, on the Wanderers v No Names match at Kilburn, the *Field* reported that a worse ground had never been witnessed, long grass completely preventing all attempts at dribbling and the goals judiciously placed so that a ditch intersected the centre of the playing area. Seven of the Wanderers team had arrived in time for a 3 pm start.[97] On another occasion, the Wanderers team, including the Alcock brothers comprised "only seven men, then eight and two 'emergencies'".[98] The days of professional groundsmanship and a professional attitude to kick-off times and even turning up at all belonged to the next generation.

It is clear from a number of sources that Charles Alcock's style of football was inclined to the robust. At a time when the average height was about six inches shorter than it has become today, he stood 5ft 11in tall and weighed 13st 6lb[99] and press reports frequently contain such comments as "Mr Alcock, as usual, required a great deal of looking after by his opponents".[100] W G Grace, better known for his exploits in another sport, tells a story told by Alcock against him:

The other story - also against myself - I must give in Mr Alcock's own words - my version of it spoils the joke. "Once," he says, "W G played football on Clapham Common, when the Wanderers were playing a match against the Rovers. I was centre-forward, and had got the ball right in front of the Rovers' goal, and was just going to kick it between the posts when, in his great rough sort of way, W G bowled me over and kicked the goal himself. It was" - Mr Alcock always adds - "the most blackguard thing that happened to me during a long sporting career."

He then goes on to comment on Alcock's own style of play:

All I can say is that my behaviour on that occasion was not half as bad as Alcock's when playing at the Oval v Scotland. In those days you were allowed to use your shoulders and the way Alcock used to knock over a fellow when he was trying to pass him I shall never forget. A friend of mine said Alcock made catherine-wheels of those fellows.[101]

Geoffrey Green relates:

...the famous story about a match between the Wanderers, the Champions of early football, and the Old Etonians at Kennington Oval. Alcock, the Wanderers' captain, tried out a special charge of his own against "Quintus" Lubbock, one of the great half backs of the day. "By heaven! Alcock," cried out the towering Lubbock. "If you do that again I'll hack your legs off!"[102]

The matter was settled without the intervention of any referee and with the acquiescence of the other players.

He was a centre-forward and regular goal-scorer from club to international level and the press was generally complimentary about his play:

We cannot abstain from saying that the play of Mr Morley of Barnes and Mr C Alcock of the Club elicited great applause from the spectators of whom there were a large number present. [*Bell's Life* March 1863]

Mr C W Alcock seized an opportunity which was given him and quickly scored the first base for the Wanderers...

Mr C W Alcock again got hold of the ball and after an excellent "run down" the whole of the ground, once more landed it securely against the Westminster's goal-posts [*Field* 12 January 1867]

A well-aimed kick on the part of C W Alcock resulted in the fall of the Hitchin goal [*Field* 28 November 1868]

A few minutes before time a side kick by C W Alcock resulted in another reverse for the Oxonians [*Field* 5 December 1868]

the School goal...surrendered to C W Alcock, after a brief run, followed by a good side kick [*Field* 9 October 1869]

another for the same side by C W Alcock, a cleverly executed run by that player [*Field* 13 November 1869]

...their goal succumbed to a long and good run down by C W Alcock [*Field* 11 December 1869]

W G Grace said that as a centre-forward, Alcock had no superior and that he played the Rugby game well enough to represent Blackheath on one occasion.[103] Not all comments about some of Alcock's contemporaries were as complimentary, one being "as usual more noticeable for the length and height rather than the accuracy of his kicks."[104]

Charles Alcock and his colleagues, public schoolboys past and present, civil servants and military men were, weather permitting, playing most Saturdays and not infrequently in mid-week. They were attached to a number of clubs and it was not unusual, for instance, for Alcock to turn out for the Old Harrovians against the Wanderers. In its summary of the 1866-67 season, the *Field* mentions that around 180 matches had been played in the London area and relates that to "the comparatively feeble state of the game in 1860" when only two clubs (Crusaders and Dingley Dell) played external fixtures.[105] Scratch and ad hoc teams and games were not infrequent, such as the Westminster Holiday team,[106] even Eton and Harrow v The World.[107]

The emphasis was on enjoyment: the public school ethos was still dominant and the game and the manner in which it was played was more significant than the result:

The esprit de corps that characterised the Wanderers in those early days were truly remarkable. I can vividly recall the details of a visit I made to Gresham Street one Friday afternoon to get a goalkeeper to play against Queen's Park at Glasgow the following day.

"Can you play tomorrow, G------?" was my salutation.

"Yes," was the reply; "where?"

When I responded "At Glasgow," he said cheerily:

"All right! When do we go?" It was then late in the afternoon.

"From Euston at eight."

"I shall be there," he returned with a smile.

And he was there...

They were glorious days in the way of enjoyment, those of the late Sixties and throughout the Seventies. Then it was the game pure and unadulterated. No gates to speak of - down our way at least. It was real sport sans exes, sans records, sans everything. Those were the days primeval, long before the turnstiles had begun to sing their merry song to the tune of the club manager, years prior to the era of luxurious travelling, of saloon carriages and sleeping berths, and every possible comfort. To go to Glasgow - a railway journey of over 800 miles there and back - for an hour and a half's football and at one's own expense was not in a way grateful and comforting. How we did it is not as easy to say. But it was done, and plenty of fun it brought with it, even if one had to travel through the night in draughty carriages with hard seats - in fact, a severely economical style, to which the new footballer - good luck to him! - is happily a stranger.[108]

Forest

The Alcock brothers were founder members of the Forest Football Club at the end of 1859, the year that Charles left Harrow. That is the date recorded in Alcock's *Football Annual* and seems more likely to be correct than 1857, which Jackson gives in *Association Football*. Alcock was a founder member of the Club and in 1857 was only fourteen and still at Harrow. It was one of the first and John was its first captain. As Alcock himself wrote later:

It was the winter of 1859-60 that really saw the first game of the great football revival. Great things, it is said, from trivial things spring. The trivial cause in this instance was the humble desire of a few Old Harrovians, who had just left school, to keep up the practice at all events of the game at which they had shown some considerable aptitude. From the primitive commencement of a mere kickabout under the shadow of the Merchant Seamen's Orphan Asylum at Snaresbrook sprang the Forest Football Club, the progenitor of all the now numerous clubs playing football of any kind throughout the kingdom.[109]

The Sheffield Club, established in 1855 by a group of former Harrovians, pre-dates it, but Alcock claims that it "secured bold advertisement in its early days more by its Athletic Meeting than by serious football".[110] When the Forest Club came into existence, there were, he says, "only a few odd teams, mostly composed of old public schoolboys with a very limited card of matches confined to the metropolitan area".[111] Forest's rules were based on those of Harrow School, one of the essential differences of which was that a goal (or base) was scored if the ball passed between the posts irrespective of height.

The Forest Club had its own ground. A few hundred yards away was Forest School, "a popular rendezvous for football clubs of the better class". After four years, during which time they remained undefeated, a private ground proving to be too expensive a luxury, Forest Football Club was metamorphosed into the Wanderers, but not before it had done sterling, pioneer work in kick-starting a game which, over forty years, was to challenge and overtake 'King Cricket' as the nation's prime spectator sport. The Forest Club was briefly revived as a separate entity in 1869, but seemed to have few fixtures beyond those with Wanderers and Forest School which continued at least once a year until 1874.[112]

Adherence to a single club for the enthusiastic footballer, however, was the exception rather than the rule. Most would have a main club, then turn out anywhere else they could get a game. Against Forest School for instance, as well as playing for the Forest and Wanderers Clubs, Alcock is known to have appeared for Mr A F Kinnaird's team, Upton Park and Crystal Palace. On occasions he would raise his own team and sometimes would be at a disadvantage when playing for instance at Charterhouse where the game was played in the cloisters and they suffered from lack of practice in playing in an enclosed space and on a hard pavement.[113] Notwithstanding these diversions, away from his insurance-broking in the City it was the Wanderers which absorbed Alcock's time and attention, despite the obligations of a wife and growing family.

Wanderers

The Wanderers emerged from the antecedent Forest Club, as a fully-fledged Club in its own right in 1864. It was, said Alcock, using the metaphor that Wilson and Guillemard had adopted in naming their cricket club:

> the transmutation of the Forest chrysalis into the resplendent butterfly - the Wanderers, a name to conjure with in the early days of the Association game.[114]

While the name of Butterflies was avoided, the colours were not. Wanderers played in orange, violet and black. From the beginning they were Alcock's Club:

> "After leaving school, did you join the Wanderers?"
> "Well, I started the Wanderers' club, so that I can hardly be said to have joined it. I was captain of the team when we won the Association Cup..."[115]

THE FATHER OF MODERN SPORT

Among the founder members were A G Guillemard, also associated with the Butterflies Cricket Club, and E E Bowen a long-serving master at Harrow, A Pember, President of the Football Association, and several others who were to distinguish themselves in football and other circles. Their first match was against the Officers at Aldershot, and reports in *Bell's Life* and *The Field* on 12 November illustrate the informality and general sociability of the game at the time:

WANDERERS v OFFICERS - At Aldershot camp. At 12 o'clock the army, having lost the toss, kicked off and the game was kept up with great energy until 2 o'clock without a goal having been obtained by either side. By mutual consent, however, it was agreed to continue play until 2.30 pm, shortly before which time a splendid kick from A Tebbut secured the only goal and a victory for the Wanderers. H Green and W Cutbill by their forward play were of great service to the Wanderers, while the indiscriminately impartial kicking of "St Patrick" and the "Oh-don't know-who" (emergencies) caused great amusement on the side of the Army. The forward play of Col. Clifford, VC, and the goalkeeping of Messrs Campbell and Parr deserve special mention. After the termination of the game the Wanderers were hospitably entertained by their military opponents, to whom, for the kind treatment and warm reception they experienced, the Wanderers tender their warmest thanks.[116]

This was very obviously officers and gentlemen, the essence of the game at the time as it emerged from the public schools. The harmonisation of the game played by the "toffs" with that played by the "lower classes" would come later.

As the name of the Club suggests, unlike their predecessors, the Wanderers did not have a home ground, playing largely away with "home" matches on the public areas of Battersea Park where the hours of play were determined by the park-keepers and the time for closing the gates. Their early matches were played while the FA was still in the process of rationalising the rules of the game and they played Forest School "under a happy mixture of Rugby, Harrow and Charterhouse rules", as a result of which "The illustrious Wanderer who attempted to run with the ball and signally failed, having his shirt-sleeve torn off, has promised not to do so again."[117]

THE SPORTSMAN

As Honorary Secretary and captain, Alcock had an autocratic role. The rules of the Old Harrovians Football Club provided that:

> The Hon Secretary, if playing, shall be Captain of the Team, and on him shall devolve the duty of selecting the different elevens and when absent of appointing a Captain to act for him.

There is no reason to suppose the rules of the Wanderers would be very different. A letter to the *Sportsman* following the failure of the Old Etonians to appear for a fixture at Battersea Park in December 1866 illustrates his role in the club, as well as giving an insight into the mind of a budding journalist, albeit perhaps one who has yet to develop the art of précis. He was not, however, alone in that.

> Sir - I send you the following particulars in answer to a letter signed "Senex" which appeared in your Tuesday's paper and also in reply to various letters which I myself have received from Individuals who visited Battersea Park on Saturday last, to witness the match between the "Wanderers" and Eton College advertised in your paper to take place on that day. In justice to myself as well as to the unfortunate individuals who had the courage to face the at all times gloomy water trip to Battersea Park in such inclement weather as that of last Saturday, I feel bound to give the following explanation of the part I took in the matter: - The match with Eton was arranged by me as early as October 21, and I received a letter from the School Captain that the proposed date (Dec 15) would suit him. Having heard nothing more since that date, I wrote to Eton on Tuesday last to inform their captain that I had succeeded in obtaining the ground at Battersea Park for the match and asked him to reply that he was satisfied with the hour arranged for commencement of the game (2.30). I received no reply to that letter but chance taking me up to Battersea on Friday last to witness the match between Eton and Civil Service, I was informed by one of the Eton Eleven that in consequence of accidents which had happened to "one or two" of the school eleven it was extremely doubtful whether the match would "come off".
>
> The School Captain being absent, I was compelled to see the Captain acting for this match (v Civil Service) who said he was merely acting captain for this, and could settle nothing with regard to the "Wanderers" match. On further discussion, as I was anxious to have a match, if possible, even at the eleventh hour, I offered to give the Etonians two well-known old Eton players

to equalise the sides, but received the same reply "Can settle nothing"! Finding that the rest of the Eton team were equally helpless in the matter of a settlement, and finding "can settle nothing" was the only reply I could get, I was reluctantly compelled to withdraw the match and send notices to that effect to the Wanderers who had promised to lend their assistance on this occasion. After this explanation, it will be seen on which side the fault lies. I have no doubt that had I not fortunately been present at Battersea on Friday and been personally known to one of the Etonian team, we should duly have made an appearance in the park on the following day at the appointed time to find ourselves "sole monarchs" of the ground set apart for the match. I cannot conclude this letter without expressing my astonishment that a school like Eton, with so many players to select from, could not collect eleven righteous men to save its reputation from the stigma this affair has cast upon it. There must "be something rotten in the state of" Eton.

Apologising for the length of this explanation and trusting you will be able to find space for it in the columns of your influential paper.

I remain, Sir,
yours faithfully,
The Captain of the Wanderers, London. Dec 19 1866

So the Wanderers had an extra afternoon to do their Christmas shopping. A notice of cancellation of the match was sent to the *Sportsman*, but an explanatory note by the Editor in reply to Senex's complaint stated that it had been "crowded out" of Saturday's impression. The Honorary Secretary and Captain of the Wanderers, however, could not have made a greater effort, firstly, to have a match of some kind and, that effort having failed, to let all concerned know of the cancellation. Now in his mid-twenties, the maturing Charles Alcock was already beginning to demonstrate a seemingly endless capacity for work and organisation, along with a rare ability to combine vision and detail that would serve him well in his later administrative positions.

An expanding fixture list for the following season, 1867/68, included "weeks" at both Oxford and Cambridge and matches against Charterhouse, Civil Service, an Eton Eleven, Forest School, Hertfordshire Rangers, Harrow School, Old Harrovians, Harrow Chequers, London Athletic Club, No Names, Oxford University, Upton Park and Westminster School.

THE SPORTSMAN

From the beginning of the 1869-70 season, the Wanderers home matches were played at the Oval, a fact overlooked in the history of the ground by Nick Yapp who dates the first football matches as 1870.[118] The error is understandable as it derives from Alcock himself originally.[119] Indeed, there was a Surrey Football Club as early as 1849,[120] the driving force behind which was William Denison, then Secretary of the Surrey Club. Membership was restricted to members of the Surrey Cricket Club, the Surrey Paragon Club, the South London Club and the Union Club and matches were purely internal (There were no other clubs to play at this early date), but certainly football was played at the ground at least twenty years before Yapp suggests and a time when the man given credit for introducing it was still a child in Sunderland. When the Wanderers transferred there, it was, says the *Field*, "the means of collecting a numerous attendance of spectators"[121]. The fact was not lost on the Wanderers' captain who three years later would have a larger say in what happened on those few acres of south London which were the home of the adolescent Surrey County Cricket Club.

It was perhaps singularly appropriate that, having been heavily involved in the creation of the FA Challenge Cup, Alcock should be the first winning captain. Wanderers can perhaps be considered a little fortunate in reaching the final as a result of only one win, 3-1 against Clapham Rovers in the second round (or second ties as they were known at the time). Their first round opponents, Harrow Chequers, had scratched; in the third round they drew with Crystal Palace and the rules of the competition at the time allowed both sides to proceed to the next round which happened to be the semi-final where Palace went down 0-3 to the Royal Engineers who had arrived there via a walk-over against Reigate Priory and victories over Hitchin and Hampstead Heathens. Meanwhile, Queen's Park, Glasgow, made their first trip to London to meet Wanderers in the other semi-final.

The match ended in a goalless draw, though Alcock twice came close to scoring, the first effort requiring the intervention of the umpires to determine that it had passed over the tape. Queen's Park declined the offer of an extra half-hour and because of their inability to travel again to London (the rule switching the venue for replays had not yet been introduced) scratched from the competition, leaving the Wanderers to proceed to the Final on Saturday 16 March to meet Captain Marindin's Royal Engineers.

Despite the Engineers being favourites, the Wanderers won by a single goal scored by "A H Chequer", a pseudonym for M P Betts. Alcock did manage to get the ball between the posts, only to have it disallowed because of a handling offence by one of his team-mates. The trophy was presented at the Club's annual dinner. In 1872/73 Wanderers were exempt until the Final Tie, the only occasion that the FA Cup has been a "Challenge" trophy pure and simple. They opted to play at Lillie Bridge, the only time apart from the 1886 replay, that the Final was moved from the Oval during the first twenty years of the competition. Alcock played no more Cup Finals, but he did referee the 1875 Final and subsequent replay as well as the 1879 Final.

By this time his playing days were over and so, effectively, were those of the Wanderers. Old Boys teams began to dominate the amateur scene and the etiquette of the day for those leaving school or university was that the club entitled to first choice of a footballer's services was his Old Boys Club[122]. The stranglehold of the old school tie remained but was soon to be challenged by the northern professionals. Adhering to the dribbling game which was now being superseded by "passing on", the Wanderers followed their triple triumph of 1876, 1877 and 1878 by losing 7-2 in the first round of the 1878-79 competition to eventual winners, Old Etonians. Their last appearance in the competition they had dominated in its first decade was the following season when they lost 3-1 in the third round, again to Old Etonians. Thereafter they played one match a season for three or four years, then went out of existence.[123]

Representative Football

Club matches were all very well and enjoyable, but it was inevitable that some players should seek something with a more competitive edge and Alcock became involved in county matches and in contests between the London and Sheffield Associations. The initiative came from Sheffield, but London responded enthusiastically and football's first representative match took place in Battersea Park on 31 March 1866.[124] The match was played under "London Rules" which were still not finalised and London won by "two goals and four touchdowns" to nothing. E C Morley scored the first goal in representative football. C W Alcock was the first player to be ruled offside.[125]

There was a dual purpose, firstly for players to test their abilities in a more competitive situation and, secondly, to test the Rules of the Association which, after four years debate, were now approaching general acceptability, though they still differed from the Sheffield Rules in several particulars, most significantly on the question of offside where the rules of the northern association allowed a player to remain onside provided one player was between him and the goal.

The first County match was Middlesex v Surrey and Kent on 2 November 1867. Alcock, resident in Islington at the time, played for Middlesex. The match should have been played at Beaufort House, but, because of what the press called "an unaccountable disagreement between Lord Ranelagh and the Hon sec of the Amateur Athletic Club", the teams were "compelled to take refuge in the wilds of Battersea Park".[126] It had not been possible to alert all the players to the change of venue. Some turned up late; others not at all.

Nonetheless, it was the first *bona fide* inter-county match, a complete novelty, and won the approval of the press:

> Football has lately increased to such gigantic dimensions, that it needs something more than ordinary club matches to bring out the rising talent. The names of the players who were engaged in this first contest - who, we are informed are the officers of the Football Association - desire impartially to perform their duties, to select the best players without regard to public schools or especial cliques, and we must congratulate them on the efficient manner in which they have commenced their work.[127]

The first London v Sheffield fixture was soon followed by others. Two fixtures per annum were played, one under Sheffield Rules, one under London Rules, and later when a third match was added with a switch of rules at half-time.[128] This state of affairs went on until 1876 when, after ten years of disagreement, the Sheffield Association brought their rules into line.

Until his retirement from the game in 1875, Alcock regularly captained London and had arranged that from 1872, London's home games were played at The Oval. The last of these was in 1890 by which time the nature of association football had changed out of all recognition. Symbolically, perhaps, it was brought to a premature end by fog with Sheffield leading 2-1.

From representative inter-Association and inter-County matches, it is a short step to international matches, but there is an intermediate stage of regional matches. The first North v South match, inspired perhaps by the equivalent first-class cricket contest which had first been played in 1864, took place at The Oval on 17 December 1870. Alcock took advantage of his birth qualification to play for the North, but this was one of the very few occasions in his playing career when he was not captain. That role was assumed by C L Rothera of Notts. In a close game, the North twice seriously threatened the Southern goal with 'a fine long kick from the foot of T C Hoonan...and again by a well turned kick from C W Alcock, the result of a sharp run along the upper side of the ground.'[129]

However, it was all to no avail as the South scored the only goal of the match with three minutes remaining.

Pseudo-Internationals

Before the first full international with Scotland in Glasgow in November 1872 there were a number of pseudo-internationals which, although recorded in the press as 'England v Scotland' were not fully representative as the Scotland teams were largely restricted to those with a Scottish connection - in some cases, quite loose - who happened to be living and working in the London area. There were five of these matches in all, spread between March 1870 and February 1872, but football historians differ in their treatment of them and secondary sources are mostly wrong and incomplete. Geoffrey Green, in the encyclopædic four-volume *Association Football*, mentions only those of the 1870-71 season[130] (as does Tony Pawson) while W G Gallagher in the same publication covers the last four, but gives the result of the match played on 19 November 1870 as 4-0 to England when it was in fact 1-0. He is correct in the results of the remaining matches - a 1-1 draw the following February[131], then 2-1 and 1-0 to England in the 1871-72 season. The website of the Association of Football Statisticians states that the second to fifth matches were played in 1870-71 when in fact they were spread over two seasons, while that of the Museum of the Scottish Football Association, objecting to the use of the term 'Scotland' on the not unreasonable grounds that the team was chosen by the English FA, claims that Scotland lost all four. They did in fact draw in February 1871 and had two draws in the full "series" of five matches spread over three seasons. Percy Young in his *A History of British Football* mentions the first one, but makes no reference to the others.

There are perhaps four reasons for the first match being disregarded by some historians: Firstly, no contact was made with any cross-border source. It was not until the November 1870 match was being arranged that the *Glasgow Herald* was used as an avenue of recruitment for players. Secondly, the match was postponed for a fortnight because of heavy frost on the originally scheduled date of 26 February 1870 and may have been somewhat lower profile when it was eventually played. In reporting the postponement the *Field*, more accurately than subsequent reports, records the match as 'England v Scotch'. Thirdly, it was the following match which spurred the rugby fraternity into action, claiming that it was not a genuine international, Scotland did not excel at the association game and would challenge England to a proper international match under Rugby rules, north of the border. Fourthly and finally - and perhaps most significantly - Alcock himself is a source of the error, in his *Surrey Cricket: Its History and Associations* stating that the first 'unofficial' international was on 19 November 1870. He has conveniently forgotten the match on 5 March, perhaps a classic case of selective memory, as according to the *Sportsman*, it was his mistake that led to the Scots' only goal in a 1-1 draw. 'owing to a reprehensible excess of confidence on the part of the England captain, the English goal which had been left thoroughly unprotected fell to a long and rather lucky kick by R E Crawford...'[132] Match reports in nineteenth century newspapers were not attributed and it is highly probable that Alcock, as football sub-editor of the *Sportsman*, was himself the author of the report.

However, a late goal by A Baker spared England's blushes or, as the Sportsman puts it rather more graphically, "saved England from the odium of defeat". Alcock was not in fact in the team selected for the match which was postponed, but played in the rearranged match in a team which showed two changes from that originally selected. For good measure, he captained the side.

The significance of the matches in the Alcock story, however, is that, as part of his early administrative career as the newly appointed Honorary Secretary of the Football Association, he was heavily involved in the organisation of the matches and the selection of the teams, and now well into the second half of his playing career, he captained 'England' in all five matches. All the matches were played at the Kennington Oval.

In the second match, his club is recorded as Harrow Pilgrims. In the first match it was Old Harrovians. As his principal club remained the Wanderers, it is tempting to speculate whether the choice was accidental or a ploy to give the Harrow/Wanderers caucus additional votes on the selection committee, the teams for all five matches being selected "by a committee formed of the captains of the chief Association Clubs". This time England won 1-0. Alcock was involved in the goal and came close to scoring himself.

Unlike some club games earlier in the decade, the match started promptly. Scotland were weakened by the absence of W H Gladstone and Charterhouse School's declining to release J T Inglis. The English Eleven, according to the press, represented the cream of association players:

> After a well executed run by the captain of the side, R S F Walker was lucky enough to accredit England with a well-earned goal, the result of good backing up and concerted work by the two players immediately interested…Once even the ball was driven against the posts of the Scottish goal by a side kick from the foot of C W Alcock, but no material triumph was recorded.[133]

For the next match, too, on 25 February 1871, Alcock played as a representative of Harrow Pilgrims, although the team seem to have played only one match and that against the Wanderers. This third pseudo-international ended in a 1-1 draw before an attendance of around 600. The fourth match of what the *Field* had decided was now "the series of matches which have now become firmly established for decision twice during each season under the auspices of the committee of the Football Association" took place on 18 November 1871, following what had now become the traditional invitation in the press to those "desirous of taking part in the match" to communicate with Mr Alcock or Mr Kirkpatrick. It was "a contest worthy of the reputation of the players engaged".[134] Alcock, having now abandoned both the "Old Harrovian" and "Harrow Pilgrims" labels now appears with a more appropriate "Wanderers" appendage. Having won the toss and compelled the Scots initially to play into the sun, he led England to a 2-1 victory, albeit against a side weakened by the absence of A F Kinnaird and Quintin Hogg, and with the aid of a goal which the Scotch captain claimed was offside, but the umpires ruled was legitimate. Fog and frost late in the match made conditions "cheerless" for the spectators and "dangerous" for the contestants.

The final match, before "full" internationals took over was held, again at The Oval, on 24 February 1872 when - interesting how the nuances of words can change, even over a hundred years - the "inefficient representation of Scotland" (Lieutenant Renny-Tailyour of the Royal Engineers was unable to play owing to an accident) contributed to a 1-0 Scottish defeat, the only goal coming from future President of the Football Association, J C Clegg, who "was enabled by a clever kick to land [the ball] safely in the centre of the goal".[135]

The match was not given undue prominence in the press. Although banner headlines were not yet in vogue, some significance might be attached to the length and positioning of match reports and, while the *Field* certainly expends more words on this match than any other on the same day, its position on the page is scarcely prominent as it nestles somewhat incongruously between Blackheath Club v ICE College (Cooper's Hill) and Derby School v Tatam's team.

By this stage the pseudo-internationals were perhaps beginning to lose something of their novelty value; but, along with the first rugby internationals and the appearance of Queen's Park, Glasgow (or Green's Park, according to one of the *Field's* typesetters whose knowledge of football north of the border was less than complete) in the later stages of the Association Cup, they played their role in paving the way to full internationals. As a player, journalist and administrator, Charles Alcock occupied centre stage.

A number of the participants in these early contests were to distinguish themselves in other spheres including Lord Kinnaird, later President of the FA, and according to the *Football Annual*, "without exception the best player of the day capable of taking any place in the field"; Quintin Hogg, philanthropist and founder of Regent Street Polytechnic; W H Gladstone, eldest son of the Prime Minister and himself MP for Whitby and earlier for Chester (the only sitting MP to appear in a home international, albeit an unofficial one); and G G Kennedy, long distance champion of Cambridge University and later police magistrate at Marlborough Street.

Full Internationals

Charles Alcock should have followed his Cup Final triumph with an appearance as captain in the first full international between Scotland and England played on the ground of the West of Scotland Cricket Club at Partick on 30 November, St Andrew's Day, 1872. He had, however, been injured in an Old Harrovians v Old Etonians match two weeks earlier.

No mention is made of this in reports of the match and there is some inconsistency in other sources, the *Football Annual* blaming an injury to the back and the *Sportsman* a sprained knee. The former, of which Alcock was Editor at the time, reports a very evenly contested match, won by the Old Etonians 2-1, then says:

> We regret to add that a severe injury sustained in the match has incapacitated the Harrow captain from any further active service in the football field.

That was something of an exaggeration. He was playing again by early 1873, appeared intermittently in the 1873-74 season when, doubtless because of FA and Surrey commitments, he passed on the Secretaryship of Wanderers to R K Kingsford. He continued to play until the 1875-76 season, but whatever the injury sustained in 1872, he was unable to play in that first international. However, he acted as one of the umpires for the match, having travelled to Glasgow overnight with the four players whose commitments had not allowed them to travel with the remainder of the team the previous day. Scotland was represented entirely by the Queen's Park Club.

Injury again prevented Alcock from playing the next two internationals, the "return" at The Oval in February 1873 (although the previous week he had been fit enough to captain Surrey against Middlesex, being now resident in the former) and in Glasgow in 1874 and it was not until 6 March 1875 that he played his sole international on what was by now virtually his own back lawn of Kennington Oval. Continuous rain during the morning reduced the number of spectators and resulted in a heavy ground. The occasion was a colourful one, England opting to play in their club shirts (and they were drawn from seven clubs) while Scotland adhered to their traditional blue jerseys and white knickerbockers.[136] Alcock captained the side and his first decision was to begin the match with ten men, W H Carr, his goalkeeper, having missed a train in Sheffield. Subsequently, the captain was involved in the first goal and scored the second in a 2-2 draw.

An infringement of the handling rule by Scotland gave England a free kick which, as usual, they entrusted to Birley. A well-directed aim just enabled Alcock to reach the ball, and, after being transferred to Bonsor and Wollaton, the last named secured a goal for England to the exuberant delight of the spectators. An objection was lodged to this score on the ground that Wollaston was offside, but the umpires did not allow it...

Scotland equalised. But then...

two corner kicks aroused the enthusiasm of the on-lookers to fresh outbursts. Neither of these had the right direction, but the next was entrusted to Von Donop, who most skilfully planted it a few yards in front of the Scotch posts. There it was breasted by the English captain, and he pertinaciously adhered to it until he had got it securely over the Scottish goal-line.[137]

Once again, Scotland equalised and although England had the better of the last twenty minutes, there was no further scoring and honours remained even.

He played little more after that international and the following season, 1875-76, was his last, though he did make an isolated appearance in a Rugby Veterans v Soccer Veterans match in 1880 (It comes as no surprise that he arranged the fixture and recruited both teams. N L ('Pa') Jackson was later to record that though he could not recall the result, everyone thoroughly enjoyed it in spite of the grievous bruises they all sustained).[138] He had been selected for England on three previous occasions (1872, 1873 and 1874). Says the *Football Annual*:

(Alcock) has been chosen Captain of the English Eleven in all four matches, but owing to severe accidents, only able to take part in the fourth. A hard-working forward player and usually a safe shot at goal.[139]

Twenty years later, he recalls missing only two, having been, he says, "laid up on both occasions".[140]

In 1875-76, although he "played splendidly" for the Wanderers against Queen's Park, "the whole of Queen's Park was brilliant in the extreme" and won 5-0 before an attendance of 10,000, he no longer appeared in the *Football Annual's* "Chief English Players" and the boots were at last hung up.

"I was," he says "very fond of the game and was very sorry indeed to have to give it up owing to an accident, for it was my chief means of recreation."[141] He was, however, in other capacities off the field of play, to take the game far beyond being a recreation, to a point where it became a competitive, professional and international business.

Alcock the Referee

When football was a gentlemen's game played by gentlemen, referees were not required. Sometimes, there were two umpires who judged on matters of fact and any decisions required on points of law were taken by the captains. For example, the *Field* reports the following on the settling of a disputed goal in the November 1866 Civil Service-Wanderers match:

> ...at the last moment Mr Phipps made a good run down to the Civil Service base, and the ball was got through somehow; but it was objected that the goal-keeper had first been handed over, and the ball afterwards handed through. The captains of the sides afterwards met, and at the wish of the captain of the Civil Service team, it was arranged that the disputed goal should be considered to count in favour of the Wanderers who were therefore winners of the match.[142]

It was a time when the result was secondary to the game itself. Indeed nineteenth century press reports did not carry the result separately and often have to be combed in some detail to discover when the goals were scored and by whom.

A player breaching the Rules was expected to acknowledge the infringement. An *obiter dicta* attached to the Harrow Rules instructed: If you inadvertently break a rule...stand away at once.

The possibility of deliberately contravening a rule was not even admitted. As trophies and money were introduced and, as a result the game became more competitive, that Garden of Eden scenario was abandoned and referees introduced to enforce the Laws with the umpires literally sidelined to become linesmen or touch judges, depending on the code.

Having acted as umpire in the first international when he was unfit to play because of injury, he refereed the 1875 Final and replay between Royal Engineers and Old Etonians, a match which brought the former their only Cup Final triumph, as they won 2-0 on Tuesday 15 March, following a 1-1 draw the previous Saturday. Again in 1879 he refereed the Final when Old Etonians beat Clapham Rovers 1-0. He was later to become the first President of the Referees' Association.

1872 Annus Mirabilis

1872 was a year which saw the births of the FA Cup, international football, C B Fry, K S Ranjitsinhji and J T Tyldesley. Only with the first two of these had Alcock any connection, but it was a pivotal year in sport and in Charles Alcock's career. From now on, the two would be almost inextricably intertwined. Globetrotting diplomats and politicians apart, few years can have been busier for anyone. In November, shortly after completing the editorial work for the fifth issue of the *Football Annual*, he was attending meetings on birth and residential qualifications for county cricketers between playing club and representative football matches, captaining London against Sheffield, organising, recruiting the team for and umpiring a full international football match in Scotland. Earlier in the year he had played in an international match, captained Wanderers to victory in the FA Cup, been appointed the first paid Secretary of Surrey County Cricket Club and become the first (and indeed, only) editor of *James Lillywhite's Cricketers' Annual*.

In its edition of 24 February the *Sportsman* of which Alcock was football sub-editor carried in the same column information on four seemingly unrelated items - England v Scotland at the Kennington Oval that afternoon, the Annual General Meeting of the Football Association the following Wednesday, London v Sheffield the following Saturday and two days after that Wanderers v Queen's Park, Glasgow in the semi-final of the FA Cup. Alcock was captain of England, London and Wanderers, hon sec of the Football Association and, holding the same office with Wanderers, responsible for ticket distribution for the semi-final. Later in the year, on 10

April, the newspaper carried on the same page a summary of the Wanderers' results for the football season just ended, news that the Surrey County Club were to appoint a paid Secretary and an announcement of the impending publication of the *Cricket Calendar* for 1872, edited by Charles W Alcock - Who else? If the *Sportsman* had deferred all this news for a week and at the same time chosen to carry birth announcements, the indefatigable Alcock could have made yet another appearance. His fourth child and third daughter, Charlotte Mabel, was born on 15 April. He was half way through his family, past half-time in his playing days, but still at the beginning of his journalistic and administrative career. Rarely can there have been a better example of the maxim that if a job is to be done properly, then it should be given to a busy man.

REFERENCES

74. *Cricket* 28 February 1907
75. *Scores and Biographies* Vol IX p 22
76. *Scores and Biographies* Vol VII p 359
77. *Wisden* 1980 p 112
78. Bettesworth *Chats on the Cricket Field* p 26
79. The match was against the Paris Club in the Bois de Boulogne: Butterflies won by 8 wickets.
80. Bettesworth *Chats on the Cricket Field* p 401
81. Bettesworth *Chats on the Cricket Field* p 401
82. *Field* 16 March 1867
83. *Field* 16 March 1867
84. 2 August 1862
85. *Who's Who of Cricketers* p 464
86. Bettesworth *Chats on the Cricket Field* p 19
87. *Cricket Lore* Issue 4 - May 1992 - p 5
88. Bettesworth *Chats on the Cricket Field* p 24
89. *Scores and Biographies* Vol X p 235
90. *Scores and Biographies* Vol XII p 688
91. Attributed to Lord Harris - Eric Midwinter *Cricket Lore* Vol 3 Issue 3 p12
92. *Football Annual* 1873

93. Alcock *Football: The Association Game* p 31
94. *Football Annual* 1881
95. Pawson *100 Years of the FA Cup* p 5
96. 9 November 1867
97. 7 December 1867
98. v Clapham Common 2 February 1867 - reported in the *Field* a week later
99. *Scores and Biographies* Vol VII p 359
100. *Field* 24 November 1866
101. Grace *'W G' Cricketing Reminiscences and Personal Recollections* p 321
102. *Association Football* iii p 8
103. *'W G' Cricketing Reminiscences* p 320
104. *Field* 30 January 1869
105. 20 April 1867 p 301
106. *Field* 10 January 1867
107. *Field* 10 January 1867
108. Alcock in *The Book of Football* p 256
109. Alcock *The Association Game* - quoted in *Butler The Official Illustrated History of the FA Cup* p 35
110. *Victoria History of the Counties of England: A History of Essex* Vol II pp 612-4
111. *Victoria History of the Counties of England: A History of Essex* Vol II pp 612-4
112. Adrienne Reynolds *Forest School and the FA Cup* (Forest School Magazine 1998)
113. *Field* 9 November 1867
114. Alcock *The Association Game*
115. Bettesworth *Chats on the Cricket Field* p 27
116. Quoted by Jackson in *Association Football* p 310
117. Quoted by Jackson in *Association Football* p 312
118. Yapp *A History of the Foster's Oval* p 139
119. Alverstone & Alcock *Surrey Cricket: Its History and Associations* p 434
120. Goulstone *Football's Secret History* p35
121. *Field* 16 October 1869
122. Pawson *100 Years of the FA Cup* p10
123. Jackson *Association Football* p 313

124. *Association Football* Vol I p 56

125. Geoffrey Green *History of the Football Association* p 42

126. *Field* 9 November 1867

127. *Field* 9 November 1867

128. Alcock *Association Football* p 22

129. *Field* 24 December 1870

130. Vol I p 22

131. Vol IV p 7

132. *Sportsman* 8 March 1870

133. *Field* 26 November 1870

134. *Field* 25 November 1871

135. *Field* 4 March 1872

136. James *England v Scotland* p 28

137. *Sportsman* 9 March 1875

138. Jackson *Sporting Days and Sporting Ways* p 52

139. *Football Annual* 1875

140. Bettesworth *Chats on the Cricket Field* p 27

141. Bettesworth *Chats on the Cricket Field* p 27

CHAPTER 4

WRITER AND EDITOR

CHARLES ALCOCK'S OBITUARY in *The Times*[143] pays appropriate tribute to him as an administrator and player of cricket and football, but makes no mention of his journalism, writing and publishing. Yet, however posterity may judge him, there can be no doubt, once his brief flirtation with the family marine insurance business was over, that he saw himself primarily as a journalist. His death certificate describes him as "Secretary, Surrey County Cricket Club". The informant was his widow who clearly saw that post as one which had provided a steady income and occasional bonus, while earnings from journalism and publishing had been the icing on the cake. Eliza outlived him by thirty years and on her own death certificate the balance is to an extent restored when she is described as the widow of "a journalist and Secretary of Surrey County Cricket Club". His grave, rededicated in 1999 - albeit on the initiative of the Football Association and Surrey County Cricket Club - describes him as "An Inspiring Secretary of the Football Association 1870 - 1895 and of Surrey County Cricket Club 1872 -1907". Yet, in Census returns, on his marriage certificate and his children's birth certificates, he is not described as either of those.

On the 1861 Census of Population, when he was still living with his parents in Chingford, he is described as a shipbroker, as he is on his marriage certificate, in December 1864. On the birth certificate of his first child, William Edward Forster, in October 1865, he is an insurance broker, but by the time his second child, Elizabeth Maud, is born, in September 1869, he is a Reporter and thereafter, from 1870 to 1878 on the birth certificates of his other six children and on the 1871 Census, he is a Journalist. On the 1881 Census, by which time he had been Secretary of Surrey for almost a decade, he was a Publisher & Journalist; 1891 Journalist & Author and 1901 J P for Surrey and Journalist.

So it is clear that Charles saw himself primarily as a journalist and his simultaneous Secretaryship of two major sporting organisations as subsidiary activities. It may be that as a Victorian from a status-conscious family and honed in the public school tradition, he saw more virtue in being a self-employed, self-made man at the cutting edge of sports reporting and leader writing than as the servant of the committees of two major sporting bodies. However, the record is there to demonstrate that he succeeded supremely in all three domains as well as fulfilling in later years, his civic duties as Councillor and Magistrate.

The British Library catalogue has thirteen Charles W Alcock entries, although some are re-issues and one, on the Northern Rugby Union, seems to have crept in by accident. However, one of his minor publications is not included and neither his prolific newspaper work, nor chapters written for a number of books, qualify for inclusion. So, had he done nothing else with his life, his writing alone would have been sufficient for him to have left his mark on his own and subsequent generations.

His first venture into paid work away from the insurance world was in the late 1860s when he began to work for the *Sportsman* and the *Field*.[144] In 1872, simultaneously with his appointment at Surrey, he began editing *James Lillywhite's Cricketers' Annual*, affectionately known as the 'Red Lilly' from the colour of its cover.

The 'Field' and The 'Sportsman'

Nineteenth century newspapers, like nineteenth century sport, were a product of the industrial revolution. Newspapers in the previous century had had limited circulation, but the introduction of mass production techniques and consequent price reduction, aided and abetted by the reduction in the tax on newsprint in 1836 and its total abolition in 1861, brought them within the range of an increasingly literate public. Before radio, television and the telegraph and telephone, they had replaced the town-crier as the main means of conveying information, sporting and otherwise. Just as Alcock was alive to the expanding sporting scene, he was alive to the possibilities of publicising it through the embryonic mass media.

In his interview with Bettesworth, Alcock says that when football began to develop, he took up newspaper work and became athletics sub-editor of the *Sportsman*, then football sub-editor of the *Sportsman* and the *Field* and later covered cricket for the *Sportsman*.

The latter was established in 1865 reflecting the boom in sporting interest in that decade, and pledged to improving the standard of sports reporting and providing a professional service to its readers:

> ...our creed in sport is catholic; our position independent; and our resources as large as enterprise or research can make them.
>
> Horace has said that the fountain of all good writing is to know something about the subject, but this, so far as we can see, has not always been a principle adopted by all who have come forth to instruct the public in sporting matters. No one is or will be admitted into our establishment from the writer to the typesetter who is not capable of avoiding the gross errors, which so frequently disfigure accounts of sporting transactions.[145]

Alcock was almost certainly not involved in the *Sportsman* from the beginning in any significant way. His address on the Wanderers membership list for 1865-66 is that of the family ship-broking and insurance business, 155 Fenchurch Street, so it is reasonable to assume that his major professional commitment still lay there. He may have had a minor involvement, however. Articles and correspondence were very rarely attributed and even when they were, the identity of the author was usually concealed under a nom-de-plume such as 'Floreat Etona', 'Juvenis' or 'Rugbiensis', the literary antecedents of 'Disgusted of Tunbridge Wells'. Alcock was certainly among the early correspondents of the newspaper, signing himself as 'Captain of the Wanderers', rather than concealing his identity behind the anonymity of a pseudonym.

Interestingly, one of Alcock's predecessors at The Oval was a pioneer of sports journalism. William Denison, Surrey's first honorary secretary, has been called the father of daily newspaper cricket reporting, his reports appearing regularly in the *Times* in the 1840s. Ahead of the Lillywhite publications, he produced the *Cricketer's Companion* which ran for four years in the same decade.

The *Sportsman* was initially published on Tuesdays and Saturdays, but within a year "at the urgent solicitation of numerous subscribers"[146] it introduced a regular Thursday edition. There had been occasional special editions on Wednesday and Thursday for the St Leger, for example, and horse racing formed a major part of its copy as it had and continued to do for the *Field*. At the time of its expansion there were "several important additions to its literary staff". It is possible that Alcock was one of these.

The Field was a well-established weekly publication, dating from 1853 and appearing every Saturday, and its double sub-titles of *The Farm*, *The Garden and The Country Gentlemen's* Newspaper leaves no doubt about its areas of interest and its intended market. Before that there was only one newspaper dealing with sport, *Bell's Life*, established in 1822 and continuing until 1886 when there was more competition from the *Field*, the *Sportsman*, the *Sporting Life* and increased coverage of sport in the *Times* and *Daily Telegraph*. Cricket had been covered for some time by the *Field*, but football began to squeeze its way in from around 1860, and while, in a very detailed annual index, cricket merits a separate heading, football, with the exception of 1864 when it is given a heading of its own, continues into the 1870s, when a couple of dozen matches a week are covered, to be listed under 'Pastimes', suggesting that while cricket might be an appropriate pursuit for a country gentleman, football is rather more marginalized.

Within five years, space for cricket coverage had become a problem for the *Sportsman*, but *omnia cum pretio*, Alcock, now dealing with cricket for that newspaper, was prepared to sell it:

SATURDAY AFTERNOON AND MINOR MATCHES

While anxious to allot space to all matches according to their importance we are so overwhelmed with scores as to be quite unable to continue publishing them, as hitherto, in tabular form. We shall therefore be necessitated in future to give short paragraphs containing the number of runs made by each batsman, and the totals put together by their respective teams. If, however, any club desire to keep a complete record, we are prepared to receive and publish their full scores at a nominal charge of 2s which may be sent to the publisher of THE SPORTSMAN. This arrangement only applies to minor matches and not to those of public interest which will meet with the fullest attention.[147]

Scoresheets to aid the submission of the scores were available at 9d per dozen (10d post free!).

The Football Annual

As football increased in popularity and the laws began to be codified and unified, Alcock added another dimension to his journalistic activity by launching the *Football Annual* in 1868. It was published with the sanction of the Association. The Lillywhite publications were well established in cricket and *Wisden* had started in 1864, but this was the first attempt at anything parallel in the newly established winter game. That it filled a market need, Alcock had no doubt, writing in the 1873 edition:

> Five years have proved the necessity for a work recording the doings of each football season. Indeed the speed with which every copy of the edition of 1872 was disposed of, showed, beyond doubt, that the utility of the annual was fully recognised...
>
> The Editor has endeavoured to make the 1873 Annual more complete in every way, and ventures to solicit the help of football players in making the annual a full and reliable record of all football matters.

In the early stages, it covered both association and rugby codes and followed the example of the Lillywhite publications by providing hints on play as well as details of clubs, results and commentaries. The history of the Football Association (necessarily brief at this stage) was included, plus information on all the known football clubs in England, notes on the chief English players and a section on football in Scotland. It was an invaluable reference book, containing for each club details of the date of formation, number of members, location of ground and dressing room (if any) and distance from nearest railway station, name and address of the Secretary, club colours and a summary of the previous season's results - though a bit of careless proof-reading in the 1873 edition has left blank spaces against Played, Won, Lost and Drawn in the Wanderers section. The 1874 edition covers a wider range and embraces football in Ireland and in India. In 1879, delight is expressed that the game in Scotland has expanded to the extent that the Scottish Association Challenge Cup has attracted 126 entries less than ten years after the supporters of the rugby code had suggested that their game was dominant and there was no opportunity to practise the "dribbling game" in Scotland. The entry for the equivalent competition south of the border was 43 clubs. The *Annual* comments especially 'on the complete revolution that has been worked in Scotland since the commencement of the crusade, headed by the redoubtable Queen's Park Club of Glasgow and it goes without saying that the Association rules are now paramount when, only a short time ago they were practically untried'.

The recognition of the increasing strength of Scottish football is not without significance. Scotland was to win the next five internationals against England. Also significant, in view of the switch of emphasis that was to take place in club football in England was the entry for the Lancashire Association, showing seven clubs in Blackburn and three in Darwen.

The *Football Annual* matures alongside the game itself and Alcock recognises both quantitative and qualitative progress, commenting on the way participation has increased and tactics improved, as dribbling yields to passing and the power-base moves from the southern public schools to the Northern professionals and to Scotland:

What was, ten or fifteen years ago, the recreation of a few has now become the pursuit of thousands, an athletic exercise carried on under a strict system, and, in many cases, by an enforced term of training almost magnified into a profession. Whether the introduction of so serious and almost business-like an element into the sport is a healthy one or not, this is not the place to enquire, but there are many old football fogies who recall with no small satisfaction the days when football had not grown to be so important as to make umpires necessary and the "gate" the first subject for consideration...[148]

Increased gates, however, meant increased potential for crowd misbehaviour and the Editor is not slow to become involved and not only criticise the miscreants themselves, but issue a warning voice on the circumstances that are likely to lead to this early form of football hooliganism:

The cowardly conduct of a few roughs at Sheffield led to the resignation of Mr W Pierce Dix, a gentleman who had for years done loyal service to the dribbling game as Hon Sec of the Sheffield Association, but it must be borne in mind that, though players are not to be held responsible for the conduct of those who are looking on, for the behaviour of men who are influenced by the insatiate passion for betting, and who have no real sympathy for the sport itself, that it was the action of Mr Dix in opposing the introduction of a class of fixtures got up solely for the benefit of the players themselves, and certain to lower the tone of the game that exposed him to an unmanly and unwarrantable attack. The question of professionalism at football is too wide in its bearings to be treated with the care that it requires in a brief review such as this, but it will be well for those who have the interest of the game at heart to recognise the existence of a problem that will in all likelihood have to be mastered before long.[149]

Like *Wisden* and *James Lillywhite's Cricketers' Annual*, the *Football Annual* is more than a book of record in that it reflects and forms opinion, recognises trends, promotes discussion on law changes and provides hints on how to play the game for forwards, half-backs, backs and goalkeepers. Referees and selectors are, as ever, targets of criticism:

...had the referee had only an ordinary knowledge of the provisions of the off-side rule, two, if not three of the goals given them by his casting vote would never have been allowed...
The English Eleven was drawn from so many clubs, some of them playing an entirely different game, that anything like cohesion, placed together on the field as they were for the first time, was impossible.[150]

Advertising revenue was received from various sports warehouses and Alcock does not miss an opportunity to advertise his other publications, for instance, the *Cricket Calendar*, *Football*, *Football, Our Winter Game*, and *James Lillywhite's Cricketers' Annual*.

Football, Our Winter Game

An unpretentious little work on Football called "Football, Our Winter Game" by Charles W Alcock has been issued from the Field office. There is no gentleman more competent to write on this manly sport, no better judge of the game, and no one has done more to increase its popularity then the Hon. Sec of the Football Association.

The Hour May 11th 1874

impartiality and good sense which characterise his remarks

Sporting Gazette May 16th 1874

the best and most useful little book on football we can have

Nottingham Guardian June 1874

Such were some of the notices for Alcock's first book and the advance publicity states that similar notices "all of a highly favourable nature" have appeared in *Bell's Life*, the *Sporting Life* and other sporting papers. Were they justified?

It is an erudite little book which begins by quoting Machiavelli, possibly a role model for the maturing administrator and author: 'he who will see what shall be, let him consider what hath been, for all things in the world, at all times, have their encounter with the things of old.'

He then proceeds to look at ancient Greek and Roman ball games and their relationship to football, dwelling on the game of 'harpastum' which some sports historians have seen as one of the precursors of football. The book also looks at 'mob football', Shrove Tuesday festivals and subsequent more refined versions of the game including the School House v School match in *Tom Brown's Schooldays*, before including some hints on play, the rules of the association game and the rugby game and advice on football boots.

Much of what he said on the historical side has been repeated by subsequent writers and the validity of the links with classical times are perhaps a little tenuous. But he was nevertheless the first to make them. Joseph Strutt in his encyclopædic chronicle of sports and pastimes published in 1831 makes little reference to football or cricket, so at least, for all its questionable historical accuracy *Football, Our Winter Game* is the first attempt to show how the rabbit got into the hat. It was, says Jackson, "the first attempt at making football history".[151]

James Lillywhite's Cricketers' Annual

Frederick Lillywhite, father of John and James, had started his *Guide to Cricketers* in 1849; overlapping, then superseding this first of the famous series of reference books was the "Green Lilly", *John Lillywhite's Cricketers' Companion* which began life in 1865, was subsequently retitled under *John and James* from 1880 to 1882, then *James* until 1885 when it was discontinued. In 1872, the third Lillywhite, the 'Red Lilly', *James Lillywhite's Cricketers' Annual* was launched, running alongside the *Companion* for thirteen years, incorporating it in 1886 and continuing until the end of the century. Its editor throughout those twenty-eight years of its existence was Charles W Alcock, described thus in 1872, then as "Charles W Alcock, Secretary, Surrey County Cricket Club".

The *Football Annual* had had the field to itself, but the *Cricketers' Annual* was introduced into a market that included the *Cricketers' Companion* and a *Wisden* which had just produced its ninth edition. The prolific and industrious Arthur Haygarth was to produce eight volumes of his monumental *Scores and Biographies* between 1876 and 1879, and while these would not have been a direct competitor to the *Cricketers' Annual*, since they were books of historical record dealing with matches from 1855 to 1873, they were indicative of an expanding market in cricket literature. The new adrenalin-fuelled young Editor lost no time in justifying a new annual publication, boasting that he was well favoured with the active co-operation of the best authorities on cricket matters. "We boldly challenge comparisons with any of our rivals," he says confidently. It was a significant contribution to the literature of the period, although curiously, Irving Rosenwater, in an otherwise comprehensive review of cricket writing in the 1870s, gives it but a cursory mention.[152]

Alcock's opinions were not invariably unchallenged. Following a controversial dismissal of 'Hit the Ball Twice', Alcock had expressed the view that "the wilful striking here means striking with intent to score off it". *Baily's Monthly Magazine of Sports and Pastimes* countered:

> This is a wholly unauthorised gloss of the commentators. Not even Mr Gladstone could so distort the meaning of a simple English word 'wilfully', or make it comprehend an intention on the part of the striker to do some particular thing not even hinted at in the law. If the law meant all this, the law should have said so in plain English: but as the law says nothing of the sort, we decline to accept the arbitrary amendment of an individual commentator as of any weight whatsoever.[153]

Three separate editions were produced in the first year. As well as coverage of MCC, County and Public Schools cricket, the Chief Clubs were also included, as was a feature on W G Grace in 1871. There were hints on batting, allegedly by Grace himself, though Derek West takes the view that Grace was insufficiently literate to write it and suggests it was 'ghosted' by the author of *The Cricket Field*, James Pycroft. Pycroft himself contributed a similar feature on fielding and James Southerton wrote about bowling.

For all of its existence it ran alongside and was both complementary to and a rival of *Wisden* which, scanty in its earlier days and carrying little more than basic results with minimal commentary, soon developed into an authoritative publication on county and MCC cricket, but *Lillywhite* consciously spread its net wider to include club and public schools cricket as well as hints on how to play the game.

Photographs in the form of sepia prints were included from 1876. From 1889 they were integrated in the text. Despite the rivalry with *Wisden*, Alcock remains gentlemanly and complementary. Of the 1891 publication, he says:

> Of the twenty-eighth edition it only needs to be said that it is fully up to the standard of the best of its predecessors, the highest possible testimony to the accuracy of the statistics, as well as the variety of the information.[154]

Wisden was eventually to win the contest, but in 1880, having sold 8,000 copies the previous year, the *Annual* was to claim that it had "surely taken first place among the records of the game".

Cricket

Alcock's appointments with Surrey and the FA did not diminish his journalistic activity. On the contrary, they supplied him with the material to expand it. Shortly, after the 1880 watershed in his career, he reached the pinnacle of his Editorial career with *Cricket* and the twilight saw his magnum opus the encyclopædic *Surrey Cricket: Its History and Associations*. All the while he continued other routine publications.

In 1882, he launched *Cricket* sub-titled *A Weekly Record of the Game*, which he was to edit until his death in 1907. Published until 1894 by W R

Wright, then by Merritt and Hatcher, it bore beneath the masthead a quotation from Alcock's fellow, though not contemporary, old Harrovian, Lord Byron: "Together joined in cricket's manly toil", the last line of Byron's poem *Cricket at Harrow*, the last quatrain of which captures the essence of the public school sports ethos, later developed in fiction by Thomas Hughes and Talbot Baines Reed:

> Our sport, our studies and our souls were one:
> Together we impell'd the flying ball;
> Together waited in our tutor's hall;
> Together join'd in cricket's manly toil.

The educational background of the Editor suffuses the publication. It is well written, invariably grammatically correct and teems with literary allusions to Shakespeare, the classics, Matthew Prior, Milton, Sheridan etc etc. It appeared weekly in the summer and monthly throughout most of the winter. Thursday was its publication date and there are several references to news items reaching the Editor too late on a Wednesday night and having to be held over till the following week's edition. All this was alongside Alcock's two other jobs, yet another example of his eternal industry. Alfred D Taylor in his *Catalogue of Cricket Literature* confirms that 'Cricket enjoys the distinction of being the only paper in the world solely devoted to the game.'[155]

By that time it had been so for nigh on a quarter of a century. It was, Rowland Bowen says, "undoubtedly the best general cricket magazine that has ever appeared".[156] That was in 1970. The *Cricketer International* and *Wisden Cricket Monthly* have since then competed for a share of the mass market and the introduction of colour and the advance of printing technology have made them both attractive publications. A hundred years ago and more, *Cricket* stood alone.

From the start the magazine was a success. Even allowing for a certain amount of self-adulation, the Editor was clearly pleased with the first issue, reporting "an amount of appreciation that has far exceeded our most sanguine expectations", the "extreme cordiality with which our first effort has been received" by "the thousands who recognise in cricket the national game...That there is room for a representative journal in connection with cricket, the exhaustion of our first issue conclusively proves".[157]

THE FATHER OF MODERN SPORT

It was unashamedly a commercial venture and the Editor's business acumen was also in evidence a hundred years before "marketing" became the buzzword of cricket administration. On page 1 of the first issue, Alcock was addressing potential advertisers in the following terms:

"Cricket" presents an unequalled medium for announcements in connection with the game. The scores of most of the principal Clubs will appear exclusively in its columns, and there is already a large number of subscribers, including most of the leading players of the day. "Cricket" will be filed for reference in the Pavilions of all the principal Clubs, and it will thus appeal to every class of cricketer.[158]

Advertising rates were £3 3s for a full page, £1 15s for a half page, 18/6 for a quarter page and 2/- for a single column inch.

The Editor is quite willing to endorse commercial products, such as Sutton's seed:

"The Committee desire me to say that they have every reason to be satisfied with the Grass Seed you have supplied to the ground for the last few years". C W ALCOCK Esq Secretary[159]

Only four years later, however, in another publication, we discover that

Carter's Grass Seeds ONLY have been used on the Surrey Cricket Ground, Kennington Oval, for the last seven years

(Signed) C W ALCOCK April 1894 Secretary. [160]

Nor did he shy away from advertising a number of the multitude of quack remedies that characterised the columns of the Victorian press. That one tablet could cure every disease known to mankind may give rise to a degree of scepticism, but the reader is encouraged to believe that Frazer's sulphur tablets are effective in dealing with impurities of the blood, eczema, acne, psoriasis, erysipelas or other skin disease, constipation or other gouty disease. On top of all this, it promoted a clear and good complexion. Dr Carter Moffat's Electric belt at 5/6 would cure bronchitis, rheumatic gout and back pain. LIRINE was regularly advertised as a cleaner for boots. In capitals, at a distance, it looked like something else.

The magazine was also used for promoting other Alcock publications, such as *Football: Our Winter Game* its initial success encouraging the Editor to launch into something similar for the winter game, a sister journal under the title of *Football*. Gradually, ancillary commercial ventures became part of the operation and by the mid 1890s, the magazine was advertising for sale Report Sheets, Order of Going In cards and two more Alcock publications, the *Cricket Calendar* and *Famous Cricketers and Cricket Grounds*.

In a less inflationary age, the selling price remained at 2d throughout its forty-two year existence. The magazine was also available by post to any address in Great Britain for 4/- for a season of 20 weeks. Files for binding were available and a full, annual index prepared. H Perkins, Secretary of the MCC pays the following tribute to the Editor:

> I think it is highly desirable that a Cricket paper should be published weekly under responsible authority. I consider no one more qualified than yourself, and you shall have my hearty support.[161]

Cricket embraced a range of literary styles. At one end of the scale was a 19th century tabloid-equivalent journalese, coupled with a certain Victorian preciousness:

> ...the mighty men who made, or at least maintained their reputations on its greensward.[162]

Tom Emmett is referred to as "the evergreen", correspondents are "esteemed" and players bat or bowl "in capital style"[163] and a lost ball becomes "the leathern truant".[164] At the other end of the scale, as in the Obituaries, for example those of Fred Burbidge and the Earl of Bessborough, it could be refined and dignified.

Of the former, he says:

> He was in a sense my mentor during the early days of my secretarial career, and it was from him that I sought inspiration in moments of doubt and trouble...Surrey cricket was a gainer by many years of useful life, as it will be a great loser by his death...I can speak of him too in all sincerity as kindness itself, thoroughly straightforward and upright in everything, loyal in the extreme, the same in every relation of life, a true friend in the best sense of the word.[165]

And of the latter:

From the time I first knew him at Harrow... nearly forty years ago, it was my privilege to have almost unbroken relations and, as I am proud to remember, continuous friendship. How enduring was his interest in Harrow and every one who has been educated at the dear old place, none but Harrovians can know - certainly none can realise....

Gentleness itself he was the perfect type of an old English Gentleman. Simple in tastes, always kind and sympathetic, cricket cannot afford to lose patrons of his class and disposition. Still, the good that men and particularly good men and true do lives after them. That is a consoling reflection.[166]

The next month, a poetic tribute followed:

> Keep fieldsman watchful, batsman resolute
> But make our hearts as loyal as his own
>
> Harrow, what service from that narrower soul
> We give the hill where hopes and courage move
> Can rival his, who spent, ungrudging, whole,
> For thee, with thee, his seventy years of love?
> Eager in boyhood; then a hero great
> In fields of sport, from vulgar flaunting free;
> Tried in life's longer labours, tasks of state;
> But most himself when caring most for thee.[167]

From a twenty-first century viewpoint, that can rank only as sanctimonious hogwash. But the appropriateness of the style cannot be denied.

The subject matter is always directly relevant to the game and the many debating points surrounding it. The Editor, now with a decade and a half's successful journalistic experience behind him, is at pains to give a balanced view, while providing an opportunity for the expression of all shades of opinion. That does not, however, prevent him from expressing strong views of his own and the matters dealt with in the first issue, are not without relevance a hundred and twenty years later. There had been suggestions of match-fixing in Australia and Alcock's Editorial outlines some of the differences between the Australian and English approaches to the game. Public school spirit shining through, he says:

> ...the Australian bookmakers succeeded in bribing two English professionals to sell a match, and were only frustrated by the honourable conduct of a third man, who refused to be bought and disclosed the conspiracy.
>
> ...men bet highly on that which interests them deeply. At home, we want to see good cricket, and are not overwhelmed with mortification when we lose, or puffed up with pride when we win.
>
> We play for play's sake far more than for victory; and it is only at University matches, when local patriotism is interested, that a few sovereigns change hands. The result is that it is worth no man's while to buy or sell a match; and we may trust that the colonial vice will never take firm root at Lord's or at the Oval.
>
> What cricket is today we all know; the chief vice is that there is too much of it...[168]

There are Hints to Junior Bowlers from H F Boyle which suggests that eight to ten yards is a long enough run-up for fast bowlers. The third Surrey Challenge Cup is about to get off the ground. Clubs paid to have their scores inserted. There is a regular 'Pavilion Gossip' section (Main news in the first edition was that W G Grace has mumps), supplemented in later years by 'Between the Innings', letters to the Editor and an enquiry column (an early day example of Cricinfo's 'Ask Philip'):

> Queries sent to us on any subject connected with Cricket will be answered at once. Question and reply will be inserted in full, and thus useful information will be given on many points of general interest to players.

Cricket's high standards were to be a feature of cricket literature for well over a quarter of a century. Nor did it shy away from allowing its readers to express strong, controversial and eccentric opinions. In 1899, one of its correspondents was clearly of the opinion that Abel should not have been omitted from the Test team:

> ... the famous selection trio (who, when they have completed their labours, ought to join Barnum's collection of human freaks)...the pachydermatous cheeks of that astonishing trio...[169]

THE FATHER OF MODERN SPORT

In an editorial on "The decadence of Cricket" the dilettante approach to the game is condemned:

The carpet knights who now do battle for fashionable clubs are indeed well contented if "play" is called at half-past twelve instead of eleven o'clock. Instead of a plain and substantial luncheon of half-an-hour an interval of twice that time is by no means infrequent for the sumptuous repast which now has to be prepared and instead of getting at once to work another delay has to be made to allow the player the luxury of a cigar.[170]

A serious threat to cricket is seen in the pastime of lawn tennis ("a sport it is not"), an "effeminate amusement" offering the opportunity of "those pleasing little social amenities sure to occur when the players happen to be of opposite sexes". The attitude was perhaps partly conditioned by a certain resentment that while Alcock was in the process of making the Oval a national sports centre, across the river MCC was launching a new sport, the establishment of its Tennis Committee in 1875, preceding by a couple of years the extension of the All England Croquet Club to embrace lawn tennis:

...an increasing tendency to seduce from the practising nets the boys and youths who ought in years to come, to recruit the ranks of the batsmen and bowlers at our public and other schools.

At Harrow, where a long and noble tradition has made cricket the one serious business of life, the danger has been recognised and lawn tennis is strictly forbidden. At Eton, on the other hand, courts abound, and though it may perhaps be rather an unfair inference, there is last years defeat at Lord's as the inevitable result.

The authorities at The Oval where cricket has always been the first and only thought, have with prudence refused to encourage its rival in any way, and it has been a great surprise to many that the Marylebone Club, the head and front of our national game, has gone so far out of its sphere as not only to allow but really to encourage lawn tennis on a ground that has always been sacred to cricket.

"This evil" seems to be playing a role once played by cricket itself and indeed football in distracting medieval warriors from their archery practice. While it is recognised that local cricket clubs can derive an income from lawn tennis and there is no right to oppose lawn tennis in the abstract, it is strongly argued that it has no common interest with cricket, "the best and most manly of our out-door sports". Not for the first or only time is the emphasis placed on the "manliness" of the game and not for the first or only time does Alcock use his Editor's privilege to plug Harrow at the expense of Eton or The Oval at the expense of Lord's.

Other topics receiving regular and detailed coverage in the pages of *Cricket* at this time are the lessons that can be learned from the Australians, the importance of fielding and bowling, standards of umpiring, opportunities for saving time by switching from four- to six-ball overs,[171] the new (1883) Code of Laws, especially the new Law X on throwing. Australian cricket as a role model has long been accepted, few cricket followers remember overs of anything other than six balls and throwing is far more tightly relegated. Other esoteric schemes did not, however, come to pass - such as the time-saving probably baseball-inspired 'American Plan', proposed by the Philadelphia Club, which envisaged a game of four innings, each innings with three turns and teams switching places at the fall of every third wicket. The visiting team would have choice of innings, there would be 10-ball overs and a 25-run penalty for slow play.[172] The seeds of one or two twentieth century experiments can be seen there, but the Plan would have made cricket a totally different game and traditionalists will not regret the fact that it was given short shrift.

The introduction of the declaration into the game was keenly debated in *Cricket's* columns. John Shuter's action in deliberately throwing away wickets for tactical reasons is defended. It was a tactic previously used by Lord Harris and other captains to terminate an innings quickly:

> I quite agree with the suggestion I have seen from several correspondents that it would be well to introduce into the Laws some clause giving the right to terminate his innings at any period, if he should think fit.[173]

The follow-on law and methods of deciding the championship county before it settled down in 1890 to something approaching its present format were other subjects which kept the correspondence columns filled. Balance is retained, however by the introduction of the occasional humorous streak:

THE FATHER OF MODERN SPORT

Anybody will do to umpire. We can recall one country umpire who gave two wrong decisions in the course of a match, and sometimes more; for his conscience was active and his observation faulty, yet he was the stock umpire of the neighbourhood, for he kept a conveyance, and would always drive three players to an out match in which he was engaged.[174]

An article satirising the rise of socialism, reproduced from the *St James Gazette*, envisaged a time when Madame Tussaud's would become the Democratic Portrait Gallery and Lord's the People's Free Circus Arena. Stumps would be drawn at 7.30, the players having voted not to continue under the Eight Hours (Prevention of Hard Labour) Act.[175]

There are detailed profiles, portraits, "chats" and interviews with the leading players of the day, such as the one with K S Ranjitsinhji who details the differences between cricket in England and in India.[176] The increased statistical consciousness of the late nineteenth century is reflected by the contributions of F S Ashley-Cooper and his "At the Sign of the Wicket: Curiosities of First-Class Cricket".

The Editor was prepared to use the columns of the magazine to further his administration. Just as he had used the *Football Annual* to compile a list of football clubs, so he used *Cricket* to identify and list cricket clubs:

NOTICE TO SECRETARIES

The Editor is desirous of preparing for the use of cricketers generally a List of Cricket Clubs throughout the United Kingdom, with the names and addresses of their Secretaries. In order to make this as complete as possible he invites the co-operation of secretaries, and any assistance with a view to the completion of a reliable list will be highly appreciated.[177]

Thirty years before the Club Cricket Conference had a similar idea and long before the ECB was advertising itself "developing cricket from playground to Test arena", Alcock was covering a similar range in his magazine. Nor was this just a bright idea that was never fulfilled. A List of Secretaries of Principal Clubs appeared in November of the following year.[178]

A century before its distinguished successor the *Cricketer* had added the suffix *International* to its title, *Cricket* was covering the game on a global scale.

Australian and South African cricket were covered in some detail, as was inter-provincial cricket in Canada. Its circulation was world-wide and there was a carefully graduated pricing structure covering virtually every corner of the globe - 5/- in summer and 6/- for the year for the USA and Europe; 6/- and 7/6 for Australia, New Zealand and South America and 7/- and 8/9 for Borneo, Ceylon, China, India, Japan, Hong Kong, Siam and Zanzibar.

Much of what it reported was expatriate cricket from places where imperialists had established it, like Ceylon, and others, which would not be the first to spring to mind in a cricket context, like Lisbon, Valparaiso and Cairo where in early 1886 the 1st Battalion Royal Fusiliers, the Second Battalion Duke of Cornwall's Light Infantry, the 19th (Prince of Wales's Own) Hussars and the Citizens of Cairo were involved in fairly regular encounters.[179] In 1887 a Canadian team toured England and there was a reciprocal tour of an Irish team to Niagara Falls in late 1888.[180]

The seriousness of some of the matches is questionable, such as "England v Scotland" in Shanghai in October 1883 when "the only excitement was whether the 'canny Scots' would avoid an innings defeat" (they didn't), but the occasion was enlivened by a "sprinkling of ladies who, as a rule, do not exhibit much interest in Shanghai, but who seem thoroughly to appreciate the tea and cake".[181]

The tour of the Parsee cricketers of 1886, which Alcock had organised, was covered, including the farewell address of their captain, D H Patel:

It was not with the object of gaining victories that we made the voyage to England, but we desired to pay homage to the centre and home of a noble game, and we desired to learn some useful lessons in its play...

...we Parsees are among the most loyal subjects of the Queen of England and Empress of India...

are unanimous in favour of British rule for they consider it best, not only for themselves, but for all the different communities of India.[182]

There was perhaps an ulterior motive. The Parsees were looking for some financial support to help them acquire a plot of ground for a gymkhana.

Prior to the 1888-89 tour of South Africa, *Cricket* produced a map for the guidance of readers showing Cape Colony, Basutoland, Transvaal and

Zululand and subsequently carried very detailed reports of the matches. Printing technology moved with the times and about the same time photography was introduced.

Not all overseas cricket was expatriate, however, and not all was of the standard expected on the playing fields of counties, clubs and schools. A correspondent from Nicaragua wrote:

> I have instituted your favorite old game, cricket, among the natives, but they are such a lazy race that half-an-hour of it completely does them up. We call ourselves the Anglo-Nicaraguan cricket team and I have no doubt you would manage to put us all out in half-an-hour, provided you escaped from your innings alive, as the native bowling is very uncertain.[183]

The worldwide interest continues with scorecards of Madras v Combined Natives, Suva v Fiji Bicycle League and, also in Fiji, Professions v Commerce and Old Residents v New Residents[184] and, perhaps more seriously and significantly, the power struggle between the Australian Cricket Council and the Melbourne Cricket Club.[185]

That conflict, however, was confined to the debating chambers and communication channels of the bodies concerned and as far as is known, was unarmed and free from physical violence. By contrast, a report from Samoa[186] bore the news that:

> Disturbances are reported from Tutuila where the natives continued to play a match against the king's order. A half-caste official essayed to stop the game, but the natives rejected his interference and brought forth their guns.

The notion of cricket as a global game, transcending time and space, is colourfully presented, not without a little hyperbole, in the Christmas Day issue of 1884:

> A Christmas number of CRICKET! And why not? Like Shakespeare, our national game is not of an age, it is for all time. Its dominion is one over which the sun never sets. It has no seasons, never a day but the bat is meeting ball somewhere in one latitude or another. While cricketers here are doomed to a period of inaction, chilled to the marrow by a pitiless wind which searches through the best of wraps, and penetrates into every cranny,

beneath the shadow of the Southern Cross the game is being busily followed under the genial influence of a clear atmosphere and the powerful rays of a sun such as we poor benighted creatures in the fatherland read about but very seldom see.

Notwithstanding cricket's worldwide appeal, however, there were some areas of the globe, rather nearer to home, where cricket was unknown, still less understood:

Mr Alcock, the secretary of the Surrey Club, sent Prince Christian, at Kissengen, a wire letting him know the result of play in the test match between England and Australia. The telegram ran "England, 576; Australia 220 - five wickets." When the Prince had the telegram posted on a tree for the benefit of English visitors, a Dutch official who knew English took the telegram to mean that war had broken out between England and the Transvaal, and this was the news of the fatalities in the first battle. He rushed off and told the Roumanian Minister of Finance, who was staying there, and was on his way to England to negotiate a loan for his state, and therefore heard the news with the greater alarm. The Minister told somebody else, and so the report spread, getting more terrible every moment. Crowds gathered round the fateful telegram and discussed it, and the proprietor of the Hotel de Russie breathlessly informed his guests that war had broken out; he knew it was true because the Roumanian Minister had heard it by telegram from his Government. A local paper bettered this in the afternoon by informing its public that owing to "amazing indiscretion of illustrious personage", a telegram had been placed before the public which revealed the fatal results of the first encounter.[187]

As well as being a distinguished journalist himself, Alcock was a mentor and adviser to younger practitioners. Writing some fifty years later Sir Home Gordon in his *Background of Cricket*[188] acknowledges the debt he owes to Alcock as well as revealing him as a shrewd and cost-conscious editor - 'canny', as they would say in his native Sunderland:

My cricket journalism began directly I left Eton. Charles Alcock, the kindly secretary at The Oval ran a magazine called Cricket. He invited me to contribute paragraphs for which he never suggested payment, but revised with drastic skill, thus offering me tuition in how to deal with topics.

The magazine had several changes of office, moving its headquarters in 1885 from 17 Paternoster Square behind St Paul's Cathedral to 41 St Andrew's House in Doctors Commons and later to 168 Upper Thames Street. At the time of Alcock's death in February 1907, there had been 741 issues of Cricket; F S Ashley-Cooper took over as Editor and by 1911 there had been 889. A 'New Series' began in 1912 under the editorship of J N Pentelow, though the Byron quotation "Together join'd in cricket's manly toil" remains, as does the Shakespearean "The abstract and brief chronicles of the time" under 'Pavilion Gossip' and the sub-title "A weekly record of the game", so there was not very much that was actually "new". For a while, although remaining *Cricket, A Weekly Record of the Game* on the cover, inside it became *Rugby Football and Cricket* and was issued weekly in the winter as well as the summer. Bizarrely there is no rugby football in it. After two years of the "New Series", it was superseded by the *World of Cricket* and A C McLaren had joined Pentelow as Editor. The new magazine was short lived, being not alone in being brought to an end by the First World War in November 1914. Six and a half years later, on 30 April 1921, Sir Pelham Warner launched the *Cricketer* which continues today as the *Cricketer International*. It is beyond argument that their ancestry was Charles Alcock and Cricket.

Football

The launch of *Football* was advertised in *Cricket* in May 1882. It would contain:

> results of all the principal matches throughout the kingdom, with special reports of the more important, and in addition will have interesting articles in connection with the sport.[189]

The Northern clubs and their veiled professionalism were beginning to make an impact on the FA Cup which would never again be won by a purely amateur team. As a spectator sport, it was making rapid strides and while it had not yet caught up cricket in popular appeal, it was well on the way to so doing. The popularity and commercial success of

Cricket clearly persuaded Alcock there was a market opportunity. Compared with its sister paper, however, it was short-lived. From the content, it is not clear why the magazine did not last longer. It was jointly edited by Alcock and 'Pa' Jackson at the same time as the latter was founding the Corinthians. Possibly the pressure of Alcock's other responsibilities was a factor, possibly competition from the *Referee*, according to Jackson, the best Sunday paper for sporting news,[190] but within six months, Jackson was sole editor and the magazine became *Pastimes* with a wider remit than football. At the same time he was diversifying his journalistic interests, joining H M Oliver and T T Prime in the ownership of *Midland Athletics*.

The intentions of *Football* were clear enough:

> The want of a Journal specially representing the interests of our National Winter Game has long been an admitted fact, and as Football is becoming more popular every year, the necessity for such a periodical becomes more apparent…
>
> It is proposed to allot every week a certain portion of space to each district, and as the reports of matches taking place in these divisions will be collected and forwarded with notes thereon, by responsible gentlemen connected with the various Associations and resident in the respective neighbourhoods, the Editors can promise a full and complete list of all the principal contests throughout the United Kingdom.[191]

The same erudition which characterised *Cricket* is apparent here. The masthead contains a quotation from Martial (Folle decet pueros ludere folle senes[192]) probably more comprehensible to public school boys than Northern professionals and the contents are topical and informative.

The equivalent of 'Pavilion Gossip' is 'Stray Kicks' and editorial policy is clearly set out. It is not dissimilar from that which featured in early issues of the *Sportsman*:

> We frequently have letters complaining that some reports of matches are incorrect. I would strongly impress on our contributors the necessity for omitting all personal remarks from their reports, which should be written impartially, rather favouring the opposing side than otherwise. FOOTBALL is intended to be a true record of matches played, and if correspondents do not strictly adhere to the facts they detract considerably from the value of our

journal, besides perhaps perpetuating an ill feeling which their opponents would otherwise easily have forgotten.[193]

FOOTBALL is open for the ventilation of grievances (real or supposed) in connection with the game; but we do not bind ourselves to any line of argument adopted by our correspondents. We like to hear both sides of the question.[194]

The first issue contains a retrospective view of the 1881-82 season in both the association and rugby games and in subsequent issues umpires and referees, rough play, gate money, county football are all subjected to the editorial pen. The cult of celebrity was for the following century, but serious injuries to players are recorded with good wishes for a speedy recovery. 'Midland Meanderings' was a regular feature and there are reports on activities in Scotland, Sheffield and the Universities.

It was well received. One correspondent wrote:

You have succeeded in producing a "Society" football journal fit to place on any drawing-room table, where it would be instructive and ornamental.[195]

There was a lively correspondence column with complaints *inter alia* about admission charges at the Oval. A shilling was not begrudged for international matches or Cup Finals but for Old Wykehamists v Old Westminsters or Clapham Rovers v Notts Forest, sixpence was quite enough. One correspondent was unfortunate enough to travel on the same train as the victorious Blackburn Olympic side and their followers after the 1883 Cup Final:

...there was a plentiful supply of whiskey with which "the Cup" was frequently filled. The players were decorated with light blue ribbon and a blue flag was displayed at the carriage window. The Cup was exhibited at every station, and altogether had "a rare time of it". What a fortunate thing that Challenge Cups are not endowed with senses.

Times were changing and while Olympic were congratulated on winning the trophy, there were a couple of snide comments about their week's training before the Final as well as that of Blackburn Rovers and Darwen before the Lancashire Cup Final, though possibly from Jackson, rather than Alcock:

We shall soon hear of special trainers and doctors attached to the staff of each of the principal northern clubs.

Surely our pastime was never intended to degenerate into a contest for which three weeks' professional training at the seaside is necessary![196]

It was in the columns of *Football*[197] that the establishment of a new Association Club was announced. It would play only the strongest matches and its fixtures would be played principally on Wednesdays. There was some probability that it would amalgamate with the old 'Wanderers' and so a club historical in football annals would be revived. N L Jackson, Hon Sec of the London Football Association would arrange fixtures some of which would be with strong provincial clubs. The announcement does not mention the Corinthians by name, but this is clearly a reference to the foundation of the club which was to play a significant role on the football stage well into the following century.

The magazine and the 1882-83 season came to an end with a poem by Isa Craig:

> Stick to the rules of the game
> Whether losing or winning
> Fair play and no malice
> Will keep the ball spinning.[198]

There was no suggestion that it would not continue.

Football, The Association Game

Much of the wisdom propounded over the years in the *Football Annual* is distilled in *Football, the Association Game* published in 1890, then amalgamated in The "Oval" Series of Matches in 1894 with Charles J B Marriott's *The Rugby Union Game*.

The book is less historically orientated than *Football, Our Winter Game* and deals with the formation, growth and progress of the association, then moves on to "modern football" and gives general hints on play and specific hints for the goalkeeper, full-backs, half-backs and forwards.

It was part of a series dealing with a whole range of sports, including cricket, lawn tennis, rackets, golf, hockey, sailing, swimming, boxing, wrestling, fencing, cycling, athletics and gymnastics - all part of a brave new world of sport and sporting competition of which Alcock had been one of the major creators.

Surrey Cricket: Its History and Associations

If Charles Alcock had done nothing else with his life, this publication, referred to in his correspondence simply as 'the Surrey book', would have stood as a suitable memorial to him. Yet it was the fact that he did so much with his life that he was able to write six of its eighteen chapters under his own name and contribute to, advise on and edit the others. The volume runs to over 500 pages, is well illustrated, has ample supporting statistics and a detailed and comprehensive index. Alcock's own experience enabled him to contribute chapters on the history of the Club, ground development, Surrey captains, the Australians at the Oval and football at the Oval. In addition, he persuaded historian and statistician F S Ashley-Cooper to write two chapters - on Surrey cricket from 1598 to 1845 and 'Cricket Curiosities', Surrey captains John Shuter and D L A Jephson to produce a few words and collaborated with his President on school and village green cricket.

While the book contains a few minor historical inaccuracies, it remains an appropriate monument to a county where, as the chapter on Early Surrey Cricket is at pains to point out, cricket precedes that at Hambledon by a hundred years and more, and to a man who was largely responsible not only for putting that county on the map, but for redrawing the whole map.

The book, published by Longman's in 1902 and still referred to at The Oval as the 'Old Testament' is Alcock's main literary achievement. His correspondence with E V B Christian who produced the chapters on 'Surrey v England' and 'Extraneous Matches at the Oval' survives and reveals Alcock as a well-organised, deadline-conscious Editor keen to have his pound of flesh on time and at minimum cost:

Things have got rather behind as I have had two nasty bronchial attacks which have spoiled my work completely. I am waiting longingly for a day or two of mild weather.

Would you be prepared to do one chapter for £5 or the two for £10? They will have to be quite lengthy and the pay, I know, is not attractive.

I want to get the book out as early as possible as I can in the summer and the earlier you could let me have the copy the better. If it would save you trouble to see me here on your way to the City I am generally here at 10 o'clock and would be so on Friday if you sent me a note to Hazelwood Richmond Surrey to say you were coming.[199]

Diplomatically, yet forcefully, he got things done:

No desire to rush you. But printers are very anxious to have pages back as early as possible. I should be glad therefore to have them returned tonight if practicable.[200]

Although jointly edited by Alcock and Lord Alverstone - at the time President of the Club and Lord Chief Justice of England - who contributed a chapter, it would be a mistake to assume a 50-50 division of labour. Unsurprisingly, despite not being in the best of health when the book was being prepared, it was Alcock who undertook the lion's share of the work.

When, asked to look at the manuscript of the 'Extraneous Matches' chapter, Alverstone commented in a marginal note: "This is a good chapter but the gentlemen and players matches should be further searched for interesting events and curiosities", Alcock, in passing this on to Christian, effectively advises him that the instruction is to be disregarded. "I merely send this for your information," he said. "I have sent on Chapter to Longman". There is no doubt who is in charge.

Revealing himself once again as a man of vision, in sending Christian his cheque and thanking him for his contribution, Alcock says: "I am not without hope that some day it may be possible to have full scores of Surrey matches from the first". A hundred years on, that hope has been metamorphosed into an expectation, but it still has to be fulfilled.

The book was reviewed at some length in the *Times Literary Supplement*[201] by the Hon Robert Lyttelton, one of several Lytteltons with an Eton and Cambridge pedigree. He was an occasional cricketer with I Zingari and represented the University at tennis, rather than cricket.[202] The review is mildly critical of Ashley-Cooper's contention that Surrey rather than

Hambledon is the real cradle of cricket, not on the grounds of chronology (Surrey cricket was demonstrably earlier) but on the grounds of the quality of play. That apart, however, it concentrates on regurgitating the contents rather than informed criticism though it is complimentary to the extent that in this "substantial volume":

> Lord Alverstone and Mr Alcock and other contributors have produced a book of the greatest interest to all cricketers, both old and young

and

> Lord Alverstone and Mr Alcock are to be heartily congratulated for this book, which is most admirably edited and it is a most interesting volume.

Other Publications

Improvements in photography gave rise to two parallel publications in 1895-96, *Famous Cricketers and Cricket Grounds* and *Famous Footballers and Athletes*. Both were first published in the *News of the World*, one cricketer, cricket ground, footballer or athlete at a time, though there were also a few team photographs. They were then amalgamated into what were little more than picture books, albeit well-presented ones, with minimal and often inaccurate biographical detail. His *Cricket Stories: Wise and Otherwise*, published in 1901 is a series of light-hearted anecdotes, Shakespearean quotations applied to cricket and material previously used as fillers in *Cricket* and elsewhere.

Alcock also had a number of contributions to sporting literature in publications where his name did not appear on the title page. For instance, he contributed to the chapter on cricket to the *Victoria County History of Surrey*, was responsible for that on football in the equivalent production for Essex and wrote on 'The Principal Clubs of the Past' in *The Book of Football* published in 1906. He contributed an essay on *Cricket under Queen Victoria* for the Diamond Jubilee Edition of the *Illustrated Sporting and Dramatic News*, produced an article on The Oval for *Ludgate Monthly* in August 1891, covered the success of the Corinthians in the *Handbook of Athletic Sports* and also wrote the Preface for a small book which appeared in 1890 under the title of *Old Cricket and Cricketers* by H H Montgomery DD, Bishop of Tasmania. The connection with Alcock was that Montgomery had been Vicar of Kennington before promotion in the church's hierarchy saw him move to a post on the other side of the world. The Preface is more than notional, more than merely using a name to boost sales, and Alcock's erudition is apparent as he deals with what might have been the game's ancestor in the middle ages, the reference in John Derrick's History of Guildford, the development of the game through Hambledon, the White Conduit Club and MCC, the involvement of Surrey and Kent, cricket's use as a vehicle for gambling in the eighteenth century and its "rescue" by the public schools. With an allusion to Dickens and a reference to Surrey's pre-eminence, he concludes on a topical note:

'Recent legislation has, however, given the power to a captain to terminate his innings in the last stage of a match and I am going to exercise the privilege in the present instance to declare mine at an end.'

The *Cricket Calendar*, a small, pocket-sized publication, was taken over by Alcock from G Kelly King shortly before the start of the 1871 season. In fact, Alcock comments in his Preface, dated 3 April, that he assumed control on 25 March and had ten days to collect and arrange matches for insertion, as well as transferring them to the hands of the printers. It comes as no surprise that he did it. Except for the occasional italicised historical note, the *Calendar* ignores cricket retrospective on the grounds that it has all been recorded elsewhere and concentrates on fixtures and lists of players, clubs and officials, while at the same time making provision for the owner to record personal performances. Alcock and Jackson preceded their joint Editorship of *Football* with the *National Football Calendar* for 1881. Few copies have survived.

Surrey's Centenary publication[203] pays tribute to Alcock's "tremendous influence on the Club's affairs" and refers to his being "instrumental in originating the tours of the Australian sides", then adds almost as an afterthought, "He was also Secretary of the Football Association, the slower tempo of affairs in those days permitting this dual service." Even allowing for the shadow of the Second World War, that last remark verges on generational prejudice and chronological snobbery and is certainly misleading. The tempo of affairs may have been slower for some, but hardly for Charles Alcock whose industry was such that it is arguable that he contributed more to the administration of both Surrey County Cricket Club and the Football Association than any of his successors in either body as well as writing and editing a substantial body of sporting literature.[204]

REFERENCES

142. *Field* 24 November 1866

143. 27 February 1907

144. Bettesworth *Chats on the Cricket Field* p 20

145. *Sportsman* 12 August 1865

146. *Sportsman* 14 July 1866

147. *Sportsman* 20 July 1871

148. *Football Annual* 1881

149. *Football Annual* 1881

150. *Football Annual* 1882

151. Jackson *Association Football* p 145

152. *Journal of the Cricket Society* Autumn 1979

153. October 1872

154. *Cricket* 30 April 1890

155. *Cricket* 29 March 1906

156. Bowen *Cricket: A History of its Growth* p119

157. *Cricket* 17 May 1882

158. *Cricket* 10 May 1882

159. *Cricket* 27 March 1890

160. Frontispiece to Read *Annals of Cricket*

161 *Cricket* 10 May 1882

162. *Cricket* 22 April 1886

163. *Cricket* 29 April 1886

164. *Cricket* 7 June 1888

165. *Cricket* 29 December 1892

166. *Cricket* 28 March 1895

167. *Cricket* 11 April 1895

168. *Cricket* 10 May 1882

169. *Cricket* 7 September 1899
170. *Cricket* 22 June 1882
171. *Cricket* 28 April 1887
172. *Cricket* 17 April 1890
173. *Cricket* 9 June 1887
174. *Cricket* 19 July 1888 quoting from 'The Badminton Magazine'
175. *Cricket* 19 June 1890
176. *Cricket* 18 April 1895
177. *Cricket* 16 September 1886
178. *Cricket* 24 November 1887
179. *Cricket* 25 February 1886
180. *Cricket* 20 September 1888
181. *Cricket* 28 February 1884
182. *Cricket* 19 August 1886
183. *Cricket* 28 October 1886
184. *Cricket* 26 January 1899
185. *Cricket* 15 September 1898
186. *Cricket* 30 April 1891
187. *Cricket* 7 September 1899
188. p 36
189. *Cricket* 1 June 1882
190. Jackson *Sporting Days and Sporting Ways* p 67
191. *Football* 4 October 1882
192. It is good for boys and men to play ball games. Follis is a fourth declension noun, meaning a leather bag and, by extension, a pair of bellows and, presumably, a ball. A further meaning is a purse, so the line could, with a little imagination, mean that it is good for boys and men to play for money - a topic not without interest in the 1880s
193. *Football* 24 January 1883
194. *Football* 1 November 1882
195. *Football* 11 October 1882
196. *Football* 29 March 1883
197. *Football* 4 October 1882
198. *Football* 11 April 1883
199. Letter from Alcock to E V B Christian 20 February 1901
200. Letter from Alcock to E V B Christian 20 March 1902

201. Letter from Alcock to E V B Christian 20 June 1902
202. Bailey, Thorne, Wynne-Thomas *Who's Who of Cricketers* p 640
203 and 204. *Surrey County Cricket Club Centenary* 1845-1945 p134

CHAPTER 5

ALCOCK AND THE FOOTBALL ASSOCIATION

CHARLES ALCOCK'S FOOTBALLING career was a natural progression from playing for his club, his county, his region and finally his country. Such a path is far from unique and has been trod by many a sportsman and sportswoman en route to the ultimate sporting achievement of playing at international level. Where Alcock's route differs from the traditional one is on the negative side, that he did not precede it by representing his school, but on the positive side, that he not only trod the path, but created it for himself and others to follow. So, his playing and administrative careers run almost parallel in that he founded the Wanderers Club and was its first Honorary Secretary and captain, he launched the FA Cup and captained the first team to win it and he instigated and played international football. The organisation, playing and recording of sports are three separate functions, normally undertaken by three separate bodies. Alcock did the lot.

He was not one of the founding fathers of the Football Association, but his elder brother was. After two years he replaced John on the Committee; five years later he became honorary secretary, then paid Secretary from 1886. On his retirement from that position in 1890 until his death in 1907, he was a Vice-President, so just as there were always Starkadders at Stella Gibbons' Cold Comfort Farm, so for almost the first half-century of the FA's existence, there was always an Alcock involved in its administration.

The Football Association was established in 1863, two years before the Salvation Army, and although the two organisations were to develop rather different histories, both have their roots in the public school tradition of muscular and militant Christianity in which John and Charles Alcock and the founding fathers were nurtured.

'Mob' Football

Although now completely international, even at senior club level, and a reflection of modern multiculturalism, in its early days football was tribal and local with a wide variety of rules and customs. It is after all a simple and easily conceived game comprising two teams attempting to propel an object at a target. The means of propulsion, the size and nature of the target, the number of players and the ways of preventing the opposing team reaching their objective provide scope for debate and disagreement which evolve into different versions of the game with different rules. Some form of football was played in China at the time of the Han Dynasty, the Romans had a game called 'harpastum'[205] and by the Middle Ages there were various versions serving as a bone-crunching outlet for rivalries between towns and villages.[206] It was from time to time subject to prohibition, partly because of its violence and partly because it distracted the participants from more useful pursuits such as archery.

There were parallel prohibitions in Scotland. An Act of James I's Parliament in 1424 provided that 'no man play at the football, under the pain of fifty shillings to the lord of the land, or to the sherrif in his neglect.'[207]

By Tudor times in England the game was more "a friendlie kind of fyghte than a play or recreation - a bloody and murthering practice than a felowly sport or pastime"[208] and in 1660, Bristol magistrates felt obliged to ban a number of activities associated with Shrove Tuesday celebrations, namely, "the ancient sports of the season - cock-throwing, dog-tossing and football-playing in the streets".[209] It was all ad hoc and disorganised and possibly had more to do with fertility ritual than with the organised game which was to emerge two centuries later. At Corfe, for instance, it was the custom for the ball, a common fertility symbol, to be supplied by the member most recently married.[210]

Organised Football

Popular mythology is that what James Walvin and others have called "the people's game" was originally a violent, disorganised affair until taken over by the public schools in the nineteenth century, cleaned up and given back to the people. Like most generalisations, that is largely true, but not the whole truth.

As well as its 'folk' origins, organised football has some of its roots in the soil of public schools and William Hornman, Headmaster of Winchester College (the oldest of the public schools and the one with the longest footballing history) in a 1519 publication *Vulgaria* refers to sport at the College and says 'We wyll playe with a ball full of wynde', perhaps an appropriate precursor of the FA. Various codes developed, largely in the public schools and the toss of a coin at the start of a match was often not only for choice of ends, but to determine under which set of rules the game would be played. At a time when the game was more casual and its adherents more versatile, such a choice was frequently between the rugby and association codes.[211]

By the early nineteenth century, the game seems to have been played very little. Joseph Strutt in *The Sports and Pastimes of the People of England* in 1831 says:

> Foot-ball is so called because the ball is driven about with the feet instead of the hands. It was formerly much in vogue among the common people of England, though of late years it seems to have fallen into disrepute and is but little practised. I cannot pretend to determine at what period the game of foot-ball originated; it does not, however, to the best of my recollection appear among the popular exercises before the reign of Edward III, and then, in 1349, it was prohibited by a public edict; not, perhaps from any particular objection to the sport in itself, but because it co-operated, with other favourite amusements, to impede the progress of archery.[212]

There was a body of organised football outside the public schools, not least in the Sheffield area, and John Goulstone argues that:

> one could quite convincingly trace soccer's main ancestral line before 1867 back to Sheffield in 1857 - and earlier still to football practised in south Yorkshire, particularly in the game's Pennine strongholds around Penistone and Holmfirth.[213]

Developments in Sheffield, however, cannot be entirely divorced from the game in the public schools, the Sheffield Foot Ball Club owing its origins in 1855 to a group of Old Harrovians,[214] although there is evidence that Eton had some involvement too.[215] J C Shaw, joint founder of the Hallam Football Club and subsequently President of the Sheffield Football Association, had been born in Penistone. He met Alcock at the first 'Sheffield v London' fixture. It was a meeting of significance. Although its origins owed something to Harrow School, the Sheffield Association had developed independently of its sister association in London and it was not until 1877 that the Rules were amalgamated.

The Alcock brothers were founder-members of Forest Football Club, "the first formal club of its kind", though it was in fact pre-dated by the Sheffield Club, established in 1855 which had independently drawn up its own set of rules in 1857, and forerunner of the Wanderers Club which was to dominate the FA Cup in its early years.[216]

Foundation of the Football Association

On Monday 26 October 1863 at the Freemason's Tavern in Great Queen Street, London, representatives of the leading clubs met and resolved "That Mr Pember do take the Chair" and "That the Clubs represented at this meeting now form themselves into an Association to be called 'The Football Association'. E C Morley of Barnes was appointed Honorary Secretary. The clubs and their representatives on what football historians have come to regard as a significant date and venue were:

Barnes - E C Morley and P D Gregory
Blackheath - F H Moore and F W Campbell
Blackheath School - W H Gordon
Crusaders - H T Steward
Crystal Palace - F Day
Forest - J F Alcock and A W Mackenzie
Kensington School - W J Mackintosh
No Names, Kilburn - Arthur Pember
Perceval House, Blackheath - G W Shillingford
Surbiton - H Bell
War Office - E Wawn

These were rough and ready beginnings and it would be unrealistic to claim that the fledgling association was at this stage representative of all areas of the game. There was no provincial interest and, although the participants had a public school background, the public schools themselves were not included, nor was Cambridge University despite the steps they had already taken towards a standardised code of laws. Some 'unattached' players were present as was B F Hartshorne of Charterhouse but as an observer.[217] The captains of the major schools were asked for their support, but it took a few years for the Association to bed down and become a representative body by which time Blackheath were already on their way to establishing a different game and Charles Alcock was on his way to being a major influence principally on association football, but also on the Blackheath offshoot.

Towards a Uniform Code of Laws

The establishment of the Football Association was in part a response to pressure to establish a uniform code of Laws for the game of football. "Mob Football" was lawless in every sense of the term, the public schools all had their own versions as did those areas outside the public schools where there were attempts at organised football. Such variations did not matter as long as the game remained "internal", but if the clubs and schools wished to play against one other, then there was a need for agreement and compromise.

Rules were in vogue both in sport and politics and the origins of those for a number of sporting organisations, in areas such as coursing, golf and archery, can be traced to the 1860s. The Queensberry Rules for boxing were introduced in 1867 and the first Geneva Conventions signed in 1864.

Strutt gives a brief outline of the rules of the pre-eighteenth century game:

> When a match at foot-ball is made, two parties, each containing an equal number of competitors, take the field, and stand between two goals, placed at the distance of eighty or an hundred yards the one from the other. The goal is usually made with two sticks driven into the ground, about two or three feet apart. The ball, which is commonly made of a blown bladder, and cased with

leather, is delivered in the midst of the ground, and the object of each party is to drive it through the goal of their antagonists, which being achieved the game is won. The abilities of the performers are best displayed in attacking and defending the goals; and hence the pastime was more frequently called a goal at foot-ball than a game at foot-ball.[218]

When the Surrey Club formulated its Rules, it was more concerned with who could participate than what should happen on the field of play:

1. The Club to consist only of such gentlemen as are members of the Surrey Cricket Club, the Surrey Paragon Club, the South London Club and the Union Club.
2. That a subscription of five shillings by any one of the above-named gentlemen shall entitle him to all the privileges of the 'Surrey Foot-Ball Club'. That the money so subscribed shall be appropriated to the defrayal of the expenses of the club, namely the cost of the balls and ropes, and the payment of a person who shall keep the balls &c in proper condition. The members shall dine together at the end of the season, and any surplus of the subscriptions which may be then be in hand, after the payment of all expenses, shall be applied to such dinner.
3. That the days for practice be (weather permitting) every Wednesday and Saturday in the afternoon, commencing the first week in October, and continuing until the last week in April in each year, the play to begin at three o'clock.
4. That the sides shall consist of not more than twenty-two each; but if that number of members shall not be in attendance, then of any smaller number, to be arranged by those present.
5. That wilful kicking shall not be allowed.
6. That the ball be tossed up in the centre of the ground, and the game be determined in favour of the side which shall first kick the ball over the 'goal rope' of their opponents. Should the ball be kicked over the fence on either side of the ground, then the ball, when regained, shall be tossed up in the centre of the ground in a line with the place where it went over.

The first attempt at codification of the Rules with the emphasis on playing rather than membership was at Cambridge University in 1846 by Messrs H de Winton and J C Thring when deliberations with the major public schools (timed bizarrely at seven hours 55 minutes) produced the Rules which with few amendments became the Association Rules and formed the basis of those of the game which came to be known as association football.[219] No known copy survives, but it is a reasonable assumption that they would not be very different from those issued sixteen years later by Mr Thring, under the heading of 'The Simplest Game' when he was an assistant master at Uppingham.

They were as follows:

1. A goal is scored whenever the ball is forced through the goal and under the bar, except it be thrown by the hand.
2. Hands may be used only to stop the ball and place it on the ground before the feet.
3. Kicks must be aimed only at the ball.
4. A player may not kick at the ball whilst it is in the air.
5. No Tripping Up or Heel kicking is allowed.
6. Whenever the ball is kicked beyond the side-flags, it must be returned by the player who kicked it, from the spot where it passed the flag-line, in a straight line towards the middle of the ground.
7. When the ball is kicked behind the line of goal, it shall be kicked off from that line by one of the side whose goal it is.
8. No opposite player may stand within six paces of the kicker when he is kicking off.
9. A player is "out of play" immediately he is in front of the ball, and he must return behind the ball as soon as possible. If the ball is kicked by his own side past a player, he may not touch it, kick it, nor advance until one of the other side has first kicked it or one of his own side, having followed it up, has been able, when in front of him, to kick it.
10. No charging is allowed when a player is out of play - i.e. immediately the ball is behind him.[220]

The Sheffield Association had its own rules, based partly on the Cambridge ones, but also incorporating Etonian and Harrovian elements. There were differences between the Sheffield Association laws and those of the London Association and in a number of instances the Sheffield ones have prevailed. These include the free-kick, the corner-kick and the throw-in being taken by the side opposite to the one which put the ball out of play.

As early as 1859, *Bell's Life* was running correspondence notionally on the desirability of uniformity, but in practice providing newspaper space for the debate between public school factions and between the game as played at Rugby school and that which was to become the association game. In response to Floreat Rugboea and Juvenis, An Old Wykhamist wrote:

> Anxiously as I desire to see the day when all the great schools of this country may be bound by the same common laws of football; as now is the case in the sister game of cricket; still, sir, I cannot but regard any attempt to give the Rugby rules a wider field of act as at once an ill-advised measure and a step in the wrong direction..[221]

A joint committee was proposed and while Rugbeians accused Etonians of a "funky spirit" because of their wish to outlaw shinning and hacking, Red Jersey concluded that it was almost impossible to arrive at a uniform set of rules and the debate became personal and more to do with inter-school rivalries than a positive attempt at harmonisation:

> The manner in which he attempts to raise Rugby's reputation at Winchester's expense is unworthy of any public schoolman.[222]

In practice what the correspondents of *Bell's Life* were notionally seeking was already in place and had been for thirteen years and, in any case, the Editor had had enough:

> We have received many other letters on this subject from public schoolmen, but they are so mixed up with abuse of each other that we consider them better unpublished and the correspondence closed. The inference seems to be that it would undoubtedly be unadvisable for different schools to meet at this game. We should have seen with pleasure some proposition for a generalisation of the rules, but there seems to be no disposition to concession on either side.

There was, however, at least one externally generated attempt to have the laws of the game harmonised and notwithstanding the Editor's closure of the correspondence, the following week, he published the following letter from Fred Lillywhite:

> Mr EDITOR - It is my intention to publish in the next edition of the Guide to Cricketers the laws and sports of all the athletic games which are enjoyed

in this country. Among them, of course, will be football: therefore if Eton and Rugby, as well as colleges and schools will form themselves into a committee and arrange that one code of laws could be acknowledged throughout the world, it would be a great benefit to all, as in the case with cricket.

It was naïvely optimistic and premature to assume that what obtained in the long-established game cricket could be achieved within a few weeks in the infant sport of football. Eventually Lillywhite had to content himself with the Eton Rules and advertising "the largest stock of footballs in England".

Throughout the early 1860s the correspondence columns of the *Field* were filled with verbose rhetoric about the respective merits and demerits of the various codes and anecdotes which pointed to the need for uniformity. One of several letters from 'Goal-stick' is not untypical and reflects the mood of the age in football circles:

SIR - A subject once warmly taken up in your columns has been allowed to die without any satisfactory conclusion. I refer to the game of football. You must remember it was shown there was a great lack of uniformity in the rules of football - Eton, Rugby, Winchester and Harrow were all different, and that on that account it became hard at the universities or elsewhere to play a match where the players has each been used to a different game. There can surely be no reason why football, like cricket, should not have its fixed rules.

…A striking instance of this may have been observed at a "Harvest-home" …where the gentlemen present eagerly mixed with their uncouth brethren, and played the best game they could. Gentlemen from Eton, Harrow, Leamington, Cambridge &c were present, and seemed to the best of his power to play his own game. Occasionally, some scientific player would bully the ball through a mighty labyrinth of iron-studded boots and corduroy trowsers [sic] in a manner wonderful to behold, only to be rewarded for his trouble and wounds by beholding on issue from the mêlée a flagrant "cool kick" grating to his feelings…

It may perhaps be objected that football is never played except at schools, and that a game of football would create as great a sensation in a country village as a game of marbles or a-whoop would be in the quadrangle at Eton College. Such I think would not be found to be the case. Cricket we see warmly taken up in some villages during the summer months; and I think that the gentlemen of any parish need only show the way, and football would be embraced with equal warmth during the autumn and winter. Football is in the spring of its existence for this year, and we trust it will not see its winter without a modern Solon rising to form a code of laws for it.[223]

It is quite possible such a code existed and was ignored. There was a club called Dingley Dell whose name may owe more to *The Pickwick Papers* than any specific geographical location. They played few fixtures (those they did play were mainly against Surbiton), were not among the founder members of the Football Association, but they were, according to the *Field* "the best club of the season, apart from the public schools".[224] They did, however, have a set of rules, based on a ten-a-side game, which the *Field* saw as "comprising the principal rules, and omitting all the peculiarities of the different systems",[225] leading the newspaper to suggest that:

> It would be a favour to the lovers of football if they would publish a copy of their rules, since they seem to be admirably adapted to form the basis of a general code. Why should not the Dingley Dell club do for football what the MCC has done for cricket?[226]

History shows that did not happen, possibly because the members of the Dingley Dell Club were of the corduroy-trousered, uncouth brethren school and therefore less influential than their knickerbockered, refined counterparts of the public school; but, had the Dingley Dell rules being accepted at this early stage, four years of debate might have been prevented and the history of the game somewhat different. Certainly the *London Review* could not then have written two years later:

> Football was once a rural pastime which villagers played in the thickest boots, and with the least possible artistic skill. It is now a game with a code as carefully drawn as the Code Napoleon; and rival schoolmen quarrel over its niceties in the columns of THE FIELD as grave Doctors of Divinity in the Middle Ages disputed on some of the more delicate points of a theological thesis.[227]

By 1865, the *Sportsman* was able to set the debate in a historical context and recognised what the Football Association had a couple of years before but was in the midst of a four year debate to put it right. The debate had begun some time before the newspaper suggests, but that does not invalidate its comments:

ALCOCK AND THE FOOTBALL ASSOCIATION

Ever since *The Times* opened its columns in 1862 to a discussion on the advisability of establishing one uniform code of laws for the regulation of football matches, the subject has been periodically revived about the middle of the Autumn and a host of eager disputants, mostly the representatives of the basic public schools, regularly rush into print, ready to do battle against all comers on behalf of his [sic] own particular system.

Football has ceased to be the property of the public schools; it has now made its way not only into the universities but into many parts of the country and in proof of its increasing popularity we may point with satisfaction to the existence of not a few influential Football Clubs in the neighbourhood of London, where this manly and invigorating pastime is pursued as zealously and as enthusiastically as among the devotees of Rugby, Eton and Harrow...

We repeat that if football is ever to attain the high position to which the game may fairly aspire among our national sports, we must have as a condition precedent one uniform and compendious code of laws, comprehensive in its scope and universal in its application. [228]

The Blackheath Split

The first splinter groups were not long in appearing, Harrow, Charterhouse and Westminster preferred to stick with their own rules, but this schism was relatively minor compared with the secession of the Blackheath Club from the Association to form the Rugby Football Union and the amateur-professional divide of the 1880s. Blackheath occupy a unique position in being founder members of both the Football Association and the Rugby Football Union and it was the stance of what in rugby circles has subsequently become known as "The Club" that led ultimately to the popular folklore definitions of rugby union being a hooligans' game played by gentlemen, then later with the infiltration of professionalism to both codes, association football being a gentlemen's game played by hooligans and rugby league a hooligans' game played by hooligans.

The conflict between "the handling game" and "the dribbling game" predates the establishment of the Football Association and may have something to do with traditional public school rivalries, particularly those between Eton and Rugby in the 1840s.[229]

The two clauses in the rules which the Blackheath Club wished to retain were:

A player may be entitled to run with the ball towards his adversaries' goal if he makes a fair catch, or catches the ball on the first bound; but in the case of a fair catch, if he makes his mark, he shall not run.

and

If any player shall turn with the ball towards his adversaries' goal, any player on the opposite side shall be at liberty to hold, charge, trip or hack him, or wrest the ball from him; but no player shall be held and hacked at the same time.

These two rules are illustrative of how the subsequent games of rugby and association football were at this stage inextricably linked. By contrast, the Cambridge Rules outlawed hacking and it was towards these rules that the majority of the members of the Association, including John Alcock, were inclined.

The crucial date was 1 December 1863. It was the fifth meeting of the Association. There had been minor disagreements about the rules, but this was a major issue with no possibility of compromise. The exchanges were acrimonious and there were accusations of bad faith and ungentlemanly conduct. Mr F W Campbell, Blackheath's Treasurer was unequivocal in his view:

Hacking is the true football game and if you look into the Winchester records you will find that in former years men were so wounded that two of them were actually carried off the field...I say they had no right to draw up such a rule at Cambridge and that it savours far more of those who liked their pipes and grog or schnapps more than the manly game of football. I think that the reason they object to hacking is because too many of the members of clubs began late in life and were too old for that spirit of the game which was so fully entered into at public schools and by public school men in after life.

Morley, the Honorary Secretary, saw hacking as detrimental to the expansion of the game:

I object to it mostly because I think that its being disallowed will promote the game of football, and therefore I cordially agree with Mr Alcock. If we have "hacking", no one who has arrived at the years of discretion will play at football, and it will be entirely relinquished to school-boys.[230]

A proposal by Blackheath to adjourn the meeting to enable them to gather more public school support was defeated by 13 votes to 4 and the split was now irrevocable.

Ironically, it was the hacking rather than the handling question which was the main cause of the split and even more ironic was the abandonment by Blackheath of their stance on hacking within a couple of years. By then, however, there was no turning back: the dissenters were on their way to forming a separate administrative body controlling a different sport.

The Rugby Football Union was born in 1871 and Alcock was not without influence in its establishment. The following letter, dated 17 September 1869, just four days before the birth of his second child and first daughter, appeared in the *Field* on the following day, timed to coincide with the 1869-70 football season. It is prophetic and based on sound common sense:

...the game is now rapidly settling down into two - and only two - distinct codes.

An association of the various Rugby clubs, similar to that which has long guided the movements of the dribblers, would surely have a beneficial effect.

As a "dribbler", I feel something akin to presumption in making this suggestion in this matter, which affects the opposite division; but, in the interests of the game, would like to see the points of separation reduced to the smallest limits; and whether Rugby or "dribbling" rules are paramount or, as I trust will long be the case, the two styles live and flourish, matters not, as one of the most manly of our national sports continues to increase and multiply. I should like to see the matter brought home to the minds of all Rugbeians before the full tide of matches precludes the possibility of a correspondence commensurate with the subject. The eve of a new season offers a fitting opportunity. Let Rugby speak!

Subsequent correspondence supported the suggestion that a standardised code of rules for rugby was required.

Honorary Secretary

John was a founder member of the Football Association, but did not serve on the committee after 1865, being replaced by his brother who, after five years was elected as Honorary Secretary, the fourth in the first seven years of the Association. By contrast with his predecessors, Alcock occupied the post for a quarter of a century, on an honorary basis for sixteen years and then as the Association's first paid Secretary from 1886. His influence, already apparent from his position on the committee, when he had been instrumental in persuading his colleagues into a limited alliance with the Sheffield Association, now became more focused and authoritative. Geoffrey Green, historian of the FA has no doubt about his place in the football firmament:

> ...there now came C W Alcock, an old Harrovian and a true lover of sport and sportsmanship. For 25 years, he was to hold the administrative reins through a period in which the character, outlook and significance of the game underwent tremendous change. The part that he played in the evolution was of the greatest significance. Indeed, it was he who above all others gave football the first real impetus that sent it rolling over hill and dale, through town and country and finally across the seven seas.[231]

In 1871 A Stair was appointed to the post of Treasurer but the increasing administrative work load on the officers of the Association - unpaid and without a permanent office - meant that in practice he occupied an unofficial post of Joint Honorary Secretary.

Alcock's influence was in evidence, however, before he assumed the post and as early as 1867, already a distinguished footballer and founder and Honorary Secretary of the Wanderers, he was beginning to make his presence felt as an administrator, recognising after four years of debate on the rules of the game, all parties need to be involved. The *Sportsman's* report of the annual meeting of the FA includes the following:

> Mr C W Alcock was of the opinion that, in order to further the views of the association, whose movements he was sorry to see were regarded with distrust by the Universities and Public Schools, a committee meeting should be held in the month of October next, when communication should be entered into with

the Universities and Schools who should be invited to attend an extraordinary meeting. He considered a little more energy was required to establish the game on a sure footing towards which its popularity was by degrees approaching. [232]

In appealing for energy, Alcock was asking for no more than a contribution of the quality he had in abundance.

The Association Cup

Supporters of the now separated Rugby code had therefore no interest in the FA Cup which began its long history the following year. Popular football legend has it that Alcock was the inventor of the competition. Certainly it was he who made the proposal at a meeting of the FA Committee held in the offices of the *Sportsman* on 20 July 1871, and he was doubtless influenced by the organisation of the Cock House Competitions he had known at Harrow. Other members of the committee would certainly have understood the principle, the cock-house knock-out device being in operation under the same name at Clifton, Rugby and a number of others. Cheltenham College had Challenge Cups while Wellington College had inter-dormitory matches organised on a league basis. Organisational details varied from school to school, but the competitive principle was well understood.

Yet it is at least possible that the concept of a knock-out competition arose in discussion between Alcock and his close friend W G Grace who was from an early stage of his career alive to the commercial possibilities of sport and had taken over the United South of England Eleven as his sporting mercenaries. In a feature in the *Daily Telegraph* in April 1997, Bryon Butler referred to anecdotal evidence in J B Booth's *Old Pink 'Un Days*, a book with a limited print run which is essentially about the *Sporting Times*, a peripheral but colourful and satirical journal owned by John Corlett who had begun his journalistic career on the *Sportsman* as a contemporary of Charles Alcock.

Booth tells of the weekly symposia and hints that W G, who had played football with Alcock, may have had some influence on the development and administration of the game:

In the early days of his newspaper work he had been associated with C W Alcock, who held a very high position in the athletic world. Alcock sat in one room, and Corlett in an adjoining one, and the latter always wondered who were the rough looking crew who used to visit his colleague every week, and hold a prolonged sitting. One member of that "rough-looking crew" was W G Grace and another was the eldest son of the Grand Old Man.

It was at one of Alcock's weekly symposia that football, as we now understand it was born. Until then, John would declare, the game for which he had very little admiration was played only in Dorking on Shrove Tuesday, when the ball was kicked through the streets and the players spent the night in the lock-up. And the only game of football old John Corlett ever witnessed was when he was taken by his colleagues to the Oval - of which Alcock shortly afterwards became manager - to see England v Scotland, a match in which both Alcock and Gladstone's son took part, before a handful of spectators.[233]

All this may be less than accurate as a historical account and Corlett has perhaps coalesced more than twenty years of reminiscences. It was not until some years later that Alcock "held a very high position in the athletic world", but it may well be that Grace's organisational sense and commercial acumen and W H Gladstone's political mentality had some input into the idea, even if they were not the only or most significant influence.

But, even if Alcock's claim to be the inventor of the FA Cup can be challenged, there can be no doubt that he was primarily responsible for its development. Not for the only time in his career does he, to borrow a metaphor from the rival code, pick up the ball and run with it and develop an idea, irrespective of whether it was his own or not, to its maximum potential.

The Cock House competitions at Harrow and other public schools were not the only model. There was a precedent for the award of a Cup by the Sheffield Association whose area was far larger than the city itself and stretched from the Tees to the Trent. Four years earlier the *Field* had reported that:

Fourteen clubs regularly during the Sheffield season carry on a spirited football campaign; and the establishment of a prize cup for the Champion Club (won by Hallam) testifies to the support which is given to the game...[234]

ALCOCK AND THE FOOTBALL ASSOCIATION

Alcock had played for London in representative matches against Sheffield and the question of challenge trophies would doubtless have been raised in après-football discussions. It is not clear whether the Sheffield competition was organised on a knock-out basis. If it was, then it would undermine Alcock's later claim in 1881 that the Association Challenge Cup was the first of its kind.

Whatever the source of the idea, the Cock House competitions of the public schools, the original mind of W G Grace or the Sheffield precedent - and they are not mutually exclusive - Alcock's proposal "that it is desirable that a Challenge Cup be established in connection with the Association, for which all clubs belonging to the Association should be invited to compete" was received with enthusiasm. The idea was not novel, but the attempt to apply it on a national scale was. Member clubs, including the Queen's Park Club of Glasgow, between them subscribed £20 for a silver trophy, designed by Martin, Hall and Co, under eighteen inches high and inscribed "The Football Association Challenge Cup". Its design is reproduced on Alcock's grave.

For the first few years it was a competition essentially restricted to the south of England clubs, but such was not the intention. From the beginning with a view to ensuring maximum participation, there was a built-in flexibility, allowing concessions for provincial teams to reduce the amount of travelling: 'In the case of provincial clubs, it shall be in the power of the committee to except them from the early tie-drawings, and to allow them to complete specially against clubs in the same district, except in the case of final ties.'

In the first year of the competition, the concession was only partly successful. Of around fifty clubs in membership, fifteen entered, Queen's Park and Donnington being the only non-London clubs. So they were pitted against each other only for Donnington to withdraw, leaving the way open for Queen's Park to progress directly to the semi-finals or "fourth ties". After a draw against eventual winners Wanderers, they were unable to travel to London again and they too withdrew from the competition, but their presence had been enough to open the way to more serious Anglo-Scottish competition.

1873 was the first and only year in which the pure "challenge" principle was applied. Wanderers, having won the Cup the previous year were exempt until the final tie, then "challenged" by Oxford University who emerged from the pack to take them on in the second Final. Wanderers retained the trophy by defeating the University 2-1. The challenge principle was then abandoned. All teams played in the first round the following year; the runners up returned to take the trophy in 1874, a feat repeated by that year's runners up, Royal Engineers in 1875. Wanderers then dominated the competition, winning the Cup for the next three years, a feat entitling them to retain the trophy permanently, but they declined to do so, returning it the FA on condition no team should ever win it outright. They had thus won the trophy five times in the first seven years of its existence. They were never to do so again. Old Etonians, Clapham Rovers and Oxford University had a period of domination, but the days of amateur monopoly were almost over and the challenges of professionalism were appearing on the horizon.

Pseudo-Internationals

On 5 February 1870 the following notice appeared in the columns of the *Sportsman* on the staff of which was the newly appointed Honorary Secretary of the Football Association:

FROM THE SECRETARY OF THE FOOTBALL ASSOCIATION

A match between the leading representatives of the Scotch and English sections will be played at The Oval on Saturday, 19 February, under the auspices of the Football Association. Players duly qualified and desirous of assisting either party must communicate with Mr A F Kinnaird of 2 Pall Mall East, SW or Mr J Kirkpatrick, Admiralty, Somerset House, WC on behalf of the Scotch or with Mr Charles W Alcock, Boy Court, Ludgate Hill, EC or Mr R G Graham, 7 Finch Lane, EC on the part of the English. (signed) Charles W Alcock.

It was unheaded, low key and in the middle of the page, but it had the desired effect.

The match was arranged and played a year before Alcock took up his appointment as Secretary to Surrey County Cricket Club, so even as the youthful Honorary Secretary to the Football Association, he already had some influence with the authorities at The Oval and in the book written jointly with Lord Alverstone, *Surrey Cricket: Its History and Associations*, he

ALCOCK AND THE FOOTBALL ASSOCIATION

acknowledges the co-operation and foresight of William Burrup, his predecessor as (albeit honorary) Secretary of Surrey County Cricket Club. As it happens, the match was not played on the scheduled day because of a heavy frost, but took place a fortnight later. The *Sportsman* reported that:

> This match, which has for some weeks occupied the attention of the numerous section of players who follow the guidance of the Football Association, took place at Kennington Oval on Saturday last, in the presence of an assemblage of spectators such as has, in point of numbers, never being equalled, the entire limit of the ground being lined by an enthusiastic array of the supporters of the two sides.[235]

The success of the exercise gave rise to the following letter from Alcock which appeared in the *Field* on 17 September 1870:

ENGLAND VERSUS SCOTLAND

SIR - I am instructed by the Committee of the Football Association to state that these two matches of the same description as that of last year under the above title, will take place at the Oval during the coming season. The dates fixed are Saturday November 19, 1870 and February 25, 1871; and as the committee are desirous of making the matches annual fixtures of importance by investing them with more than local interest and at the same time are especially anxious to fuse into the contests something of an international character, by selecting the best players at their disposal, regardless of clubs or distinctions, I am commissioned to beg in their name and on their behalf that secretaries of clubs will as much as possible arrange their programmes for the season as to avoid collision with the matches named.

The publicity given to this communication in your paper will materially serve the interests of the committee.

Charles W Alcock, Hon Sec
Football Association
West Dulwich, Sept 16

It was six weeks later that, possibly to make the matches more authentically 'international', he wrote in not dissimilar terms to the *Glasgow Herald*:[236]

SIR, - Will you allow me a few lines in your paper to notify to Scottish players that a match under the above title will take place in London on Saturday 19th inst., according to the Rules of the Football Association? It is the object of the Committee to select the best elevens at their disposal in the two countries, and I cannot but think that the appearance of some of the more prominent celebrities of football on the Northern side of the Tweed would do much to disseminate a healthy feeling of good fellowship among the contestants and tend to promote to a still greater extent the extension of the game. In Scotland, once essentially the land of football, there should still be a spark left of the old fire, and I confidently appeal to Scotsmen to aid to their utmost the efforts of the committee to confer success on what London fondly hopes to found, an annual trial of skill between the champions of England and Scotland. Mr A F Kinnaird, 2 Pall Mall East, London, will be glad to receive the names of any Scottish players who will take part against England in the match in question.

The move was partially successful to the extent that Scotland's leading club, Queen's Park, nominated Robert Smith, a London-based member playing for South Norwood ("a persevering, but not gifted player", according to the *Football Annual*) and asked him to report back on the proceedings.[237] To have a member of a Scottish club playing for the 'Scotland' team was a marginal improvement on the March match when, apart from a few Scottish sounding names such as Kirkpatrick, Hamilton and Muir Mackenzie the only Scottish-sounding team represented was the London Scottish Rifles.

There were repercussions which led to the first Rugby International. A group of Scottish-based rugby players wrote to the *Field* and other newspapers in the following terms:

There is a pretty general feeling among Scottish football players that the football power of the old country was not properly represented in the so-called International Football Match. Not that we think the play of the gentlemen who represented Scotland otherwise than very good - for that it was so is so amply proved by the stout resistance they offered to their opponents and by the fact that they were beaten by only one goal - but that we consider the Association rules, in accordance with which the late match was played, not such as to bring together the best team Scotland could turn out. Almost all the leading clubs of the country play by the Rugby code, and have no opportunity of practising the Association game, even if willing to do so. We therefore feel that a match played in accordance with any rules other than those in general use in Scotland - as was the case in the late match - is not one that would meet with support generally from her players.

For our own satisfaction, therefore, and with a view of really testing what Scotland could do against an English team, we, as representing the football interests of Scotland, hereby challenge any team selected from the whole of England to play us a match, twenty-a-side, rugby rules, either in Edinburgh, Glasgow, on any day during the present season that might be found suitable to the English players. Let this count as the return to the match played in London on Nov 19 or, if preferred, let it be a separate match. If it is entered into, we can promise England a hearty welcome and a first-rate match.

Any communication on the subject addressed to any of us will be attended to.

JOHN W ARTHUR Captain, Glasgow Academical Club
ALEX H ROBERTSON West of Scotland FC
FRANCIS H MONCRIEFF Edinburgh Academical F C
B HALL BLYTH Merchistonian F C
J HENRY OATTS St Salvator F C, St Andrew's

The Challenge was taken up, the match played at Raeburn Place, Edinburgh, on 27 March 1871 attracting "a large and fashionable assemblage" -the first of an annual series of matches which in 1879 led to the Calcutta Cup and eventually developed into the Five and Six Nations Championship. Of more immediate concern for the Alcock story, however, was the return match which brought rugby to the Oval. Meanwhile, the "association" matches continued, those desirous of playing in the third being invited to write to C W Alcock at Grassendale, Dulwich S E.

Full Internationals

The principal difference between the former pseudo-internationals and the match played in Partick in November 1872 which led to its being regarded as the first 'proper' international was that the Scotland team was selected by the Queen's Park Club, not by the English FA. All the Scottish players were from Queen's Park and the match was played in Scotland.

ENGLAND v SCOTLAND The first match of any importance that has taken place over the border according to the Rules of the Football Association was played in Glasgow on Saturday November 30, 1872.

Though both elevens did all they knew, no decision was arrived at, neither side being able to force their opponents' lines.

England played in their traditional 1-1-8 formation, Scotland a more conservative 2-2-6. The fixture attracted a gate of almost 4,000, "more out of curiosity and patriotism than any great interest in the 'dribbling' game", said the *North British Mail* which also reported that the match took place "in the presence of the largest assemblage seen at a football match in Scotland...including a good number of ladies."[238]

There is no photographic record, the local photographer not having received a guarantee that the players would buy his prints, nor are there any of the return match at Kennington Oval the following February, as the players frustrated the efforts of the "photographic operator" by repeatedly pulling faces at his camera.

The different nature of the Scottish game pioneered by Queen's Park and subsequently taken up by other clubs, notably Vale of Leven, was later to enable Scotland to win three successive internationals, including a victory of 7-2 at Queen's Park in 1878. Some rethinking of the predominantly all-dribbling English approach would be stimulated.

A novelty whose origins most would place shortly after the Second World War first made its appearance in 1878 at Bramall Lane, Sheffield. This was Association Football by electric light. Four lamps stood on thirty-foot wooden towers at each corner of the ground and almost 20,000 spectators witnessed the novelty on what was reported as being a "crisp moonlit night".[239]

Charles Alcock not being slow to recognise commercial potential, a similar event was planned for The Oval on 4 November. It was not a success because of uneven illumination and high winds. Not for almost 120 years was there to be another attempt at floodlit sport at The Oval when the first day-night cricket match in England was to have graced the ground. Again it was not a success, a deluge causing the match to be abandoned without a ball bowled and allowing Edgbaston to become the first venue for floodlit competitive cricket in England. The problem of uneven illumination remains.

All Alcock's powers of illumination were required over the next few years as the game's popularity increased at a rapid rate, the one club in the Birmingham area having escalated to 20 in 1876 and 155 in 1880, and professionalism began to spread southwards and impose itself on an amateur game.

Christopher Wordsworth, Bishop of St Andrews, writing in *Cricket* had his reservations about the increasing popularity of the game:

As an old cricketer, I confess I feel a little jealous of the ascendancy which football - a good game for boys, but in my opinion too savage for grown up men - appears to be now assuming...football is certainly much older and was played I believe even in antient [sic] Sparta (a suitable birthplace for such a game).[240]

In 1881 an illuminated address was presented to Alcock by his colleagues in the Association. It was a typical Victorian gesture and part of the culture before the expansion of the civic honours system during the First World War.

The citation read:

That the committee of the Football Association, on behalf of the subscribers to the Alcock Testimonial Fund, do present to Mr C W Alcock, hon. sec. of the Football Association, a silver inkstand and candlesticks, with a purse of £330, in recognition of all that he has done, during the past eighteen years to establish and further the Association game, and the committee, in their name and in the name of all players scattered the throughout the Kingdom, tender to Mr Alcock the expression of their sincere thanks for the zeal and energy with which, since its foundation in 1863, he has discharged his duties as hon. sec. to the Association, and further record their unanimous conviction that the success which has attended the Association in all its undertakings and the established position the game now occupies among winter sports, are due in no ordinary degree to the loyal and untiring devotion with which he has ever sought to promote its interest and prosperity.

Alcock's reply, if no less verbose, was somewhat less abstract:

Mr C W Alcock, on rising to return thanks, said he found difficulty in finding words to express himself in return for the kindness shown him. He said that although football under Association Rules was not actually known to the general public before 1863, as a matter of fact the first football club playing under these rules was started in 1859 by his eldest brother, and he himself held the club cup for kicking most goals in 1861-62. In referring to the starting of the Football Association, he intimated that a tremendous difficulty had to be overcome, not the least of the obstacles being the notices that from time to time appeared in the Lancet dwelling on the accidents attendant on play. So narrow, said the speaker, were 'the limits of the body at one time that it was known as Kinnaird, Alcock and Fitzmaurice's Association'; and too, when the first international match was played in Scotland, the northern papers ridiculed the title of the match, there being only one Association club in Scotland. He (Mr Alcock) could look back with pride to October, 1871, when by his proposal the Association Challenge Cup competition was originated, this being the first of its kind throughout these isles, whereas now there were several. The speaker impressed on his audience the fact that Association football had started simply as a healthy outdoor recreation, and was carried on as such for a great many years; but of late things have in some directions taken a change, and perhaps gate-money has a lot to do with play being turned into a profession. The South have often been taunted on their meagre attendances, but the North have to contend against many and various internal dissensions, and indeed the time had arrived to settle the question whether the executive of the parent Association were simply to draw the ties or to legislate upon the different laws affecting the game. Mr Alcock concluded by again thanking the donors for their munificence.[241]

Alcock was not yet at the half-way point in his forty years plus of service to the FA, so it was perhaps in a sense premature as he had twenty-five years to go. His two immediate successors Frederick Wall and Stanley Rous both had knighthoods conferred. Had civic honours been awarded with the same relative liberality as they were in the twentieth-century, then the title on the cover of this book would undoubtedly be 'The Life and Times of Sir Charles Alcock'.

REFERENCES

205. Radnedge *Ultimate Encyclopedia of Soccer* p 8

206. Gannaway *Association Football in Hampshire Until 1914* p 1

207. *Field* 23 October 1869

208. Stubbes *Anatomie of Abuses in the Realme of England 1583* - quoted in Grayson *Corinthians and Cricketers* p 19

209. J Latimer *The Annals of Bristol in the Seventeenth Century* - quoted in Goulstone *Football's Secret History* p 9

210. Goulstone *Football's Secret History* p 16

211. Gannaway *Association Football in Hampshire* p 4

212. p 100

213. Goulstone *Football's Secret History* p 50

214. Fabian & Green *Association Football I* p 150

215. Dunning *Something of a Curate's Egg*

216. Obituary notice in *Richmond and Twickenham Times* 2 March 1907

217. Young *A History of British Football* pp 132-3

218. p 100

219. Radnedge *Ultimate Encyclopedia of Soccer* p11

220. Fabian & Green *Association Football* pp144-5

221. *Bell's Life* 2 January 1859

222. *Bell's Life* 16 January 1859

223. *Field* 12 October 1861

224. *Field* 15 March 1862

225. *Field* 22 April 1862

226. *Field* 15 March 1862

227. Quoted in *Field* 19 March 1864

228. *Sportsman* 18 November 1865

229. Dunning *Something of a Curate's Egg*

230. Fabian and Green *Association Football* pp 52-3

231. Green *History of the Football Association* p 47

232. *Sportsman* 28 February 1867

233. pp 60-1

234. 20 April 1867 p 301

235. 8 March 1870

236. 3 November 1870

237. Young *A History of British Football* p 152
238. quoted in *England: The Official FA History* p 9
239. Barrett *Daily Telegraph Football Chronicle* p 7
240. *Cricket* 31 March 1887
241. *Marylebone Cricket Club Scores*

CHAPTER 6

THE OVAL OFFICE

Philosophies of Administration

A DISTINGUISHED UNIVERSITY VICE-CHANCELLOR once said that the two qualities required of an administrator were an awareness of resources and a familiarity with whatever was being administered. It is possible to have both those and do a reasonable job, but if they are the only ones, our administrator may incline towards the stereotype of the faceless bureaucrat beloved of cartoonists. If Charles Alcock's qualities had been similarly limited, he would perhaps have been remembered, as most of his contemporaries at other counties, predecessors and successors at The Oval and elsewhere, as a competent and worthy Club Secretary who kept the bureaucratic machinery ticking over. He certainly did that, but would have seen it as the minimum requirement, the foundation on which he would base a structure and develop ideas that would spread far beyond his own historical and geographical limitations.

Surrey cricket and its affiliate professional touring circus, the United South of England XI, had a major impact on the cricket of the 1860s, but the county was tending to complacency and inertia and required an injection of new blood. Charles Alcock was to provide that. That he had a familiarity with and enthusiasm for the cricket is beyond question. His office overlooked the playing area and he claimed after more than twenty years in the job that he had only missed one match - and that through illness.[242] In an 1893 interview with *Cassell's Family Magazine*, reproduced in local newspapers,[243] it is clear that he is much more than a detached bureaucrat as he expresses strong views on the state of the game, including the debt of the English game to the Australians who have, he says, "brushed us up wonderfully":

> the whole secret of bowling is to get well over arm and make the ground help the ball as much as possible. Cricket...has greatly improved; there are many more good bats than there used to be; wicket-keeping generally is decidedly better; and fielding is much better than it used to be.

THE FATHER OF MODERN SPORT

His conception of cricket is directly in the Tom Brown tradition ("It's more than a game. It's an institution") and again, the public school ethos is continued into adult life. The following extract from the interview with Raymond Blathwayt was more than twenty years after his appointment, but there is every reason to believe that it is part of the vision Alcock brought with him to the job and continued to inspire him for thirty-five years. He is described as:

> a thorough good all round sportsman; an adept at most English games; a tall broad-shouldered man with iron-grey hair, a thick, grey moustache and keen kindly eyes - a typical Englishman, in short, with all an Englishman's enthusiasm, and perhaps many of an Englishman's prejudices. He believes in cricket not merely as a simple game, but as a great educational principle; seeing in the devoted cricketer, a patriot, a clean-living, straight-going specimen of manhood; and regards cricket as a means whereby England and her colonies can be knitted and welded together as they could not be by all the policy and all the theories of Imperial Federation put together.

All sound, popular journalism, but the evidence from Alcock's administration and writing is that his vision was broader than that and that he appreciated that there are lessons to be learned from, as well as taught to, overseas sportsmen. Further north and in later years, Neville Cardus was to view the game in a different light:

> There is no nonsense about 'art for art's sake' in the Saturday afternoon matches of the hinterland of the northern counties. A game begins soon after the midday dinner "buzzer" has sounded ...No time is wasted polishing the period of style. All strokes look alike on the score sheet.[244]

He is, he says later in the interview, encouraged by the spread of the game to the working classes who are now beginning to participate in the sport - "a great education for them in every possible way" - as well as being enthusiastic spectators of it, as witness the attendance of 30,760 on a Bank Holiday in 1892 and 2,000 on a Whit Monday for a 2nd XI fixture. A major county fixture such as Surrey v Notts would attract 25,000, a tenfold increase over 15 years. It was the high noon of empire, the apogee of the amateur, what cricket historians have subsequently called the "golden age".

THE OVAL OFFICE

Alcock was not merely an interested observer. He had helped to create it. There were, however, undercurrents of revolt, both in cricket and in society and the Surrey secretary, neither arch-conservative, nor zealous reformer, had managed to harness those currents and convert them into the power that had brought The Oval to its present position, while across the river, Lord's, while not entirely unadventurous, remained the bastion of the establishment at play.

His office was packed with souvenirs of the game, the ball from which Surrey scored 631 against Sussex in 1885; the ball used in the match in 1886 when Surrey beat Yorkshire for the first time for twenty-one years; photographs of famous cricketing occasions at The Oval and pictures from the early part of the century. He has been in office some 21 years, but the almost schoolboy-like enthusiasm is still there. He is in his element:

> The room in which we sat formed one of a handsome suite in the pavilion at the Oval. Great open windows admitted a flood of summer sunshine, and the pleasant sound of batting was heard now and again, and the old familiar cry came floating in -
>
> "Well hit sir; well hit indeed. Run it out," the cry we all know so well; and every now and again as he talked to me Mr Alcock would start up from his seat to watch the progress of the game with a pleasant apology for doing so.
>
> "You really must forgive me, he would say, but as long as I have played cricket, I never can sit and watch a game in silence," and he would applaud as vigorously as the rest of those who were seated round the sunny field looking on the game.

No faceless bureaucrat here. There is little in the interview that he has not said wearing his journalist's and editor's hat, but it is nevertheless compelling evidence that he saw his role as being something beyond the servant of the committee and like all strong administrators, he built a job around himself that goes beyond a job-description, which, like any other, could never include a provision that the job-holder should become an entrepreneur and visionary. He knew the rules, indeed he lay down the rules, and did not so much break them as mould them to his own image and move beyond them.

In a chapter entitled The Management of a Club in T C Collings *The Sports Library: Cricket*, published in 1900 with contributions from inter alia

Monty Noble, Lord Harris and Pelham Warner, Alcock sets out what is expected of a Secretary. To an extent, the views expressed perhaps represent what the Committee would have wished him to write, but they contain some sound common sense on the orthodoxy of Club management by one who although 'Secretary' in name was perhaps a century ahead of his time in becoming *de facto* if not *de jure* a 'Chief Executive'. It is perhaps worth a look at what he says:

'There are Clubs and Clubs. But whether small or large, good management is essential to all of them alike. Good management presupposes the hearty co-operation of everyone who has a share in the administration. An active and intelligent officer as hon secretary may and does count for a great deal, not only in the satisfactory working, but in maintaining the character of a club. But after all he is only the outward and visible sign of the administration, the mouthpiece of the real management.

'To ensure good order and a proper, as well as responsible, conduct of affairs, the management of a club should be vested in a committee. The number will naturally vary according to the size and responsibilities of a club. Where the scope is large, as for instance in the case of a county club, and it is expedient to have the principal districts represented, the managing body consists of as many as twenty-four, exclusive of the officers. For ordinary purposes, this would be quite unwieldy; for general work, a committee of nine, or, at the outside, twelve, would be sufficient. For a cricket club the fitting number would obviously seem to be eleven, which should include any officers to whom executive powers - that is, votes on the committee - are given. The committee should be de facto responsible for the real business of the club. To facilitate the conduct of the work there should be a small quorum, if only to ensure that there is no actual blank at a meeting.

'Care should be taken that the committee should be as representative of the interests of the members as possible, that is, they should all of them be practical men, which is to say that they should be conversant thoroughly with the work they have to do, in this case cricket. They are the trustees for the members of the property of the club and all the moneys should be under their control. All accounts should come before them, and, where circumstances will allow, all cheques should be brought before them for approval; these and all other details should be duly entered on the minutes of the meetings, which would therefore be an actual record of the business of the club. Where feasible, it is advisable to have fixed dates for committee meetings, rather than leave them to be called at the discretion of the hon. secretary, to which there are obvious objections. It is usual to have at least two officers - a president and a treasurer. The president in the ordinary course takes the chair at the annual general meetings, and both the treasurer and he are ex-officio (or should be) members of the committee.

'Where the business is large and the meetings are frequent it is usual for the committee to appoint out of their own number a chairman, whose business it is to preside, with a vice-chairman to act in his absence. With the ordinary run of clubs it will be found most convenient for the president to take the chair, especially if he takes an active interest in the affairs. The treasurer should be responsible for the accounts, receive subscriptions from the hon secretary, and generally supervise the financial part of the work. His signature should be essential to all cheques, which it would be well to have also signed by a member of the committee as well as the hon. Secretary. The committee, who will of course have been appointed in the first instance by the full body of members, are themselves the voice of the club, and their duty is to carry out what they believe to be the wishes of the members generally. In the case of big clubs a certain number of them retire at the annual general meeting, which it is advisable should be held at a fixed period of the year. As a general rule the retiring members are eligible for re-election. This may be, and is, perhaps, best when the committee is not of large dimensions; where it is large and there is a variety of interests it would seem advisable that a certain proportion should retire at every annual meeting, and not be eligible for re-election for, say, a couple of years. This secures a constant infusion of new blood without any real detriment to the continuity of policy or the general character of the management. The president and treasurer, if they are officers, should come up for election every year. In some clubs it is customary to have a vice-president; in many to have several. In the former case, he is an officer entitled to a vote on the committee, and, if so, should be subject to re-election at the general meeting, like the president and the treasurer. With many clubs it is the custom to have a number, according to local circumstances, of vice-presidents, who have the privilege of subscribing to the funds without a seat on the committee, and consequently do not form a part of the executive.

'The powers of the committee are regulated by the rules of the club, which have been, it goes without saying, drawn up and approved by the members at the meeting when the club was formed, and are liable to alteration at each annual meeting by due notice. These at the same time specify the responsibilities as well as the privileges of the members, the amount of entrance fee and subscription they have to pay, the penalties enforceable in the event of misbehaviour etc. on the one hand; the value they get for the subscription in the shape of practice at the nets, votes at the annual general meeting, accommodation in the pavilion and at matches for themselves and friends etc. on the other. The hon secretary, or secretary if the club is in a position to have a paid officer, is, as already stated, the mouthpiece of the committee. At times, and in emergencies, he has to act "on his own" so that he should be equal to the responsibilities of the post where decision is essential. The position of secretary is necessarily not free from anxiety, so that he should have the hearty and loyal support of the officers and the committee at all times. It is his duty to carry out the instructions of the committee, and it will be well for him if he carries them out to the letter as much as possible.

'On the other hand, on occasions he has to use his own discretion and judgement, and rightly or wrongly, as long as he does his duty conscientiously, ought to be thoroughly upheld. He is the corresponding officer of the club, should write all the letters, see to all the arrangements of the ground, to the practice, and all matters connected with it, that the ground work is properly performed, that the ground bowlers, where there are any, fulfil their duties according to the regulations laid down by the committee. He is, in fact, the working official of the club, the controlling person, and to him the committee look to see that every detail of the work is duly and properly carried out. On him depends the success of the club in a great measure, and hence the choice of a secretary is of vital importance. It has been already pointed out that he has a right to count on the hearty support of the executive; on the other hand, he should be careful to remember that he has a duty to the members. A secretary's lot is at times not altogether a happy one. But, after all, and with a certain consideration to the wishes of those he has to represent, he will, as long as he is consistent and impartial, be sure of the general support essential if the business of the club is successfully conducted.

'A little tact and judgement will make his office pleasant enough. A cricket club, in addition to a secretary, has need of a captain. In the ordinary course the captain is a regular officer, even if he has not the right to a place on the committee like the president and the treasurer. Some clubs, on the other hand, are content to have different captains, appointing one in fact for every match as it comes on. In either case the captain's duties do not in the general way extend to anything beyond the conduct of the match itself, or at the outside to a voice in the selection of the team, in addition to the direction of the team on the field. He is not an essential to the internal management of the club itself.'

A Paid Secretary

Alcock assumed appointment as Secretary of Surrey County Cricket Club on 9 April 1872. He claims not to have given serious consideration to becoming Secretary of the Surrey Club, but to have been, in the management speak of the following century, "head-hunted" at the instigation of V E Walker, a member of the Surrey committee, who had been his contemporary at Harrow. So, not for the first or last time, the old school tie network was much in evidence:

> "...In the course of time I became Secretary of the Surrey County C C, but I really don't know how this came about. Of course, I knew a few men who had seen me doing work for the Sportsman, but I must own I never had the slightest idea of being chosen as the Surrey secretary. V. E. Walker was really my sponsor, and when William Burrup retired I found myself succeeding him in April 1872..."[245]

The time was ripe for the appointment of a paid Secretary. As early as 1865, a letter to the *Sportsman* from "A Surrey Man" expressed the view that:

> The Surrey Club has become a great machine, too large for any one man to manage; and until we get a paid Secretary working under a committee, willing to undertake responsibility, things will not mend.[246]

The Editorial response was supportive:

> It is very kind of any gentleman to undertake the duties of an honorary secretary of a cricket club - and, in the case of such an extensive one as Surrey, those duties must be more than usually onerous, and possibly thankless - but it is more than anything else his paramount duty to guard against partisanship; and while doing his utmost to further the interests of his own club, to take especial care that no offence be given to others. It is difficult in the case of the private and unsalaried official to call upon him to render an account of his stewardship, but in the case of the paid one no such difficulty exists and the remedy for any grievance can be at once and easily had. [247]

THE FATHER OF MODERN SPORT

John Bennion Booth in *Old Pink 'Un Days* relates that:

Up to the time Alcock took the reins of management of the Oval the Surrey Cricket Club had been run in a very amateurish way by a Mr Burrup, a bookseller on the Royal Exchange. On one occasion after Jupp and Humphrey had each scored his "fifty" Burrup, as was then usual, took them out something cooling in a cup. Henry Feist, in the Daily Telegraph, made graceful mention of this and referred to the beneficent Burrup as "the welcome Ganymede". This pleased Burrup immensely, who had not the faintest idea as to the identity of Ganymede; but on looking up a classical dictionary and finding that Ganymede was a beautiful youth who was cup bearer to Jupiter, and of by no means irreproachable character, he was furious, and commenced an action of libel, but ultimately had the sense not to go on with it. [248]

Sir Home Gordon, writing at the beginning of the twentieth century with the benefit of hindsight was able to put Burrup's period of stewardship in an historical context:

That the club suffered, as it undoubtedly did for a time, was due to the existing arrangements, or rather to the lack of proper organisations [sic] than to an official who did his best with the means and time at his command. The fact remains that when the new regime began the club was in a somewhat unsatisfactory state. [249]

The Club's origins, like those of Hambledon and MCC before it, were those of a gentlemen's club with cricket an adjunct of, and secondary to, the social element. It was not yet the professional cricket club it was to become under Alcock's influence:

Following the good old-fashioned plan adopted by the Marylebone Club of an inaugurative meeting without the practice of bat or ball, Surrey met on Friday, the 4th inst. at the London Tavern and celebrated their fourteenth anniversary in a manner thoroughly becoming a powerful, spirited and influential county club. [250]

From the early 1860s, however, the number of first-class fixtures (though retrospectively judged as such) began to increase and at a time when county cricket was not fully established and the professional touring elevens played a more significant part than a decade subsequently, Surrey, established in 1845, were in the vanguard of attempts to move the county game nearer to centre stage. By the early 1870s, however, the successful team of the sixties was beginning to break up and results continued to be disappointing. Surrey's own fortunes were at a low ebb. The years from 1866 to 1871, under a succession of no fewer than five captains, had all seen more defeats than victories and part of the intended renaissance were the appointments of George Strachan as captain and of a paid secretary. It is highly unlikely, however, that the members of the club committee which met at the Bridge House Hotel on 20 March 1872 and carried unanimously the proposal of Mr Norman, seconded by Mr Roberts, that "it is desirable to appoint a paid secretary to the County Club"[251], followed by an amendment proposed by Dr Jones and seconded by Mr Gale "that the Secretary should be appointed at the minimum rate of 200 a year", had the remotest idea of what the medium and long consequences would be. The selection process was not prolonged. There was an immediate further proposal that "Mr C W Alcock shall be recommended by the Committee to be the paid Secretary of the Surrey County Club for the current year".

The required change of rule was approved and Mr Burrup's resignation (politely and discreetly referred to by Alcock as a retirement) received at a Special General Meeting on 9 April. At a committee meeting held the same evening it was resolved unanimously "that William C Alcock [sic] of Dulwich be elected Secretary of the Club at a salary of £250 per annum subject to the New Rules passed this day". In a non-inflationary age, the salary was to remain the same for twelve years, although a £50 bonus was added after five. The New Rules are pasted in front of the minute book, the relevant one, Rule XVII, reading as follows:

> That the committee shall have power to appoint a Secretary at a salary the amount of which shall be fixed at the Annual General Meeting of each year. The office of Secretary shall be vacated only by death, resignation, or a vote of two thirds of the Committee present at a Special meeting of that Body, called for the purpose.

It was a rule that the Committee did not have to use for the next thirty-five years and a security of tenure enjoyed by few at the time, certainly not by the ground bowlers who were subject to instant dismissal for lack of punctuality.[252] In footnotes to his interview with Alcock, W A Bettesworth gives the date of the committee meeting as 6 April and of the Annual General Meeting as 6 May, but Club records (though dates are not always entirely reliable) seem clear that the dates were 20 March for the initial proposal and 9 April for the Special General Meeting. 6 April is a date repeated by Alcock[253] and by a number of secondary sources;[254] Haygarth in *Scores and Biographies* says 7 April,[255] but as 6 and 7 April in 1872 fell on a Saturday and Sunday (Haygarth also gets the date of birth wrong by two years) and Committee meetings were generally held on weekday evenings, 9 April seems the more likely. The Annual General Meeting was separate, held on 2 May 1872 and the traditional dinner afterwards made the appropriate ritual appreciative noises about the outgoing Hon Secretary.

Dr Jones proposed:

"Success to cricket" and coupled with it the names of Messrs Burrup and Alcock. Referring at great length to the eminent services rendered by the former, he said no one could have served more faithfully and continuously. In Mr Alcock he knew the members would find a thorough gentleman and a first rate judge of cricket, and as his indefatigability was undoubted they would no doubt have the undeveloped talent of Surrey brought to the front. When the name of the new Secretary was brought forward there was not an objecting voice, and he was unanimously elected.[256]

More significant perhaps was the address by the new Secretary who created a favourable impression by being buoyantly optimistic and forward-looking and using the age-old public relations technique of telling the members what they wanted to hear:

...it was now the fashion to decry Surrey and Surrey cricket, not only by the enemies of the county, but he feared by many of its well wishers, whose allegiance a series of unforeseen defeats had somewhat shaken. He asked them to unite in sustaining the club and if they could not assist it certainly to say nought to its detriment. He felt he had undertaken a great task, but trusted with the aid of a good committee to be equal to the occasion. With the names of Jupp, Pooley and R Humphrey they need not despair; they had the best wicket-keeper in the world and the best bowler in the south of England, and if well-wishers would pull together and assist him, he had no fear but Surrey would soon be found on the winning side. What they wanted to do was to make the young blood believe they would be promoted and secure places in the Eleven whilst the senior members of the Eleven should understand that as the club rose in prosperity so their positions would improve.[257]

Twelve months later *Wisden* was appropriately prophetic. Its report on the 1872 season included the following paragraph:

Mr. C. Alcock, the new Secretary, possesses youth, energy, practical knowledge of the game and great popularity among all classes of the Cricketers of the period; and by education and associations is peculiarly adapted for the important position he now occupies; and there can be no doubt that this gentleman will both merit and obtain success in his new office.[258]

"Education and associations" is clearly Wisdenspeak for the old school tie, and the presence of two of the Harrow-educated Walker family[259] on the Surrey committee was a powerful factor in an appointment which in later years might have been made by a more democratic, but not necessarily more effective, selection procedure.

But did the reality match the rhetoric? As an incumbent of the Oval Office, although he was perhaps not quite so distinguished in global politics as some of his equivalents in the eponymous workplace in Washington DC, his influence in his own area of sports administration was equivalently immense. It was not always so in the early days of his appointment, however. His predecessor, William Burrup, who had held the position on an honorary basis, remained a member of the Committee and an influential one to boot, and 'The Secretary was instructed...' is a not infrequent form of words in the 1870s and on occasions the wording of a letter is determined by the Committee. That, however, becomes less frequent as the Committee becomes more confident about the new Secretary's literacy, ability to act on delegated authority and capability as an Administrator. Membership and income too began to increase rapidly. Alcock inherited "fifty-seven practising with six hundred ordinary members".[260] Thirty years later it was over 4000 with a limit of 4250 imposed.[261]

It is perhaps unsurprising that Alcock did not make the same impact in his early days as paid Secretary at Surrey as he had in his unpaid equivalent post with the Football Association. Firstly, he was appointed from within to the latter post, having already been on the Committee of the FA for five years, so was in a position to exert more influence than he did on a body to which he had been appointed from without and which contained his still influential predecessor.

The first recorded decision under his secretaryship was to refuse the use of The Oval to the Borough of Lambeth Rifles who had asked for the use of the ground for practice. The second was that the Secretary be empowered to purchase a desk for his use'.[262]

What had happened to whatever desk Mr Burrup had used is unclear, but it is an interesting starting point to the administrative career of one who was to change the face of sport worldwide that he required the Committee's authority to equip himself with the most basic piece of office furniture.

Even in the bread-and-butter area of routine secretarial work and record-keeping his influence was immediately apparent. Before his arrival, the transactions of the committee were contained in rough minute books and are largely restricted to lists of new members, plus the occasional note on the engagement of bowlers, the purchase of bats, balls and stumps and a 'catapulta', a primitive form of bowling machine.[263]

With Alcock's arrival, matters changed. From 1872 minutes cease to be in the form of rough notes, and become more formalised with properly recorded resolutions. It also becomes obvious from the outset of his Secretaryship that he has that rare combination of gifts, the ability to pay attention to detail without losing sight of the broad picture. He is a visionary who is nevertheless still able to work with nuts and bolts. And there were plenty of those - leases, insurances, requests for the use of The Oval for a variety of purposes, an ongoing debate with Ind Coope about the terms of their tenancy of the Club House, a continuing love-hate relationship with the Surrey Bicycle Club, who used the ground twice a year, about charges for the Club's services and complaints from the neighbours about music and noise, in short routine bread-and-butter issues that pervade the minutes of any amateur or professional sports clubs. Systems too are tightened. A day of the week is fixed for paying the players rather than the haphazard random methods used by Burrup. The desirability of change was recognised by the professionals, though its implementation was not always appreciated, especially by Henry Jupp who the previous year had enjoyed the luxury of being paid three times for the Lancashire match.[264]

Relations with Players

But Alcock went much further than improving the literary quality of the minutes and tightening financial systems and also took an active part in the recruitment of players:

> Under the vigorous researches of the fresh Secretary Mr C W Alcock, a wonderful number of new and rising cricketers have been unearthed from the various clubs and villages to the Surrey side of the metropolis.[265]

Twelve months after his inaugural AGM, Alcock was able to report a successful first year:

> The Secretary…thankfully acknowledged the hearty co-operation accorded to him by every class of cricketer in the County during his first year of office; he attributed much of Surrey's success in 1872 to the painstaking action of the committee and to the excellent discipline, unanimity and good feeling that had existed among the County Eleven.[266]

1873 would be different, but his first year was not a one-season wonder and Alcock's enthusiasm for detecting new blood continued well beyond that. In his brief autobiography, Bobbie Abel recalls how he was first recruited:

> Mr Alcock subsequently came to Southwark Park and asked me if I would like to go up for the Colts, but I told him that Mr Wrigley did not think I was a good enough player, and that when I was he would recommend me.[267]

Mr Wrigley was Abel's employer, a foreman in a large hop warehouse, but on this occasion, his judgment of cricketing potential seems to have been less sound than that of the Surrey Secretary, though to be fair, Abel made little impact as a batsman for half a dozen seasons.

Alcock seems to have developed a rapport with the players fairly quickly, not only those from his own social background, but also - as one would expect from his subsequent handling of the issue of professionalism in football - with the paid cricketers who provided Surrey with its on the field reputation. He became friendly with James Southerton and in his interview with the prolific writer on cricket, W A Bettesworth, tells of the subterfuge to which the professional resorted to present a gift to Alcock:

> After he returned from a visit with one of the England elevens to Australia, he gave me a valuable gold locket for my watch-chain. His way of presenting it was quaint. I happened to mention to him that my liver was out of order. He said nothing, but on the following day came up to me and remarked, 'Mr. Alcock, I've been thinking that I have a box of pills here will cure you.' I laughed and put the box in my pocket, forgetting all about it until the evening when I mentioned to my wife that Southerton had given me some special pills. We opened the box, and found a locket, with my initials engraved upon it - from 'J.S.' The next morning I was very angry with him for spending money over me like that; but he only smiled serenely and said, 'I knew you would never accept the locket unless I got you to take it by some dodge.[268]

It is clear that Jupp bore no personal animosity towards the new Secretary for the reduction of his pay to normal proportions and some years later, Jupp had Alcock to thank for his participation in the 1873-74 tour of Australia when the hungover opening batsman literally missed the boat in Southampton. Alcock on board the P & O liner, the *Mirzapore*, at a pre-departure breakfast with the captain and team, descended a rope ladder, returned to shore and arranged for him to have a lift on the mail-tug to catch up the departing liner.[269] After Jupp's death in 1889, the Committee was generous to his surviving dependents, granting £50 to his son and £25 each to his two sisters.[270] The Club also met the cost of his funeral and memorial stone and made a grant to his widow.[271]

Furthermore, Alcock appears to have handled the case of Edward Pooley - coincidentally the two are almost exact contemporaries, sharing a year of birth and of death - with a sensitivity that enabled the Club to take advantage of the services of a world-class wicket-keeper while at the same time exercising a degree of discipline over the recalcitrant professional. Alcock had been in the post just over a year when Pooley was suspended for allegedly "selling" a match in Sheffield. Pooley's subsequent appeal against this decision, supported by six of his fellow professionals, led to his eventual reinstatement, but during his playing days and beyond, he was to appear regularly in the minutes either on disciplinary charges or in a quest for work, grants and pensions. It is fair to assume that while the Committee might deal with matters of principle, this would be one case when Alcock would need to follow his own dictum and "act on his own" in detailed investigation and negotiation. It was a particularly traumatic time too in Alcock's family life. His infant son, Charles Ernest, lost a battle with whooping cough and convulsions to die aged just under five months, ironically on 13 February 1874, Pooley's birthday, celebrated four days after his reinstatement.

Player Qualifications

The first major policy issue to land on the Secretary's new desk was the question of "what constitutes qualifications for a county player", not in the sense of academic or professional qualifications, but of what qualified a cricketer to play for one county ahead of another. Until this time the arrangements were ill-defined, random and disorganised with cricketers moving between counties almost at will. Since then the wheel has come full circle with cricket's transfer market beginning to mirror football's and players moving between counties in much the same way as they did a hundred and thirty years ago - except they do not (yet) do so mid-season. James Southerton had managed to play at various times for Hampshire, Sussex and Surrey and in 1864 and 1865, no questions were asked about Edward Pooley moving from Surrey to Middlesex and back and representing both counties in the same season.

On 12 November 1872, the *Sportsman* contained the following report:

> For several reasons prior to 1872, the impropriety and unfairness of cricketers playing for two counties had been the subject of sharp criticism among county cricketers…
>
> In 1872 "residential qualification" became so frequent and animated a point of discussion that cricket opinion culminated in a decisive desire that this vexed and growingly irritating question should be forthwith settled.[272]

Led by Surrey, counties joined forces in an attempt to tidy up the situation. It was decided:

to write to the Secretaries of leading counties (Notts, Yorkshire, Lancashire, Gloucestershire, Kent, Sussex, Middlesex and Derbyshire) asking if they approve of the suggestion to send two members of the Committee of their County Club to attend a meeting to be held in London early during the recess to consider and determine the future qualifications for a county player.[273]

The MCC stood aside:

It may be stated that early in the season the committee of the Surrey Cricket Club at whose instance the meeting was convened, communicated with the Marylebone Club with a view to securing the services of that body in endeavouring to remove the laxity which has of late existed relative to the qualifications that constitute a County player. The reply from the headquarters of cricket was that the matter was so internally associated with the counties themselves that the MCC must decline to interfere, but that they would be glad to consider any resolutions that might ultimately be confirmed by the several counties interested.[274]

So the counties, with Alcock as Secretary, set about drawing up the new regulations. Eventually, after some toing and froing between the counties and MCC about what constituted 'residence', four rules emerged, which the MCC endorsed at a Special Meeting on 7 May 1873. They were:

1. That no cricketer, whether amateur or professional, shall play for more than one county during the same season.
2. Every cricketer, born in one county and residing in another, shall be free to choose at the commencement of each season for which of the counties he will play and shall during that season be qualified for that county only.
3. A cricketer shall be qualified to play for any county in which he resides, and has resided for the previous two years; or a cricketer may elect to play for the county in which his family home is, so long as it remains open to him as an occasional residence.
4. That, should any question arise as to the residential qualification, the same should be left to the decision of the Committee of the Marylebone Club.

Although the new regulations were perhaps not absolutely watertight and allowed some amateurs to interpret the question of residence more liberally than was intended, the hand of Charles Alcock can be seen in a piece of efficient administration and while the nature of his personal contribution to the debate may be uncertain, there can be little doubt about his ability to draft legislation which was to stand the test of time, remaining unchanged (apart from changes necessitated by the 1888 Local Government Act - Cricket did not and still does not recognise the revised county boundaries)[275] until the introduction of overseas players into the county game and the nascent transfer system of the late twentieth and early twenty-first century.

The Challenge to MCC

Apart from its long-standing significance, the debate over the regulations is of importance because it marks a slight loosening of the ties between MCC and the counties. The position of the Marylebone Club as the ruling body of the game is a historical anomaly.

In a book published in 1914 to mark the centenary of the present Lord's ground, Lord Harris and F S Ashley-Cooper were able to write:

> Throughout its existence the MCC has been the recognised head of the cricketing world. During that period the game has undergone many alterations and improvements, and the Club itself has changed from an autocratic into a democratic body; but, this notwithstanding, the MCC has never been seriously challenged...[276]

Well, they would say that, wouldn't say? Whether such was the case depends on how seriously we interpret 'seriously'. The story of the Marylebone Club with its roots in the soil of Hambledon, subsequent transfer to London and metamorphosis into the White Conduit Club and subsequent pre-eminence has been well documented elsewhere. So dominant was it that the fixtures of the infant Surrey Club in the 1850s were restricted to Thursdays and Fridays to avoid a clash with more prestigious events across the river:

> The Committee of this Club have already made the following arrangements for the forthcoming season. In their selection of days, they have been careful in confining themselves to the Thursday and Friday in the week during the season of the Marylebone Club matches.[277]

By 1875, however, the MCC were complaining that counties were organising fixtures which clashed with prestigious fixtures at Lord's.

The most serious challenge was to come in 1887 with the establishment of the eventually short-lived County Cricket Council, but a quarter of a century before that, in 1863, there had been a proposal in the *Sporting Life* for a 'cricket parliament'. The newspaper took the following view:

> Some more comprehensible and responsible form of government than that which has hitherto existed for the regulation of the national game of cricket has become absolutely necessary.[278]

It was argued that the professionalisation of the game and its extension to the north of England meant that its administrative structure needed examining and that its government should enjoy a wider franchise. It is at least possible that the concept owed something to the Football Association, established a month earlier. A blueprint of a new constitution was produced showing proposed constituencies and the representation envisaged for each. In the 1860s the climate was ripe for reform. The 1832 Reform Act had begun the process of dismantling the earlier parliamentary system with its pocket and rotten boroughs and the second Reform Act of 1867 was to extend the franchise further so, for the politically aware, it required but little imagination to do something similarly appropriate in the administration of cricket. The idea received enthusiastic support in the *Sporting Life's* correspondence columns, but a planned meeting to establish a representative assembly in July 1864 failed to take place and the putative cricket parliament withered on the vine.

Had the proposal succeeded, the whole history of cricket administration might have been different. It is at least arguable that the development of cricket, unlike that of football, has been retarded because it been governed by a private amateur club, rather than an association or consensus of senior clubs and that, consequently, the introduction of competitive devices, such as leagues, knock-outs, promotion and relegation and organised internationals have lagged behind their equivalent in football by at least fifty and sometimes more than a hundred years.

Notwithstanding MCC's opposition to this initiative, its proposed introduction of a County Challenge Cup appears to turn traditional views on their head and show the Marylebone Club as the progressive visionary and the counties as stick-in-the-mud conservatives. The Rules are a truncated version of those for the FA Cup established the previous year:

1. That a silver cup be advertised for competition, to be called the County Challenge Cup.

2. That a certain number of counties, not exceeding six, shall be invited by the committee of the MCC to take part in the champion contests in each season. The counties accepting or declining must notify their intention before January 1. In the event of fewer than the number invited accepting, the Committee shall reserve the right of filling up the number after that date.

3. That the sides shall be chosen by the committees of the several counties, provided that only duly qualified players be selected.

4. That the committee of the MCC shall reserve a power to decide upon the proper qualification of any player.

5. That the dates of the matches shall be arranged, and the ties drawn by the committee of the MCC, as soon as possible after the acceptances shall have been received, and due notice thereof shall be given to the respective county committees.

6. That the matches shall be played in strict accordance with the rules and regulations in force at Lord's ground.

7. That the matches shall be played out within or under three days or be declared drawn.

8. That in the event of a draw, the county declining to play a second match shall be withdrawn from the competition.

9. That the county winning the final tie shall hold the cup that year, and shall produce it at the annual dinner.

10. That the winner of the preceding year shall have the right of playing in the following year.

11. That the winner of the final tie for three years successively shall hold the cup in perpetuity.

12. That the name of the winning county, with date of match, shall be engraved on the cup at the cost of the MCC, by whom also all the usual expenses in connection with the matches shall be borne.[279]

The experiment had failed after one season. Surrey had failed to support it; indeed had vigorously opposed it in the following terms:

Dear Sir

The Committee of the Surrey County Club have considered the rules for the County Cup which were published in Bell's Life last week, and they think it due to the Marylebone Club and to the County Clubs of England to give their reasons for not encouraging the cricketers of Surrey to join in the matches for the cup.

The Committee consider that the fact of offering a prize to the counties may tend to create a desire among cricketers for some inducement beyond the honour of victory which has proved amply sufficient for the present generation. Further that County Cricket never having been more evidently supported than at the present time, they are afraid that the new arrangement organised by the Marylebone Club may be made a precedent for "Cup Matches" in other places and disarrange the present systems of County Cricket in London and in the provinces.[280]

This was one part of a two-pronged attack on the Marylebone Club. At the same meeting, the Committee considered its response to what it saw as the MCC's interference with the carefully drawn and proposed simplified regulations on County qualifications. Having initially opted out of the debate, the MCC had then tried to extend the definition of residence and the Surrey committee, despite the superficial courtesies, bristled with indignation:

...although the Committee of the Surrey Club were empowered by the Counties to accept any trifling alterations in the rules framed, they are of the opinion that some of the alterations in the rules are of so grave a nature that they can not accept those sent by the Marylebone Club without further consulting the other counties. At the same time the Committee beg to thank the Committee of the MCC for the trouble they have taken in considering the subject.[281]

Other counties took a similar view. In the wake of the establishment of the FA Cup the previous year and at a time when Challenge Cups of all kinds were getting off the ground in both cricket and football, it seems strange that it did not succeed and that Surrey should take such a reactionary position. It was perhaps even stranger that some years later, Alcock would question the whole concept of Challenge Cups, suggesting that their existence changed the spirit in which games were played.[282] He was writing more of association and rugby football, especially in the north of England and South Wales, where the proliferation of Challenge Cups had stimulated a desire to win and necessitated tighter legislation. Perhaps, just momentarily, he had become aware of the Pandora's box that was opened with that first FA Cup draw in 1872.

On the cricket front, however, one possible explanation is that at this stage Alcock was very much the servant of the Surrey committee and, despite the new broomery in player recruitment, organisationally the Club remained conservative and unresponsive to initiatives from across the river. Other reasons may have been the prospect of observing Rule 8 and devoting three days to a replay after a three-day draw, perhaps coupled with the quality of the pitch at Lord's and, possibly most significant, the fact that W G Grace, already a figure of some influence in the game, opposed it on the probable grounds that it would be damaging to his pecuniary interest if his mercenaries, the United South of England Eleven[283], chose to represent their counties in the competition.

The only match played in this abortive competition took place on June 9 and 10. There was never going to be any need for a replay. Originally scheduled for three days, it was all over early on the second. Having unearthed "a new and very fast bowler in Mr Coles" who took 6-23 and 4-47, Kent beat Sussex to win by 52 runs as four innings were completed in less than half the playing time available. *Scores and Biographies* says that "the ground was stated to have been in a very bad condition" and "several members of the Sussex Eleven were injured by Mr Coles' very fast bowling"[284] and *Wisden* contains the bizarre scorecard entry... Not out (retired, hurt by Mr Coles' bowling) 32. So, the initiative of knock-out cricket at county level was a failure and though the possibility may have been considered from time to time, it was another ninety years before Sussex were able to improve on their runners-up position. Meanwhile, the following year, MCC replaced their competition with another concept that 130 years or so later is still the subject of controversy and debate - regional cricket - the MCC playing against each of four regions, the representatives of which were selected by the MCC Committee. The intention was "to bring out many players who, from various circumstances, may have been debarred from playing for their respective counties".[285] Wisden went on to describe the venture as "one of the novelties of 1874". It did not survive into 1875.

The Surrey committee, however, was not averse to the principle of Challenge Cup competitions, introducing one for clubs within the county in 1880. It was not a conspicuous success. There were several inter-club disputes which demanded arbitration. Mitcham arrived at the final, having required the Committee's intervention to declare them winners in their first round tie against Mostyn and grant them an extension of time for their second round match against Richmond. The other finalists, Farnham, had been awarded a first round tie when South Norwood turned up with seven men.[286] All this took up valuable committee time in a year when other items on the Agenda included the repair of the urinals in the skating-rink[287] and the possibility of an England-Australia cricket match. Within three years the idea of a Challenge Cup was abandoned and replaced by a Colts' competition.

By the mid-1870s, the scene was changing, but the MCC was not and still took the view, endorsed by Surrey some twenty years earlier, but not any more, that all other fixtures should be confined to days which did not clash with the senior club's interest:

> ...the season at Lord's is repeatedly injured by the inconsiderate clashing of fixtures on the part of the counties.
>
> The Marylebone Club representing, as it does, all parts of the cricketing world, has strong claim on the professionals. It has founded a fund for the benefit of all deserving cricketers, independently of engagements in the Club service. The ground players are seldom refused permission to play for their counties, even to the detriment of a Club match; it is not too much to expect in return that the players not holding engagements under the Club should respect the time-honoured matches at Lord's.[288]

Among these "time-honoured matches" was the traditional Whit Monday North v South fixture from which a number of Yorkshire and Nottinghamshire players had chosen to absent themselves and take engagements elsewhere. The alternative argument is that it is MCC's adherence to what is "time-honoured" and reluctance to embrace new ideas like the possibility of women members that has kept the Club and game in the nineteenth century while the rest of the world has moved on to the twenty-first.

Even in 1875, the M C C's official line was not unanimously endorsed by its members:

> Mr Willoughby rose to make his annual onslaught on the accounts…he drew attention to the match list which he described as "rubbishy"; the members could play in better matches elsewhere. As to the professional players, it was easy to explain their reluctance to play at Lord's, where they were worse treated and less liberally paid than on any other ground.

At this stage, the counties' challenge to the authority of Lord's and the MCC was of a negative, reactive nature. By the end of the decade, led by Surrey and Charles Alcock, it had become, while remaining excessively polite and courteous, positive and proactive, as there is a marked shift in the sporting focus of the metropolis.

The Commercial Dimension
- Other Sport at The Oval

The playing of other sports on The Oval had already begun before Alcock's assumption of the Secretaryship. He had been directly responsible for the Cup Final and indirectly responsible for the rugby international and the commercial advantages were not forgotten.

The resources he inherited were limited, but his apprenticeship in the city had provided him with a business and commercial awareness that enabled him to add to them. One result was that The Oval of the late nineteenth century came nearer to being a national sports centre than anything since, or indeed anything currently on the horizon, as 10 ¾ acres of Kennington which had thirty years earlier been a market garden became not only a nursery of international cricket, association and rugby football, but provided a general public with an increasing interest in both competitive and recreational sport with athletics, cycling, lacrosse, skating, baseball and, briefly, lawn tennis. Australian Rules Football was also a candidate in 1884, but finance could not be found for a tour and it was not until the centenary of Alcock's appointment in 1972 that the sport made its appearance at The Oval.[289]

Rugby had already made an appearance there before the time of Alcock's appointment, but in an indirect way he was responsible for that too. The first rugby international had been at Raeburn Place, Edinburgh on 27 March 1871. Several of Scotland's leading clubs who played under the rugby code had taken exception to the matches organised by Alcock in 1870 being labelled internationals when in effect they were scratch games between groups of friends, some of whose links with Scotland were tenuous and debatable:

> Only one member of the side representing Scotland came from a Scottish club, and the connexion of several others with the far north was somewhat problematical. It was stated, however, that one had crossed the border to shoot grouse, which was considered sufficient qualification, but it was seriously doubted if another should have been allowed to play whose sole claim was a partiality to Scotch whisky.[290]

Consequently, an open letter was sent to the *Scotsman* and *Bell's Life* stating that the majority of Scottish clubs followed not the association code, but the rugby code and would relish the opportunity of testing themselves against a representative English side.

The consequences were that first international at Raeburn Place, the formation of the Rugby Football Union and regular internationals first with Scotland, then with Ireland and Wales, seven of the first fourteen of which took place at The Oval. In its early form, rugby was a twenty-a-side game characterised by prolonged scrummages. Whatever the technical skills and aesthetic merits of such a game, it did nothing to improve the outfield of what was primarily a cricket ground and no more international rugby was played at the ground after the England-Ireland match of 24 March 1879, although inter-county rugby and the Varsity match continued after that date. The final rugby fixture was Blackheath v London Scottish in a Charity Festival on 14 March 1891.[291] The first had been on 5 February 1872, a few weeks before the FA Cup Final.

Relations with the Football Association remained good (unsurprisingly, perhaps, as the two organisations shared a Secretary who on several occasions had the dubious distinction of writing to himself) and the Committee was happy to agree to provide medals ("not to exceed two pounds each") for the Cup winners while the FA took one-third of the gate money.[292] The novelty of floodlit football was one which appealed to the committee and on 28 October 1878, it gave its approval to such an event the following week. It was not a success, but is a further indication of the innovative ideas which the committee and Alcock were prepared to introduce - and this long before the days of Development Directors and Marketing Managers. There were, however, limits. A proposal that the ground be flooded and used for ice-skating was "not entertained".[293]

The Committee had an uneasy relationship with the Surrey Bicycle Club, welcoming the gate money, though allowing the Club to keep two-thirds of it,[294] but being reluctant to allow them to build a path round the Oval.[295] At a later date, while still allowing the Club to retain the same proportion of gate money, the Committee imposed restrictions on professionals and public betting.[296] Later, the Bicycle Club was obliged to cough up £15 per meeting "in consequence of the serious damage to the ground"[297], a criterion which seems not to have been applied in financial negotiations with the Football Association and rugby union authorities. The Bicycle Club objected, but were informed that the sum included an element for preparing the ground and paying the pavilion keeper.[298]

The ground was made available to Amateur Athletics Clubs;[299] in June 1875, the Montreal Lacrosse Club were granted use of it[300] and, interest aroused, the Oval hosted a North v South of England match, advertised it widely and cashed in on half the gate money.[301] Towards the end of the same year the Committee gave in principle approval for the erection of a skating rink[302] and a hoarding advertising its presence.[303] It was a mixed blessing. There were commercial advantages (or would have been had the tenants been more inclined to pay the rent on time[304]) but one of the Secretary's more mundane duties was to deal with complaints from the neighbours about the music [305] and he had to be prepared to compromise his views on the effeminacy of lawn tennis, when the committee saw fit to let out the rink for that purpose at 6d per game.[306] Lawn tennis on grass was briefly introduced in 1880, but does not seem to have lasted.[307]

Baseball had made an appearance at Lord's in 1874, as an interlude in a cricket match between Eleven Gentlemen of MCC and Eighteen Gentleman of America. The Americans had been reluctant to play cricket, but a compromise was struck and the match suspended at 3 pm. to allow the ex-Champions, Athletic Club to play the current champions, Boston. *Wisden's* correspondent compares the game with its antecedent, rounders, but concludes that it is a "modernised, manly and unquestionably improved edition".[308] For once, Lord's was ahead of The Oval. It was not until fourteen years later that the Committee granted the use of the ground and 75% of the gate[309] to American baseball players at the end of a world tour which had seen them perform in Australia, Colombo, "under the pyramids" and in various European capitals such as Rome, Vienna, Berlin and Paris. Cricketers were asked to take note "to what a pitch of accuracy expert Baseballers have reduced ground fielding and throwing".[310] Cricket and baseball are long lost brothers, as Matthew Engel has reminded us.[311]

In 1874, "in consequence of the purchase of the lease and the increased rent" all clubs renting the ground (and there were a number) found themselves paying 25% more, an increase "reluctantly" imposed by the Committee.[312]

Alongside and also as a result of all this extraneous activity, the Club continued to expand financially, in terms of membership, and physically to meet all this activity. A new stand was built and extended, new facilities for the press and scorers were built[313] and buildings added to the skating rink.[314] The pre-1872 amateur administration of the Club was yielding to a more professional, commercially-orientated approach which was not entirely divorced from a view that the Club would benefit from a similar approach to its on-the-field activities:

> To many outsiders who for years have looked on Surrey cricket it appeared probable that if the County tried fewer Gentlemen and more professional Colts, Surrey would meet with more success.[315]

In recognition of his work on behalf of the Committee the Secretary was paid a bonus of £50.[316] It continued for a number of years until absorbed into a salary increase, which took him to £300, then £400 in the mid-80s.[317] Given the inevitable expenses of a wife and family of seven young children, it was doubtless appreciated.

The First Test Match in England

The case of the proposed County Challenge Cup seems to be the exception that proves the rule, an initiative by the MCC rejected by Surrey. By 1880, Alcock by a gradual osmosis became the leader rather than the follower of his committee. Despite their initial negative reaction, he arranged that England's inaugural home Test match (though only subsequently named as such)[318] would take place not at Lord's, the Headquarters of the game's ruling body, where all logic says it should have been played, but at The Oval which now represented a serious and successful challenge to the Headquarters of the game. The roles were, however, reversed in 1980 when the Centenary Test was, again against all logic, played at Lord's, although, as David Lemmon says, "it is hard to fathom for what reason".[319]

On the international scene, even before Alcock's time, the connection between Surrey and Australia was fairly well developed. As early as 1860 a tour had been mooted and sponsorship arranged:

The All England Eleven and Australia - Bell's Life in Victoria says - By the last mail the Secretary of the MCC[320] received a communication from England to the effect that the All England Eleven would pay a visit to Australia, for the purpose of taking the measure of the Australian cricketers, if the latter would guarantee to the eleven a certain pecuniary consideration. In consequence of this offer Messrs Spiers and Pond of the Café de Paris, have sent word to George Parr, telling him that they will guarantee the expenses of the journey overland here and back, and remunerate the players, should they make up their mind to pay these colonies a visit.[321]

Negotiations continued over the next eighteen months and in consequence in 1861-62 H H Stephenson had taken the first English team, comprising mainly Surrey cricketers, to Australia, but matches were against local sides and against the odds, though the tour did produce a "supplementary match", the almost intergalactic, rather than international, The World (in Australia) v Surrey (in Australia). Charles Lawrence, a Surrey man who had been on that Stephenson tour and settled there had brought his Australian Aboriginals to Britain in 1868, but although the tour was a success socially and in financial terms there was no suggestion that they were strong enough to take on a representative England side and it was not until March 1877 that the first Test Match was played. Although contemporary newspapers on both sides of the world billed the match as Australia v England, it was at the time officially a Combined Melbourne and Sydney XI against James Lillywhite's professional touring team and only subsequently regarded as the inaugural Test Match.

An Australian side toured England in 1878, but the MCC did not deign to arrange a return Test match and it was left to Alcock's initiative to establish Test cricket in England two years later at The Oval. In 1878, against all expectations, they had beaten a strong MCC side at Lord's in a day, bowling their hosts out for 33 and 19 and replying with 41 and 12 for 1. Spofforth had match figures of 11 for 20.

the "maddened crowd" ...shouted themselves hoarse before they left to scatter far and wide that evening the news, how in one day the Australians had so easily defeated one of the strongest MCC elevens that has ever played for the famous old club.[322]

A week after the touring side's impressive victory over MCC at Lord's, Alcock had watched at The Oval as a capacity crowd of 20,000 on the first day and 15,000 on the second caused the carriage gates to give way and several improvised entrances to be created to relieve the crush, as the spectators, eager to catch a glimpse of the tourists, spilled over on to the playing area.

The tourists went on to beat Yorkshire and Lancashire and 'not for the last time, England was left wondering why it wasn't any good at cricket any more.'[323] Professionalism and attention to bowling are the twin reasons adduced by Rupert Christiansen and later underlined by Alcock's own journalism. The Australians were more concerned with winning cricket matches than the social peripherals of the game:

THE OVAL OFFICE

An English gentleman took a slightly dim view of bowling: his caste wished to excel at batting. It was here that the art of cricket lay, providing opportunities to turn stylish defensiveness with an elegant minimum of sweaty physical effort. Traditionally, on the village green, the squire would face the bowling of his brawny armed tenant farmer: that was the image which lay at the heart of Victorian cricket in all its glow of social, moral and spiritual rectitude. The Australians had no such inhibitions...[324]

International competition in the minority sport of association football being now well established, Alcock was not slow to see similar sporting and commercial opportunities in the more popular game. It was too late to arrange anything for that year, but two years later, in conjunction with Lord Harris, he had persuaded his committee to host England v Australia at The Oval on 6, 7 and 8 September 1880 and, more diplomatically, the Sussex committee to defer the Sussex v Australia fixture which had been arranged for the same dates. The occasion was a commercial and cricketing success: 40,000 attended on the first two days. W G Grace made the first Test century for England, who, having enforced the follow-on, won by 5 wickets.

Cricket folk-lore and references to the first Test Match in England have perpetuated the story that the success of the Australians in beating a full-strength MCC side at Lord's and the Oval attendances for the Australian matches in 1878 spurred Alcock into arranging the England v Australia fixture at The Oval in 1880. That is not untrue, but it is only part of the full story. Surrey's centenary booklet naïvely states that "the arranging of this fixture was due entirely to the then Secretary of the Surrey Club C W Alcock who was for so many years instrumental in getting the Australians to the Surrey ground".[325] "Entirely" is something of an exaggeration. In reality, the path to that landmark fixture was a labyrinthine maze, skilfully negotiated by the administration and diplomacy of the Surrey secretary, with the influential support of Lord Harris. W G Grace, perhaps not entirely unbiased, said the match was arranged "through the exertions of Lord Harris, Mr Alcock and myself".[326]

The 1878 tour had not run entirely smoothly towards the end. Surrey had made The Oval available to the Australians for a fixture with the Players of England. Administrative arrangements, including players' pay

149

were left in the hands of the Australian management. Guided by the precedent of their benefit match on James Lillywhite's tour of Australia and New Zealand in 1876/77, the Players asked for £20 per man. The Australians offered £10 with the result that the team that took the field was virtually a 2nd XI and the match was concluded in under two days, Australia winning by 8 runs. Ironically, as a token of the Australians' appreciation to those who did turn out, £20 per man was paid and an additional £5 went to Edward Barratt, like Alcock a County Durham man, who had the distinction of taking all ten Australian wickets for 43 in the first innings. In addition:

> A collection was made for him round the ground by two persons professing to have obtained the permission of the Surrey authorities for the purpose. The public was sympathetic, as it always is, and these two individuals reaped a fairly good sum in response. Unhappily Barratt himself was none the richer. The pair proved to be members of the light-fingered fraternity, and decamped with their spoils unsuspected.[327]

Within two hours of the conclusion of the match, there was a major disaster on the Thames when two pleasure boats collided, the *Princess Alice* sunk and more than 700 lives were lost. Some sections of the sporting press suggested that the Australians' match against Eleven Players of England at Prince's later in the month be replaced by a match against a full-strength Players of England side with the proceeds split three ways between the Australians, the players and the Calamity Fund. It did not happen, though it has to be recorded that the Australians did make a £100 donation to the Fund.[328]

In a perceptive Editorial to the following year's edition of Lillywhite's *Cricketers' Annual*, Alcock places Australian cricket in context, saying that the idea of a visit from an Australian team was treated by English cricketers as something of a joke and there had been a reluctance to accredit the Colonials with the extraordinary advance they had made in the development of the sport. Australia was about to introduce a new era into the history of the game which the author of *Tom Brown's Schooldays* had not inaptly described as the prerogative of Englishmen.[329] There follows a detailed analysis of the Australians' play. Their great strength, says Alcock, is undoubtedly in their bowling which is "superior to any that we can show, even in the best of our county Elevens".[330] He comments in particular on Spofforth's "very high action".

However, Anglo-Australian relations were not improved on the 1878/79 tour under Lord Harris. Matters came to a head in the fixture with New South Wales on 7, 8 and 10 February. On the second afternoon, Billy Murdoch was given run out by Coulthard, a Victorian umpire who had been hired by Harris, and a section of the Sydney crowd, doubtless fuelled by alcohol and the thought of prospective gambling losses, took it upon themselves to invade the playing area. Lord Harris was physically assaulted, Hornby joined in the fray, removing one of the 'larrikins' to the pavilion and play was abandoned for the day. "The Eleven Englishmen were surrounded by a rough and excited mob, who prevented further cricket being played that day" reported *Wisden*.[331] "What will they say in England?" was the Australasian headline the following day.

There were due apologies from officials. Lord Harris diplomatically exonerated the authorities from any culpability: '...he did not place any blame on the Association, or the cricketers of Sydney, but it was an occurrence which it was impossible he could forget.'[332] In his report of the tour in Lillywhite's *Cricketers' Annual* Lord Harris makes no mention of the incident, contenting himself to say that "when stumps were drawn on the 8th New South Wales were still about 70 behind with one wicket down".

Notwithstanding the diplomacy, Australia and Australians were now in bad odour. A domestic dispute between the Victorian and New South Wales Cricket Associations about the management of the rapidly cobbled together tour did not help matters[333] and the 1880 tour seemed doomed to be a public relations and financial failure. It would have been so but for the England-Australia match at The Oval. They managed to secure only a handful of first-class fixtures, against Derbyshire, Gloucestershire, Sussex and Yorkshire (the latter without the support of the county committee) and had to be content to play matches against the odds, mostly teams of eighteen.

Writing a year later in Lillywhite's, 'Incog' said that the visit of the Australians nearly produced a permanent rupture between the cricketers of the old and the new world. Although he was an ardent admirer of Australian cricket, he took the view that the visit was "ill-advised". The commercial spirit of the 1878 tour still had disagreeable memories of *de jure* amateurs, but *de facto* professionals. 'Incog' goes on to admit, however, that "the match at the Oval proved the means of reconciliation",[334] but with a patronising condescension adds:

> It is easy to comprehend that the distinction between amateurs and professionals may be a little strange in a country of such recent growth as Australia…
>
> …it will be best for Australians to understand that this is one of our English notions, nay more, that it is one of our English laws, that anyone who takes more than his expenses is in reality a professional.
>
> We should remind the colonial managers too, to make their programme sure by sending over their own agent in time for the annual meeting of the English county secretaries, and this will remove another of the obstacles which stood in the way of the team which visited England in 1880.

He then passes on to public schools cricket, having conveniently chosen to overlook the fact that W G Grace, England's heaviest scorer in the Oval match, while notionally an amateur, was also a far heavier earner than any of his professional colleagues.

'Incog', however, did not go as far as Walter Hadow, who wrote to the Daily Telegraph:

> …it is sincerely to be hoped that we have seen the last of Australian cricket and cricketers; at any rate until they have learned the true spirit in which the game should be played.[335]

Baily's, looking back to the previous tour and "the pretentious spirit which characterised their conduct in 1878, and their objection to being considered professionals, while sharing in the profits of a lucrative voyage", nevertheless regretted the fact that no fixture had been arranged on a metropolitan ground.[336]

James Lillywhite, as Agent for the 1880 tourists, did his best to arrange more first-class fixtures, approaching Surrey in January with a proposal for a match at the Oval. The Committee was not interested:

> A letter was read from Mr James Lillywhite Junr proposing a match or matches at The Oval on behalf of the Australian cricketers engaged to visit England

during 1880. The Secretary was instructed to reply that the programme for the season was too full to admit of the Committee making further engagements.[337]

The following month, a further letter was received and dismissed peremptorily, the Secretary being instructed to reply that he had the matter before the Committee and they would further consider it.[338] The committee then turned its attention to the more important business of the report of the Challenge Cup Sub-Committee.

Lillywhite persisted, playing an additional card of the possibility of a match for charity. The committee was split and the response, while not quite as negative as it had been on the previous two occasions, was hardly encouraging:

> The question of playing a match with the Australians for a charity was brought forward and after some discussion Mr Burrup proposed and Dr Blades seconded that the Committee do not entertain the proposition of playing the Australians on any consideration whatsoever. An amendment was proposed by Mr Smith and seconded by Mr Mark Catley that the question remain in abeyance for the present.[339]

So the door remained slightly ajar. The Australians themselves chipped in, but the diehards on the Committee remained adamant:

> A letter was read from the Secretary of the Australian Eleven asking for the use of the ground for a match the proceeds to be given to the Cricketers' Fund. Mr Burrup proposed and Dr Blades seconded a resolution that the Committee having received the letter of the Australian Secretary regret their inability to entertain the proposition inasmuch as owing to previous engagements a truly representative eleven could not be secured to meet them.[340]

It was only when W G Grace's attempts to secure a match at Lord's had failed that the Committee was persuaded to seize the opportunity not taken by the Marylebone Club and stage a full international at Kennington. At the committee meeting on Thursday 15 July 1880, the following letter from the Secretary of MCC was read:

Lord's July 5 1880

My dear Sir

I write immediately to tell you what has taken place here today at Committee with regard to the Australians. Mr W G Grace came to the Committee and said that it was a great pity that the Australians did not have a match here and offered to get up an eleven against them on July 19th (ie over and under 30 here) and it was resolved that if Mr Grace can send a representative eleven of England to this Committee by Monday next, his proposition will be favourably entertained. Believe me.

Yours very truly
Henry Perkins

A further letter written four days later accompanied it:

Lord's July 9 1880

My dear Sir

I have just got a telegram from Mr W G Grace that the Australians could not in any case play here and as far as the MCC are concerned the matter is at an end.

The Committee resolved to call a special meeting on Monday 26th "to consider the advisability of allowing the use of the Oval for a match against the Australians. At that meeting, incorrectly dated 15 July in the minute book, 'It was resolved that a match be played against the Australians on such dates and on such conditions as may be subsequently arranged.' It was the sixth time the question of a match with the Australians had come before the Committee. The U-turn was complete. Having said 'No' and then 'Maybe' the lady was finally persuaded to say 'Yes'. A Sub-Committee comprising Messrs Burrup, Lucas, Strachan and the Secretary was appointed "with full power to carry out the necessary details". The extent of the contribution of Messrs Burrup, Lucas and Strachan is unclear. The Secretary, having been ill earlier in the month[341] and fully aware that if Moses had been obliged to work through a committee the children of Israel would still have been in Egypt, was left with the tasks of enlisting the aid of Lord Harris, finding a team and with a few weeks of the season to go, finding suitable dates. Possible ones were 6, 7 and 8 September, but James Lillywhite had used his Sussex connections to arrange a fixture with that county. Alcock sallied forth from the Oval office on a Kissinger-style diplomatic mission.

First port of call was Canterbury where Lord Harris was participating in the Festival, then, his support enlisted,[342] to Brighton to meet the Sussex Committee and persuade them to defer their match with the tourists till a later date, thus freeing 6, 7 and 8 September for the Oval fixture. Secondary sources and subsequent exchanges of correspondence between the two county clubs suggest that the meeting was cordial. Under Sod's Law of Archival Research, the Sussex minutes have not survived, the earliest records of the Executive and General Committee dating from September 1880. Then, telephonic communication having only just begun its journey to the sophisticated heights it was to achieve in the twenty-first century, Alcock made a trip to Scotland,[344] not for a football international this time, but to persuade A G Steel and Alfred Lyttelton to forsake the grouse moors and answer their country's call. He was less successful with three who had witnessed the Sydney riots, Emmett, Ulyett and, despite the Harrovian connection, A N Hornby, but, notwithstanding that, a team of tolerable strength was assembled. The remainder of the Committee stayed home to deal with the domestic arrangements.

It has been said that minutes can be like balance sheets and bikinis - less interesting for what they reveal than what they leave to the imagination - and it is not difficult to detect a mild committee panic underlying such entries as:

It was resolved that in consequence of the difficulty placed in the way of getting a representative eleven of England to meet the Australians the Secretary be instructed to do his best to ensure a representative eleven of Players for a match at the Oval in September in default of securing an England England [sic], progress to be reported to a future meeting of the Committee.[345]

and later:

The Committee decided that rather than the Australian match should not be played on Sept 6 7 & 8, the Secretary be empowered to pay the professional players twenty pounds each.[346]

No prevaricating between £10 and £20 now as was the case in 1878 and would be again in 1896. Detailed arrangements for the match were going ahead and large scale non-co-operation from the game's more talented journeymen was to be avoided at all costs.

Lord Harris had no doubt that Alcock's motives were partly mercenary and confesses that he was less than convinced about the venture, but was won round by Alcock's enthusiasm and diplomacy. Writing over thirty years later, he said:

> The late Charles Alcock besides being very keen about the game always had an eye for the main chance, ie Oval gate money, and appeared one day in August at Canterbury when Kent was playing there in order to implore me to waive my objections, 'help to get together a team' and captain it. To this, after much talk I consented and I had to bring a lot of pressure to bear on several prominent amateurs to return from Scotland in order to play. They did so but were nothing like in full practice. The Lord Mayor subsequently entertained both teams at the Mansion House, when I had the opportunity to bury the hatchet as regards the Sydney incident.[347]

On 23 August, the Committee decided on the admission charges for the match: 1/- for entry, 2/6 for transfer to the stand, 2/6 for horses, 10/- for carriages, £1 for drays. A week later - further panic. Large crowds anticipated, it was decided that no carriages or horses be admitted - a classic and literal example of policy making on the hoof. Forty policemen on foot and four mounted were hired.

Not for the only occasion in the game's history were the establishment view and the response of the general public in conflict. A season which had begun with some serious opposition to the very concept of a tour by Australians ended with crowds flocking to The Oval for England's first home international cricket match. The size of the actual gate varies from publication to publication - 40,000 on the first two days according to Easterbrook; 65,000 over the three according to Rae - but Alcock's foresight was justified. The events of 1880 marked a watershed in his relations with the Committee. The *de jure* position remained the same, but the *de facto* position is that the Secretary was now a leader more than a servant of his committee and the formal channels of getting things approved were separate from the informal and diplomatic ones for getting them done.

The match itself was also a success from every point of view - cricket, financial and public relations:

> The English Eleven was captained by Lord Harris, whose presence in that position was regarded as an emblem that thorough friendship was restored between English and Australian cricketers...
>
> The result was as creditable to the vanquished as to the victors, and it hardly established the superiority of English cricket which Englishmen were yet disposed to claim.[348]

Australia were weakened by the absence of Spofforth who had suffered a broken finger, batting against what contemporary reports say was a blatant thrower at Scarborough in a match with Eighteen of that town.[349] England's 420, thanks in the main to W G Grace's 152, put them in the driving seat. Australia collapsed and followed on, but Murdoch's undefeated 153 ensured England had to bat again. Requiring 57 to win, they tinkered with the batting order and lost half the side for 31, but recovered to win by five wickets. A G Steel recalled later:

> The writer had taken off his cricket clothes at the end of the Australians' second innings, thinking all would soon be over; but cricket is a strange game and he soon had to put them on again.[350]

One remarkable feature was Fred Grace's catch in the deep to dismiss Bonnor. Sadly, two weeks later, having never recovered from a chill caught on a railway journey, Fred was in his coffin.

On a lighter note, there is an anecdote, that, following W G's innings, Murdoch bet a sovereign, that he, Murdoch, would surpass it and, having done so and won the wager, wore the coin thereafter on his watch chain.[351]

Alcock, himself was in no doubt about the significance of the fixture: 'In the eternal fitness of things...the game was in every way worthy of a historic occasion'.[352] In the wake of the match, the Committee, conveniently forgetting their earlier attitude, basked in an orgy of self-congratulation. Letters were sent to "Lord Harris and the various Amateurs who represented England".[353] Mr Heartay of the London and County

Bank was presented with an umbrella for his services.[354] The professionals were conveniently overlooked: they'd had their £20. The Sub-Committee were thanked for "the excellent manner in which they carried out all the arrangements and a letter sent to the caterers "complaining of the imperfect manner in which the public visiting the Oval on the occasion of the Australian match was provided for"[355]

The letter to Lord Harris has survived. Written by the Secretary from his home address on 18 September 1880 it reads:

Dear Lord Harris

I am desired by the Committee of the Surrey Club to express to you their sincere thanks for the hearty and ready assistance rendered to them in connection with the recent match between England and the Australians.

They recognise fully the extent of the help received from you, as indeed but for you the match would never have come off, and they appreciated thoroughly the effort made by you to ensure the success of the match when it was at last fixed.

They trust that you yourself share pleasant recollections of the game, which the Australians and the public generally seem to retain not only of the match, but of the impartiality of the immense company before which it was played.

Yours truly
C W Alcock
Sec Surrey County CC[356]

An exchange of diplomatic niceties with Sussex followed, lubricated by a cheque for 100 guineas. Mark Catley, the Treasurer, who was to die shortly afterwards, wrote to the Sussex President in the following terms:

Great Suffolk Street
Southwark Square
10 Nov 1880

To the Right Honourable the Earl of Sheffield
My Lord
As Treasurer of the Surrey County Cricket Club I have been requested by the Committee to forward to your Lordship as President of the Sussex County Cricket Club the enclosed cheque for one hundred guineas in recognition of

THE OVAL OFFICE

the kind feeling which induced your Club for the good of cricket to make such arrangements as enabled ours to play the Australian match early in last September which resulted in such a brilliant success and was of the greatest advantage not only to our Club but I firmly believe also to cricket generally, and which will help to strengthen those friendly feelings already existing between ourselves and our Australian colonies.

I have the honour to remain
Your Lordship's obedient servant
(sgd) Mark Catley

Two days later, his Lordship replied:

Sheffield Park Nov 12 1880

Dear Sir
As President of the Sussex County Club I beg to tender to yourself and the Surrey Club my heartfelt thanks, not only for the cheque which is, in itself, a welcome and valuable addition to our funds but for the succeeding handsome and generous spirit which has dictated so liberal a gift.

It will always be most gratifying to the Sussex County Club to remember that their endeavours to meet the views of the Surrey Club and to enable Australia to meet England at The Oval, have met with such a cordial and generous appreciation.

I am confident that the Committee of the Sussex Club will take the earliest opportunity for expressing in the most marked manner in their power the sense of the generous conduct of the Surrey Club. Meanwhile allow me as President to tender to you and through you to the Surrey County Club my own warmest acknowledgement of an act, the liberality of which will not soon be forgotten either by our own County Club, or by the cricketing community of Sussex.

I thoroughly concur with the opinion you have expressed as to the excellent effect of the Australian match itself.

Believe me. Yours truly
(sgd) Sheffield

The great advantage to cricket generally is not reflected in the MCC's Annual Report which makes no mention of the abortive attempt to host an international at Lord's. In *Wisden's* report of the match, the compiler 'much regrets that the limited space allocated to the Australians' matches in this book precludes the possibility of giving a lengthened account of this famous contest'. Fourteen pages were devoted to the Australian tour; seventy-three to the doings of the MCC. Over time, the balance was to change.

Family Life

On the family front, it was shortly after his appointment at The Oval that, on 15 April 1872, a fourth child and third daughter, Charlotte Mabel was born and to meet the needs of a family that was growing up and increasing in numbers at approximately yearly intervals, Alcock moved to Jersey Lodge, Norwood Lane, a larger property a little nearer to The Oval. His fifth child, Charles Ernest was born there on 16 September 1873. Sadly, the baby survived just five months, died on 13 February and was buried in West Norwood Cemetery five days later. Helen Mary and Marion Frances were also born at Jersey Lodge on 11 October 1874 and 7 August 1875 respectively.

By this time Norwood Lane had become Norwood Road and, since the transfer of the Crystal Palace from Hyde Park to Sydenham after the Great Exhibition of 1851, Lower (now West) Norwood area had developed rapidly as a suburban base for the newly emerging middle classes. There then followed a move back across the river to Stoke Newington where the last and eighth child and sixth daughter, Violet May, was born on 14 May 1878. Her mother was now 38 and enough was enough.

It was about the time of the inaugural Test that the Alcock family moved again, this time from Stoke Newington to a large house at 36 Somerleyton Road, Brixton, in an area which, a hundred years later, was at the centre of the race riots which led to the Scarman Report, but at the time a highly respectable part of suburbia where his neighbours included a clergyman and senior civil servant. It was from that address that Alcock wrote to Lord Harris after the successful first Test match on English soil.

It is a story of upward mobility, both socially and professionally. The administration of cricket is an area of Charles Alcock's life, though by no means the only one where, one might draw on his classical education and say of him, as Suetonius did of Augustus, *Iure sit gloriatus marmoream se relinquere, quam latericiam, accepisset.* He found a city of earth and left a city of marble.

REFERENCES

242. Bettesworth *Chats on the Cricket Field* p 24

243. *Richmond Herald* 8 Sept 1893; *Richmond and Twickenham Times* 9 Sept 1893

244. Cardus *Cricket* p 174

245. Bettesworth *Chats on the Cricket Field* p 20

246. *Sportsman* 7 October 1865

247. *Sportsman* 14 October 1865

248. Booth *Old Pink 'Un Days* pp 60-1

249. *Victoria History of the Counties of England - Surrey* p 531

250. *Field* 12 May 1860

251. Surrey CCC minutes 20 March 1872.

252. Surrey CCC minutes 17 July 1879

253. Alverstone & Alcock *Surrey Cricket* p 324

254. Lemmon *The History of Surrey County Cricket Club* p 45 and Alcock's Obituary in *Cricket* 28 February 1907 p11

255. Vol VII p 359

256. *Wisden* 1873 p 121

257. *Wisden* 1873 p 122

258. *Wisden* 1873 p 123

259. John and V E

260. Alverstone & Alcock *Surrey Cricket* p 326

261. Alverstone & Alcock *Surrey Cricket* p 339

262. Surrey CCC minutes. 10 May 1872

263. Surrey CCC minutes : Rough minute book 1850-72

264. Obituary in *Cricket* by F S Ashley-Cooper 28 February 1907

265. *Sporting Life* 1 January 1873

266. *Wisden* 1874

267. *Life and Reminiscences of Robert Abel in the Cricket Field* p17

268. Bettesworth *Chats on the Cricket Field* p 22

269. Rae *W G Grace: A Life* p 149

270. Surrey CCC minutes 6 June 1889

271. *Cricket* 8 August 1889 p 317

272. Quoted in *Wisden* 1874 p 93

273. Surrey CCC minutes 26 August 1872
274. *Sportsman*
275. Alverstone & Alcock *Surrey Cricket* pp 330-331
276. *Lord's and the MCC*
277. Surrey CCC minutes - Rough Minute Book 1857
278. *Sporting Life* 28 November 1863
279. *Wisden* 1874 p 100
280. Surrey CCC minutes 13 February 1873
281. Surrey CCC minutes 13 February 1873
282. *Cricket* 17 May 1882 p 14
283. Rae *W G* p132
284. Vol XII p 706
285. *Wisden* 1875 p 23286.
286. Surrey CCC minutes 31 May and 10 July 1880
287. Report of Ground Sub-Committee 20 January 1880
288. *Wisden* 1876 p 19 - Report of 1875 Annual General Meeting held 5 May 1875
289. Hedgcock *Aussie Rules History in UK* www.iatc.org.au/uk250.html
290. Titley & McWhirter *Centenary History of the Rugby Football Union* p 75
291. Alverstone & Alcock *Surrey Cricket* p 439
292. Surrey CCC minutes 14 March 1876
293. Surrey CCC minutes 20 January 1880
294. Surrey CCC minutes 8 June 1874
295. Surrey CCC minutes 26 March 1873
296. Surrey CCC minutes 8 June 1874
297. Surrey CCC minutes 8 December 1879
298. Surrey CCC minutes 20 January 1880
299. e.g. Peckham Surrey CCC minutes 11 August 1873 and London Harriers 14 August 1876
300. Surrey CCC minutes 24 June 1875
301. Surrey CCC minutes 8 March 1877
302. Surrey CCC minutes 20 December 1875
303. Surrey CCC minutes 14 March 1876
304. Surrey CCC minutes 20 March 1877
305. Surrey CCC minutes 12 May and 4 September 1876
306. Surrey CCC minutes 19 July 1877

307. Surrey CCC minutes 8 December 1879

308. *Wisden* 1875 p 66

309. Surrey CCC minutes 17 January 1889

310. *Cricket* 21 February 1889 p 25

311. Foreword to Rob Steen's *This Sporting Life: Cricket*

312. Surrey CCC minutes 20 April 1874

313. Surrey CCC minutes 4 September 1876

314. Surrey CCC minutes 20 November 1876

315. *Wisden* 1877 p 147

316. AGM 3 May 1877

317. Surrey CCC Accounts

318. The first known use of the term 'Test match' was in Hammersley's *Victorian Cricketers Guide 1861/62* which, referring to H H Stephenson's tour, says "Of the thirteen matches five only can be termed 'test matches': the three played at Melbourne and two played at Sydney". Those, however, were against teams containing more than eleven players and cricket history now accepts the match played at Melbourne in March 1877 as the first Test match. *The Sydney Morning Herald* of 3 January 1883 referred to "The first of the great 'test matches' on Hon Ivo Bligh's tour, but it was only from 16 September 1884 when the *Melbourne Argus* reported that "One of the test matches was won by England, the other two drawn in favour of Australia" that the term passed into general usage (*Cricket Quarterly* Spring 1966 and Winter 1966-67)

319. Lemmon p 52

320. Melbourne Cricket Club

321. *Field* 10 March 1860

322. *Wisden* 1879 pp 26-29

323. Christiansen *The Visitors* p 182

324. Christiansen *The Visitors* p 183

325. *Surrey County Cricket Club Centenary 1845-1945* p 35

326. *'W G' Cricketing Reminiscences and Personal Reminiscences* p 170

327. Alverstone & Alcock *Surrey Cricket* p242

328. *Wisden* 1879 p 131

329. p 1

330. p 4

331. 1880 p 31

332. 1880 p 32
333. Rae *W G Grace: A Life* p 241
334. *Lillywhite's Cricketers' Annual 1881* p 17
335. 1 April 1880, quoted by Rae
336. May 1880
337. Surrey CCC minutes 20 January 1880
338. Surrey CCC minutes 9 February 1880
339. Surrey CCC minutes 10 May 1880
340. Surrey CCC minutes 31 May 1880
341. Surrey CCC minutes 1 July 1880
342. Sir Home Gordon *Background of Cricket*
343. *The Man Who Made All Seasons, Wisden* 1880 p 107
344. Gordon *Background of Cricket* p 29
345. Surrey CCC minutes 12 August 1880
346. Surrey CCC minutes 23 August 1880
347. *Memorial Biography of W G Grace* p147
348. Brumfitt and Kirby *England v Australia at the Wicket*
349. Rae p 247
350. Steel & Lyttelton *The Badminton Library: Cricket* p 317
351. Sir Home Gordon 80 not out in *The Cricketer Annual 1951/52*
352. Alverstone & Alcock *Surrey Cricket* p 243
353. Surrey CCC minutes 13 September 1880
354. Surrey CCC minutes 25 October 1880
355. Surrey CCC minutes 13 September 1880
356. MCC collection

Charles W. Alcock, The Father of Modern Sport.

Left and below: 10 Norfolk Street, Bishopwearmouth - Alcock's birthplace.

Above, right and below: Pann's Bank and Wearside, where the Alcocks had their shipyard.

Left: 17 John Street, the Alcock family residence in the 1850s.

Above: Druries' House, Harrow, where Alcock spent his schooldays.

Meeting held 26th October 1863 at Freemasons Tavern

Proposed by Mr Morley
Seconded by Mr Mackenzie
and Carried "That Mr Pember do take the Chair"

Prop'd by Mr Morley
Sec'd by Mr Steward
and carried "That the Clubs represented at this meeting now form themselves into an association to be called "The Football Association"

whereupon the following clubs were enrolled

Clubs	Represented by
N. N. Kilburn	Arthur Pember
Barnes	Geo E. Morley
6 O War Office	Ed. Wawn
Crusaders	H. T. Steward
Forest Leytonstone	J. F. Alcock
Perceval House	G. W. Shillingford
Blackheath	

Above: Minutes of first meeting of FA on 26 October, 1863
(Official History of the FA).

Right: Newspaper report of the first 'pseudo international' on 5 March 1870, taken from the 8 March 1870 edition of the *Sportsman*

ENGLAND v. SCOTLAND.

Left: Minute of FA establishing Challenge Cup, 20 July 1871 (Official History of FA).

Above: Artist's impression of first rugby international at the
Kennington Oval, played on 5 February 1872.

Right: An Alcock item
about his involvement with
Surrey County Cricket Club
and cricket publications
taken from the *Sportsman*,
10 April 1872
(By permission of the
British Library).

ENGLAND v. SCOTLAND.

ASSOCIATION RULES.

THE second international match of the season, according to the rules of the Football Association, will take place at Kennington Oval this (Saturday) afternoon. Play will commence at three and ceaso at half-past four o'clock. The following have been selected to represent the two countries:

England: C. W. Alcock, Wanderers; C. J. Chenery, Crystal Palace Club; J. C. Clegg, Sheffield Club; G. Holden, Clapham Rovers; A. C. Thompson, Old Etonians (half-back); Percy Weston, Barnes Club; R. W. S. Vidal, Westminster School; C. W. Stephenson, Wanderers (back); T. C. Hooman, Wanderers; A. G. Bonsor, Old Etonians; and C. F. Woollaston, Oxford University. Reserves: C. W. Thompson, Old Etonians, and W. S. Rawson, Westminster School.

Scotland: Quintin Hogg (captain), Wanderers; H. W. Renny-Tailyour, Royal Engineers; H. Mitchell, Royal Engineers; R. E. W. Crawford, Harrow Chequers; G. G. Kennedy, Wanderers; W. Lindsay, Old Wykehamist; M. Muir-Mackenzie, Old Carthusians; H. S. Ferguson, Royal Artillery; C. E. Nepean, Oxford University; W. H. Gladstone, M.P., Old Etonians; G. Barker, Royal Engineers. Reserves: H. H. Stewart, Cambridge University; E. Elliot, Harrow Chequers; W. H. Primrose, Civil Service; and R. Smith, Queen's Park Club, Glasgow.

ASSOCIATION CHALLENGE CUP.

WANDERERS v. QUEEN'S PARK, GLASGOW.

THE above match will be played at Kennington Oval on Monday afternoon, March 4, from half-past three until five o'clock. The Scotchmen will be represented by R. Gardner (captain), R. Edmiston, J. Hepburn, W. Ker, H. Leakie, J. Smith, R. Smith, J. Taylor, J. E. A. Walker, R. Wotherspoon, and J. Weir. The Wanderers will in all probability be C. W. Alcock, A. C. Thompson, C. W. Stephenson, A. G. Bonsor, C. W. Thompson, R. E. W. Crawford, Hon. T. H. Pelham, R. C. Welch, C. F. Woollaston, F. H. Wilson, and H. H. Stewart. A dinner will take place at the Oval after the conclusion of the match, at which the Glasgow eleven will be present. Members of Association clubs are invited. Application for tickets may be made to the hon. sec. of the Wanderers Football Club, Boy-court, Ludgate-hill, E.C.

FOOTBALL ASSOCIATION.

WE are requested to remind officers of Association clubs that the annual general meeting will be held at the Arundel Hotel, Arundel-street, Strand, London, on Wednesday evening next at seven o'clock.

SHEFFIELD v. LONDON.

THE third match of the present season will be played at Bramall Lane, Sheffield, on Saturday next. The game will be divided into two equal periods, the first to be played according to Sheffield, the second according to London rules. The elevens will be selected from the following:

London: C. W. Alcock, T. C. Hooman, C. J. Chenery, C. W. Stephenson, A. Morten, R. E. W. Crawford, Percy Weston, Percy Currey, R. C. Welch, F. B. Boden, E. H. Elliot, and D. Allport.

Sheffield: J. Marsh (captain), A. Wood, J. C. Clegg, W. E. Clegg, W. H. Carr, J. Hollingsworth, G. H. Sampson, C. Mills, H. Ash, Butler, and Horton.

Only fine weather is required to produce an immense "gallery."

Left: Four news items in the *Sportsman*, 24 February 1872, all involving Alcock. (By permission of the British Library).

Above: Sketches of first association football international in
Glasgow, 30 November 1872 (Official History of FA).

Above: Frontispiece of Alcock's book
Football: Our Winter Game, 1874.

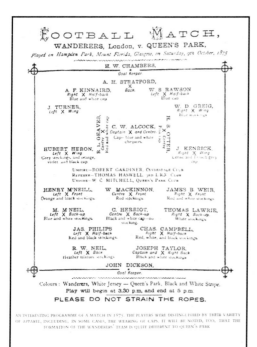

Left: Programme for
Queen's Park v
Wanderers, 9 October
1875.

Above: Football at Kennington Oval.

Above: Football by electric light at Bramall Lane, Sheffield,
14 October 1878.

In Affectionate Remembrance

OF

ENGLISH CRICKET,

WHICH DIED AT THE OVAL

ON

29th AUGUST, 1882,

Deeply lamented by a large circle of sorrowing friends and acquaintances.

R. I. P.

N.B.—The body will be cremated and the ashes taken to Australia.

Above: Mock obituary in the *Sporting Times* of September 2, 1882 creating the Ashes (By permission of the British Library).

Above: Sketches from the 1883 Cup Final, where Blackburn
Olympic beat Old Etonians to lift the Cup.

Above: 1880 Test Match (Surrey CCC).

Above: Letter from Alcock to Lord Harris after
1880 Test Match (Reproduced by kind permission of the
Committee of the Marylebone Cricket Club).

Left: 16 Stanhope Road, Streatham, where Alcock lived in the mid-1880s, and where his eldest son died.

Above: Hazelwood, 16 Ennerdale Road, Richmond - before his death in Brighton, this was Alcock's last home. His widow continued to live there until her death in 1937.

Left and below: The last resting place of Charles W. Alcock in West Norwood Cemetery.

C.W. ALCOCK

AN INSPIRING SECRETARY
OF THE FOOTBALL ASSOCATION
1870 — 1895
AND OF
SURREY COUNTY CRICKET CLUB
1872 — 1907

CHAPTER 7

THE COMPETITIVE DEVICE

IT WOULD BE AN EXAGGERATION to say that Alcock 'invented' the League and Knockout systems of competition which today are taken for granted. A league system where each match was not an end in itself but part of a wider system had been established in baseball in 1871 and the knock-out cup device certainly owed something to the Cock House Cup system used at Harrow and other public schools. But in his hands and through his proactive administration, the ideas spread like a forest fire and became the established norm by the end of the century. Even the idea of a knockout competition for County Cricket Clubs, seen as too revolutionary by the conservative forces opposed to the for once pioneering MCC had become reality in the form of the Gillette Cup by 1963.

It would be misleading to suggest that sport began in the nineteenth century. The Greeks, Romans and Chinese had long sporting traditions and long before Queen Victoria came to the throne in 1837, some sort of cricket had been played, as had "mob football". Athletics, prize fighting and horse racing especially were well established, but would not have flourished were it not for widespread and heavy gambling. It was in the last third of the nineteenth century, however, that the Victorian penchant for organisation, classification and 'rational recreation' led to codification and formalisation. The Victorians organised their society by class and it was a small step from that concept to that of organised leisure which included not only sport but brass bands, amateur dramatics and church-based organisations. In *The Sports and Pastimes of the People of England*, published in 1831, Joseph Strutt separates Rural Exercises practised by Persons of Rank from Rural Exercises generally practised. It was a significant distinction. A number of sports trace their governing bodies to the mid to late nineteenth century and the establishment of competition is a natural extension of that organisation.

Challenge Cups

The FA Challenge Cup, originally played for by a small number of southern amateur clubs with the occasional entry from the provinces and dominated in its early years by Alcock's Wanderers, was by the end of the 1870s attracting the interest of those outside the narrow social band of past and present public schoolboys and their associates and becoming something of a holy grail for the northern working class clubs, still notionally amateur under the rules of the Association, but effectively sowing the seeds of professionalism which, after a long and often bitter struggle, would be legalised in 1885.

The numbers entering the competition had steadily increased from fifteen in 1872 to 54 by the end of the decade. The first challenge to southern monopoly came from Nottingham Forest and Darwen in 1879. The former reached the semi-final beating Sheffield, Old Harrovians and Oxford University on the way, but it was the mill-workers of Darwen who stole the limelight. After being 5-1 behind to the Old Etonians with fifteen minutes left, they fought back to earn a 5-5 draw and a replay which, under the rules of the competition as they then stood, took place on the same ground. In straitened financial circumstances, helped by a contribution from their opponents, the FA and public subscription, after their first trip had been financed by the citizens of the town, they again travelled to the Kennington Oval and again they drew, this time 2-2, but physical and financial resources exhausted, they succumbed 6-2 in the second replay (the quick fix penalty shoot-out was more than a hundred years away; indeed, the penalty kick itself still had to hit the rule book). Old Etonians went on to beat Nottingham Forest in the semi-final and then went on to lift the trophy. Old Etonians won the Cup again in 1882 when legend has it that their captain, Arthur Kinnaird, stood on his head in celebration in front of the pavilion. If the rumour is true, it was a gesture of symbolic significance, for from that point the whole ethos of amateur football was turned on its head. Never again would the Association Cup be won by an amateur side. The Darwen team had included two Scotsmen, James Love and Fergus Suter. They were significant pointers for the future of the game.

Darwen had made an impact and paved the way for near neighbours Blackburn Rovers and Blackburn Olympic to get their hands on the "little tin idol" in the not too distant future. Olympic were the first team to take the Cup out of London. Significantly and symbolically, their opponents were Old Etonians who made little impact on the competition in subsequent years.

The *Eton College Chronicle* took a dim view of Olympic's approach to the game, suggesting that their victory was due to the sharp practice of preparation and training:

> So great was their ambition to wrest the Cup from the holders, that they introduced into football play a practice which has excited the greatest disapprobation in the South. For three weeks before the match they went into a strict course of training...

The criticism was identical to that which Flanders and Swann directed at foreigners:

> They've simply no notion of playing the game.
> They argue with umpires; they cheer when they've won.
> And they practice beforehand which ruins the fun.[357]

Flanders and Swann were deliberately satirical. The *Eton College Chronicle* was in deadly earnest. The gilt of the jeunesse dorée was being challenged and tarnished by the guilt of barely concealed professionalism.

Meanwhile, Olympic and their supporters cheered when they'd won. The return to Blackburn was marked by brass bands and applauding crowds as the victorious local heroes were drawn through the streets of the town on a wagonette pulled by half a dozen horses. "Is that t'Cup?" asked one of the locals. "It looks laike a tea-kettle." Sam Warburton, the Olympic captain, is alleged to have replied, "It might well do to thee, but it's right welcome here in Lancashire, an' it'll ne'er go back to Lunnon."[358]

The words were strangely prophetic. Although taken back for annual presentation, that particular trophy was never again held by a London club, amateur or professional. In 1895, having been won by Aston Villa, it was stolen from a shop window where it was on display and never seen again. Over sixty years later there was a confession to the effect that the cup had been melted down and converted into counterfeit silver coins, but the story was never authenticated. There was a proposal in the FA

Council that the stolen cup be replaced by a gold one to the value of £200. It was defeated and the Council decided to replace the trophy with one as close to the original as possible. The symbolic significance was of more importance than the cash value. This second trophy was superseded in 1911 by the current one and presented to Lord Kinnaird in recognition of his twenty-one years' service as President of the FA and his earlier playing distinctions.

The Cup was the forerunner of numerous others. In Surrey, for example, a Challenge Cup was instituted in 1882-83, a Junior Competition in 1886-87 and a Junior League in 1898-99.[359] Hampshire's first Challenge Cup had been earlier when Captain John May of Basingstoke Football Club put up a trophy for competition in 1879.[360] There were numerous similar examples throughout the country.

By 1888-89, it was clear that the organisation of the competition was in need of some streamlining and an element of seeding was introduced. Indeed, as much had been suggested by *Football* six years earlier:

Several complaints are made by first-class clubs against the admission of second and third class teams to the Association Challenge Cup competition. Hitherto the Football Association have refrained from taking any steps in this direction, but I hope this will be considered before next season. It is preposterous to allow a club whose eleven would stand no chance against the second eleven of the club it is drawn against to bring their opponents perhaps a hundred miles only to effect a result that is a foregone conclusion.

The revised rules provided that all ties in any round would be played at the same time on the same date. Preston's 26-0 victory over Hyde was the catalyst for exempting clubs with strong professional staffs from the early stages where weaker opposition would mean lower gates. The last 32 clubs in the competition would comprise the previous year's semi-finalists, eighteen clubs selected by the Council and ten to emerge from district qualifying competitions. The Association had turned from its original object of promoting sport to developing a business, The fun had gone and commercialism had taken over. Major Marindin resigned the Presidency in July 1889, his departure regretted by amateurs and professionals alike who, if they failed to see eye to eye on many matters, paid tribute to his fair-mindedness.

THE COMPETITIVE DEVICE

There is something in elimination competitions that appeals to the human psyche, whether it be in the final stages of the World Cup competitions which most major sports now have or games of musical chairs at children's parties. Geoffrey Green analyses it as follows:

What was and is the secret of the Cup? What has been its lure?... In the beginning, of course, it offered something to play for in a pattern that was then made up merely of friendly games. It was an impetus. Then it became a challenge. And as the challenge grew the impetus became the greater. We have seen how this little Cup inspired competitiveness, inspired the growth of new teams and set the whole game alight.

We have seen, too, how the desire to win it led to greater rivalry and with that expanding rivalry the encroachment of professionalism. In a word, indeed, the Cup changed the whole face of football...

It comes as a breath of a fresh air as the Old Year hands over to the New, a wonderful, breathtaking tonic that comes to sharpen and uplift the country in deep mid-winter...

The League programme may well be considered as the backbone of football. But it is the Cup that makes that backbone tingle with a thrill.

It is the character of the Cup, and the lure of the unknown, that grips. In the League, two sides can leave the field with honours equal and the points shared...But in the Cup there are no such half measures...[361]

Twenty of the first twenty-one Cup Finals were held at The Oval, the one exception being that of 1873 (the year of the only genuine "challenge" trophy) when it was held at Lillie Bridge and the crowds gradually increased from 2,000 when Wanderers beat the Royal Engineers to 25,000 in 1892 when the professionals had taken over and West Bromwich Albion beat Aston Villa. The ground had seen a power shift in the game from the amateurs to the professionals and then from the Lancastrian strongholds of Blackburn and Preston to their midland equivalents of West Bromwich Albion and Aston Villa.

Throughout all these changes, Alcock remained in charge at The Oval with a strong, hands-on, influential style of management. The authorities at The Oval were, however, becoming concerned about the potential damage to the cricket square. No football was played there in 1893 to allow repairs to the turf and in June 1895 the membership of the Surrey County Cricket Club voted by 1095 votes to 453 to discontinue football at The Oval. Not for the only time there was a direct conflict between cricket and commerce. Alcock remained appropriately neutral, to an extent a victim of his own success, alive to the advantages of exploiting the Oval to its maximum potential whilst ever mindful that its primary purpose was that of a cricket ground:

> What the future may have in store, of course, no one can foretell. But even the most enthusiastic believer in football can hardly conscientiously gainsay the fact that the discontinuance of football has made for the unmistakable improvement of the Oval in its chief mission as a cricket ground. One may regret, as many undoubtedly do, that the exciting contests in which the giants of football in generation after generation took part are numbered now among the things of the past. But necessity has no law. And in this case, one can honestly say, even though a footballer, that it was a stern necessity.[362]

The decision was not taken without serious consideration by the Football Sub-Committee, established in 1892 to examine the conflict between income and damage to the ground. Receipts were reducing because the proportion of the gate accruing to the Club was becoming smaller. On the other hand a number of members subscribed largely because of the football. Initially there had been an uneasy compromise as the Committee recommended:

> That football be continued at the Oval for the present - but having regard to the proper preservation and improvement of the turf for cricket purposes, it should be played only under the following restrictions:
>
> 1st. That no match be played on the centre turf, excepting the final tie, and that subject to the approval of the General Committee.
> 2nd. That no football be played on the ground more than once in the week, except by the special permission of the General Committee specially convened for that purpose.
> 3rd. That the receipts to the club from football on the ground in no case be less than half of the gross receipts, the Corinthians and the Final Tie excepted, without the special sanction of the General Committee.[363]

The membership had at first in 1894 voted in favour of the retention of football by 1108 votes to 727, but the following year, a petition from 35 members requested a special meeting and, after advice from the Committee, the verdict was reversed. The Secretary wrote to the membership in the following terms:

> In consequence of the great injury occasioned to the turf by football during the past season and the great expense thereby occasioned to the club, the Committee of the Surrey Cricket Club after due consideration, unanimously resolved that "in their opinion football should not be played at the Oval".

It was the end of an era. Since 1881, the total attendance for football at the Oval had been over a million, filling the coffers of both the host club and their tenants. If they thought it was all over, it was and, apart from a brief period in the 1950s when the ground was used by Corinthian Casuals, and cricketers' pre-match kickabouts, football has not been played at the ground since.

So, the Cup Final had to look for a new home. For two years, it had a peripatetic existence, finding a temporary base at Fallowfield and Goodison Park before settling down at the great natural bowl of the Crystal Palace where in 1901 110,820 saw Sheffield United and Tottenham Hotspur, the survivors of 220 entrants, draw 2-2. Less than thirty years earlier, the equivalent figures had been 2,000 and 15; twelve years later, when Aston Villa beat Sunderland 1-0 there were over 120,000 spectators, a world record at the time, and 457 entrants. In one generation the idea sparked off in part by an internal school competition had grown to proportions undreamed of by those pioneers in the offices of the *Sportsman* in 1871.

Geoffrey Green finds it impossible to overemphasise its significance and influence:

> Organized football, indeed, developed from an amusement of the leisured classes to the sport of nations. The influence of the Cup in all this wonderful growth is almost incalculable. It was the spark that set the whole bonfire of football alight…It altered the whole pattern and the whole purpose of the game.[364]

Cricket, as ever, was much slower in adopting the knock-out principle and following the short-lived MCC experiment of 1873, it was not attempted again - at least by teams at first-class level - for another ninety years. The conservative nature of the game's governing body was one reason, but a further one was that cricket by its nature produces more unfinished matches than football and, even among leisured amateurs and full-time professionals, replays and perhaps second replays would not be a practical proposition, especially if played over three days. Some modification of the rules would be required.

There had been earlier experiments, not so much with the knock-out principle in mind, but with a view to brightening up the game and producing a definite winner. In an article in the *Journal of the Cricket Society* in Spring 2000 J F Bailey traced the beginnings of limited overs cricket to South Africa in the First World War when The Reef met The Town at the Wanderers, Johannesburg, on 14 March 1915. The plan was to divide the batting time equally between the two sides, the first innings running from 10.30 to 2.25 and the second from 2.35 to 6.00. Someone seems to have got the arithmetic wrong, but the intention to disregard wickets and avoid a drawn match was nevertheless clear. The emergence of a clear winner made the formula appropriate for a knock-out competition, albeit with the need for the Duckworth-Lewis method and its precursors for deciding the winner in weather-affected matches.

Bailey is incorrect, however, in seeing the South African experiment as the first time-limit contest. More than a decade earlier, there had been a not dissimilar attempt at this kind of cricket in England, albeit over four innings of 4 ¼ hours each and a further novelty of 60-yard boundaries. Wickets would be disregarded and the result determined by runs alone. The one match played under the experimental rules (Yorkshire v Notts at Headingley in 1904) ran its course without their being implemented as neither side managed to bat for 4 ¼ hours.[365] The match can be seen as an administrative aberration, an idiosyncratic venture to attract spectators or perhaps as a precursor of limited overs cricket, 60 years ahead of its time.

The Football League

The establishment of the Football League in 1888 was one of the few significant sporting events of the late nineteenth century in which Charles Alcock was not directly involved. He was a pioneer of international competition in cricket and both codes of football and had both metaphorically and literally kicked off the Association Cup. The new venture arose from the desire of the professional clubs of the North and the Midlands to establish a regular competition where all-play-all in addition to the well established and growing one where one stroke of ill fortune could mean elimination and an anti-climactic end to the season.

The idea was not new. In the USA, baseball had been on the scene rather earlier than football. The New York Knickerbockers Club had been established in 1845 and drawn up a set of rules. Professionalism was introduced in the mid-1860s to a less class-conscious society than was to struggle to accept it on the other side of the pond twenty and thirty years later. 1869 saw the first all professional team in the Cincinnati Red Stockings. The National Association of Baseball Players, the ruling body of the game, was strictly amateur, but the financial success of the Red Stockings caused it to be superseded by the National Association of Professional Baseball Players which established an all-professional league in 1871, the National League in 1875 and the American League in 1883. All preceded the Football League by a number of years. The Oval had been made available for American baseball players in the same year the Football League was established and the sport had been seen at Lord's in 1874. So, there was certainly cross-fertilisation between the two sides of the Atlantic and an Alcock influence on the establishment of the Football League is at least conceivable. Although the inspiration behind the League was William McGregor of Aston Villa, had it not been for Alcock's enlightened and progressive approach to professionalism, the conditions would not have been in place for the new competition to be established and association football may very well have gone the way of rugby football and split into separate amateur and professional codes.

It was not McGregor's intention that the League should be in competition with the FA but rather that it should be complementary and provide an organisational framework for matches outside the Association Cup. He wrote to Aston Villa, Blackburn Rovers, Bolton Wanderers, Preston North End and West Bromwich Albion, inviting them to nominate other clubs:

Every year it is becoming more and more difficult for football clubs of any standing to meet their friendly engagements, and even arrange friendly matches. The consequence is that at the last moment, through cup-tie interferences, clubs are compelled to take on teams who will not attract the public.

I beg to tender the following suggestion as a means of getting over the difficulty. That ten or twelve of the most prominent clubs in England combine to arrange home-and-home [sic] fixtures each season, the said fixtures to be arranged at a friendly conference about the same time as the International conference. This combination might be known as the Association Football Union, and could be managed by a representative from each club.

Of course, this is in no way to interfere with the National Association, even the suggested matches might be played under cup-tie rules.[366]

The minutes of the Football League of 22 March 1888 expressed an intention 'to improve the present unsatisfactory state of club fixtures and to render them more certain of fulfilment and interesting in character'.[367]

So, the League became an organisation within an organisation, its co-existence with the senior body, generally peaceful, but with the occasional clash of interest.

The County Championship

Within a year cricket had followed the example of the winter game and the Secretaries of the first-class counties had agreed on a method of determining an order of merit the following season. While the formation of the Football League had been one catalyst, the triple tie for the 1889 'Championship' when Nottinghamshire, Lancashire and Surrey had each finished with 10 ½ 'points' on the informal basis of one for a win and half for a draw. Correspondence in *Cricket* [368] and other newspapers debated whether a draw was really equivalent to half a win and suggested various forms of tie-breaker including ones used much later, such as the number of wins and the "head-to-head". Some even went so far as to suggest categorisation into first, second and third class counties with end-of-season challenge matches to determine promotion and relegation.[369]

The idea of a 'champion county' was far from novel, but until this point, the holder of the title had been decided by the press with some input from

THE COMPETITIVE DEVICE

W G Grace and, unsurprisingly, at a time when counties played different numbers of matches and on occasions two or more counties had similar records, the verdict was far from unanimous. The emphasis was on an *ex post facto* decision and neither the press nor the counties themselves seem to have given much credence to the concept of a "title race".

The counties, both first-class (at the time Gloucestershire, Kent, Lancashire, Middlesex, Nottinghamshire, Surrey, Sussex and Yorkshire) and the newly emergent ones were seeking more of a say in the running of the game. The short-lived Cricket Council was a spirited attempt to have one, but vested interests caused its demise in 1890 after an existence of only three years.

Surrey's success spanned the old system and the new. They had been Champions in 1887 and 1888 (and 1886 according to the possibly biased *Cricket*, the other six 'authorities'[370] giving the title to Nottinghamshire) and shared in the triple tie of 1889. Under the rationalised system they took the title four times in five seasons between 1890 and 1894, being interrupted by Yorkshire only in 1893. The 'glory years' of the 50s and 60s had returned.

For its first five seasons the competition was based, as was the Football League, on an all-play-all basis, home and away, and the number of points determined by the simple device of ignoring draws and deducting matches lost from matches won. By 1895, however, the admission of Derbyshire, Essex, Hampshire, Leicestershire and Warwickshire to the existing nine (Somerset had joined in 1891) meant that the original basis had to be abandoned, as it was no longer possible for every county to play every other county home and away and the placings were now decided by points, as a percentage of finished games. It was as fair a method as any, but it was not until 1993, the first year when all Championship cricket was played over four days, that the all-play-all basis was reintroduced and later still, in 2000, that the 1890-94 system of nine counties playing home and away was re-established, the main difference being that there were now two divisions of nine each. The possibility of two and even three division championship was raised from time to time in *Cricket's* correspondence[371] and has been mooted on several occasions over more than a hundred years, but only at the end of the twentieth century was the nettle firmly grasped.

In 1903 the Minor Counties' Cricket Association put forward proposals similar to those in *Cricket* fourteen years earlier for a three-division county championship, ten teams in the First Division, eight in the Second, the remainder in the Third, two up, two down between all divisions, except no 2nd XI would be eligible for promotion. All would play all in Divisions 1 and 2 and these would be regarded as First Class. The scheme was shelved as being too revolutionary.

It was soundly condemned by *Wisden* Editor, Sydney Pardon:

If the second-class teams realise that if they show sufficiently marked superiority over their rivals promotion will follow as a matter of course, we shall hear no more of the proposals to adopt the system of the Football League. I have not a word to say against that body, but the system which answers very well with football would not do at all for cricket. The idea of a county with the tradition of Surrey or Notts being relegated to the second-class as the result of one bad season could not be entertained for a moment.[373]

His stance had not changed two years later when W G Grace proposed a two-division championship. The championship was a means to an end, not an end in itself and must not be made into a fetish.[374]

A century later, ECB took a long-overdue initiative and deigned to entertain such a notion, but it might just be that adherence to tradition at the expense of progress is one of the key reasons why the paying attendance of county clubs over a season is about the same as that for a second or third division football match on one Saturday afternoon.

REFERENCES

357. *Song of Patriotic Prejudice*
358. Phythian *Olympic F C* p 138
359. *Victoria County History of Surrey II* p 551
360. Gannaway *Association Football in Hampshire until 1914* p 7
361. Fabian & Green *Association Football III* p 26
362. Alcock & Alverstone *Surrey Cricket* p 445-6
363. Surrey CCC minutes 19 January 1892

364. Fabian & Green *Association Football III* p 9
365. *Cricket* 28 April and 5 May 1904
366. Young *A History of British Football* p 178
367. Gannaway *Association Football in Hampshire* p 17
368. *Cricket* 5 September 1889
369. *Cricket* 26 September 1889
370. Rowland Bowen, Wisden, John Lillywhite, James Lillywhite, WG Grace and Holmes
371. *Cricket* 29 March 1900
372. *Cricket* 26 November 1903
373. Quoted in *Cricket* 26 January 1905
374. *Wisden* 1907 p cxlvi

CHAPTER 8

PROFESSIONALISM

AT THE BEGINNING of the twenty-first century, professionalism has acquired a dual meaning beyond that of simply being paid to do a job of work: it can mean everything that is commendable about an approach to sport in the way of preparation, training and attitude, as in "a thoroughly professional performance" or it can refer to what is shabby, underhand and despicable, as in "professional foul". These nuances were already around in the nineteenth century, though at the time they were linked with social class. At its basic and crudest level, however, professionalism in Victorian Britain meant playing sport for money. It was not new. In the Athens of the sixth century B.C. which, like Victorian England, had a class structure, Solon had rewarded Olympic Games winners with cash prizes and Vergil and Homer record prizes of bullocks, wine, cloaks and money for victors of athletic events. Eighteenth century cricket had seen the aristocracy hire private professional cricketers and professionalism had long been accepted into cricket as it had in horse-racing and prize-fighting. It was new to football. None was more alive to the situation than Charles Alcock. His dual background of the industrial revolution and public school served him well.

Not everyone saw the situation in Alcock's way. Caspar Whitney, in *Sporting Pilgrimage* in 1894, expressed the view that to mix amateur and professional sport was as senseless as negroes fraternising with the refined and cultured members of the civilised world, while Trollope, in *British Sports and Pastimes* in 1868 had suggested that, while to play billiards was the mark of a gentleman, anyone who played the game well could hardly be considered a gentleman 'in the best sense'. It was part of an amateur ethic which, says Neil Wigglesworth, "preached the exclusion of the professional at any cost, an exclusion which was facilitated by the peculiarly feudal nature of English Society".[375]

Alcock, however, was conscious of the fact that sport organised exclusively under the aegis of private members' clubs and the 'closed' Old Boys' Associations was no longer sustainable, especially in the urbanised environments of the North and Midlands, and with a more realistic and pragmatic appreciation of the circumstances than many of his contemporaries, confronted professionalism not with a view to proscribing it, still less to sweeping it under the carpet but rather with the intention of recognising it and controlling it. Veiled professionalism existed in cricket and, he reasoned, would continue to do so in football unless the FA removed their blinkers and legalised it albeit under 'stringent conditions'.

Shamateurism

Professional cricket was not exempt from this trend. At a time when class was a significant factor in society and consequently in cricket, the general root of the trouble was the hypocrisy that characterised the game to the extent that the "expenses" of the "amateurs" frequently exceeded the legitimate pay of the professionals and specifically that the Australians who were notionally amateurs were receiving a share of tour proceeds which made them far better remunerated for their efforts than the opposing English professionals.

The *Cricketers' Companion* was critical of the MCC's pusillanimous, ostrich-style attitude to the issue. Continuing a theme begun the previous year, the Editor was nothing if not forthright:

> The abuse of the word "amateur" was strongly exposed at a General Meeting of the County Clubs, when the balance sheet showed that, under the grossly misapplied heading of "expenses" so-called amateurs asked for three or four times as much as is paid to professionals for wages, expenses and all. The Marylebone Club have now to define the word "expenses", and if an amateur's railway fare to the scene of action and back, no one is likely to grumble, or to advance the opinion that a gentleman receiving the amount of such fare forfeits his right to be considered an amateur, but if hotel bills are to be included, and a gentleman playing for his county is to be at liberty to drink Chateau Yquem with his dinner, and to smoke shilling cigars at the expense of the Club, and if the said Club is to be debited with £10, £15 or £20 for the privilege of retaining the services of such so-called amateurs, the MARYLEBONE NOTE is worse than useless…That a Professional's wages should be £5 and an Amateur's expenses £10 for playing in the same match is simply absurd. It is high time that this unsavoury question was fairly met and disposed of for good and all.[376]

The most famous example of this kind of "shamateurism" was, of course, Alcock's great friend, W G Grace, who financially could not afford to play as an amateur and socially could not afford to play as a professional. He was not alone and a significant example at Surrey was under Alcock's nose in the form of W W Read who held the sinecure of Assistant Secretary. Read was without a doubt one of the leading batsmen of his generation, his most memorable innings being 117 for England against Australia on his home ground and, according to *Cricket,* contending with Bobby Abel for the title of Surrey's greatest batsman. He was "the first man to discover the infinite possibilities which lay in the pull"[377] and his contribution to Surrey cricket on the field was unquestioned:

[his] brilliant record as a batsman for Surrey during a period of twenty-five years forms one of the brightest pages in the history of the county during the last quarter of the nineteenth century...the first of a succession of great Surrey amateurs.[378]

The only challengeable part of that tribute is the last word.

Read first played for Surrey in 1873 at the age of 17, Alcock's attention having been drawn to him by Henry Jupp. He was appointed Assistant Secretary in 1881 at a salary of £120 plus a railway season ticket which, said his *Wisden* obituary more than a quarter of a century later,[379] "enabled him to devote all his time to the game."[380] The appointment was, said Alcock, "one of the chief incidents in the records of the club in 1881."[381] Later in the year, the committee resolved that Barratt be reprimanded by the Secretary for his behaviour to Mr Read.[382] The nature of the incident is not recorded, but deference of the professional to the "amateur" was the only conceivable outcome.

Leave of absence was granted to him to go to Australia for the 1882-83 tour,[383] the £250 and artistically illuminated inscription of vellum he received from the Club for his "brilliant batting" in Australia being rather more than adequate compensation for any loss of earnings from his sinecure of Assistant Secretary, his salary having been increased by 25% to £150 [384] within eighteen months of his first appointment. The presentation was made on the second day of Edward Pooley's benefit match and compared not too unfavourably with the £400 or so which the match raised for a professional with twenty-three seasons of service to the county.

In 1884, the Committee decided in July that each of the professionals be paid £10 for the Players v Australia and England v Australia matches and in August that 20 guineas be awarded to Mr Read for his innings against Australia.[385] It was followed by a bonus of £50.[386] The following year £250 was given to him as a wedding present, more than twice the sum earned in a year by the average professional. To this sum was added a piece of plate to the value of £15.[387] He was, added the minutes, in apparent justification, "a cricketer second to but one in England."

By 1894, however, the Committee decided to bring the arrangement to an end:

It was resolved that a complimentary match be arranged for Mr W W Read in 1895 that if possible Surrey v England be played and that the secretary be instructed to approach the other counties on the subject.

The Committee contributed £200 to the testimonial,[388] but in making this gesture, decided to implement their arrangement with Mr Read that the Assistant Secretaryship held by him should come to an end when he ceased to be a regular member of the Surrey eleven.[389]

For the first time since 1866, Surrey played England. The match coincided nicely with the Club's fiftieth anniversary. Thanks to Alcock's efforts, it was, apart from Brown and Peel who were playing for Yorkshire against Oxford University, a full strength England side. From a cricket point of view, Leicestershire's Arthur Pougher ruined the match as a serious contest with bowling figures of 26.3-15-34-9 and 35.4-24-43-3, as Surrey plunged to defeat by an innings and 75 runs, Read contributing 3 and 1 and 0-24 in 11 overs. Financially, however, Read made over £800, including £200 from the Club. Bobby Abel in his benefit year had £621, including 50 guineas from the Club, so while gate receipts were about the same, the committee's contribution was significantly different. That Read was to all intents and purposes a professional is perhaps demonstrated by Alcock's reference to "Read's benefit" rather than the more correct "Mr Read's testimonial".[390]

Despite all this, Mr Read did not go quietly, objecting to the simultaneous termination of his playing contract and contract as Assistant

Secretary, an action that says all that needs to be said about 'shamateurism'. Logic would suggest that if he were no longer playing, he would have more time to devote to administration. The reality was that the Club had always regarded the two as co-terminous, the Assistant Secretaryship and various handouts enabling him to continue as an amateur.

A high-powered Sub-Committee comprising the President, Vice-President, John Shuter and the Secretary recommended, having discussed the matter with Mr Read:

> that in their opinion it is fair to Mr Read that the present arrangement as to the Assistant Secretaryship should be continued as long as Mr Read continues as a regular member of the Surrey eleven. The Assistant Secretaryship to be deemed to commence on the 1st of January in each year and the salary of Assistant Secretary to be paid to Mr Read up to the 31st Decr in the year in which he shall cease to be a regular playing member.[391]

Despite the fact that it had been made crystal clear two years earlier and had been an understanding for some time before that, despite the high powered Sub-Committee to review his situation and despite the Committee's generous financial treatment, Mr Read feigned astonishment:

> I am quite at a loss to understand why any such proposed alteration be made, considering that during the present season I have been a regular member of the team and scored nearly 1000 runs, and besides having for the past fifteen or sixteen years done more than any other member of the team to uphold the privilege of Surrey Cricket. I would suggest in all fairness both to yourselves and myself that the above mentioned office be continued at all events until December 31st 1897 upon the following terms viz:
>
> That the remuneration for the said office remains as heretofore £150 and railway season ticket and in addition to the extra payment of £100 and £4.4.0 for each match played which have been given to me in lieu of any increase in salary, these latter payments be made to me in the same proportions as the proportion of matches in which I take part.[392]

In the absence of the President and the Secretary, the matter was deferred. Eventually £375 was offered "in lieu of all future payments". Mr Read declined. It was not enough, he said. He had always regarded the Assistant Secretaryship as a permanent appointment. The Committee increased it to £400 to be paid by 25 March 1897 "in satisfaction of all future payments". He accepted. The saga was over. In 1905 he was engaged as coach. Sissons sums up the position as follows: "Walter Read may have batted like an amateur and been considered one socially, but he was paid as a professional."[393]

Even the Corinthians who have passed into sporting folklore as the icon of all that is purely amateur and free from professional taint cannot be totally exempted from the charge of shamateurism. They declined to pay their players, refused to take part in any Challenge Cup competitions, frowned on anything devious or underhand and refused to recognise the penalty-kick (If awarded one they would deliberately shoot wide and should - horrors - one be awarded against them, the goalkeeper would stand aside), but they were involved with Surrey in some acrimonious wrangles about their share of the gate money. In 1889, 75% was agreed.[394] This was no different from the arrangement with the Football Association, but by contrast, the gate from Old Etonian, Old Harrovian and Old Carthusian matches was usually donated to charity.

In comparison with much of the flowery prose that characterised the correspondence of the time, their approach to the Surrey committee was direct and peremptory, almost discourteous, but they were from the patrician class, born to rule, unused to not getting their own way:

Dear Alcock

Our Committee last night decided to play the following matches at the Oval, if your Committee will agree and accept the suggested terms. Oct 20 v Army Nov 17 v Notts County Dec 15 v Aston Villa Feby 9 v Derby County Mar 9 v Queens Park. Terms 75% of gross receipts (gate, enclosures and stands) to be paid to the C.F.C. I may add that these are the terms elsewhere.

Yours truly, N L Jackson Hon. Sec[395]

This was less than ten days before the first fixture was due. The fact that the ground might be required for other matches was clearly something which was not an issue for the Corinthians. The Sub-Committee agreed with some reluctance, but the Corinthians were informed that it was not proposed to erect any more stands and they reserved the right to limit the use of the pavilion to Surrey members on big occasions. The following month, it was tentatively suggested to the Corinthians that they might consider a contribution to the expenses of their matches which for the best attended could include the cost of "two sergeants, fifteen constables and an inspector".[396] Stating that the expenses of their matches were met by inter alia by Queen's Club and Essex County Cricket Club, the Corinthians wrote with an aristocratic arrogance "expressing their disinclination to pay the ground expenses of their matches".[397] They may not have been paid, but unlike subsequent generations of amateur footballers, there was no question of their "paying to play."

Association Football

At the beginning of the 1884-85 football season, the *Sporting Life* carried a hard-hitting feature, denigrating the ostrich-like opposition to professionalism of the Football Association and the hypocrisy of some of its opponents, who themselves practised veiled professionalism in the form of boot money and what the French have called payments *dessous la table*:

ANOTHER FOOTBALL SEASON

The winter game has now become, in the north, at least, as much of a business as cricket and indeed, there is, in some districts, only the slightest possible spare interval between the seasons for footballers. To the old school of players, the practice of football in August or September must seem a little strange, but the game has quite outgrown the expectation of its early followers...

The tendency of late years in the direction of paid players has been so unmistakable that the obstructive policy which has lately marked the decisions of the Association seems very unwise if not suicidal.

While the article recognised the dangers of 'veiled professionalism' and of financial inducements to entice players from other districts, it deplored the judgments of the FA which resulted in the expulsion of Accrington from the Association and the exclusion of Preston North End from the Challenge Cup and questioned the wisdom of the General meeting's rejecting the legislation of professionalism when the Committee had recommended it. The tone became more vitriolic:

PROFESSIONALISM

Not one argument, as far as we know, has been adduced to prove that open professionalism would be injurious to the game. It is not a little strange that the principal opposition to the admission of paid players comes from quarters where it has been proved that payment has been made and that the chief supporters of recognising professionalism are in the South where, as far as we know, there has been no suggestion of such practices. Every sport of any pretension recognises professionals, and it is manifestly absurd for those who have the management of football to think for one moment that they will now be able to carry out the system of repression on which to judge by their recent enactment they now propose to embark. The game has passed beyond the line of an amateur sport and there is no reason in the world why a professional footballer should not be as much respected, and occupy the same position as a professional cricketer...

There can be no possible objection to the recognised payment of men who cannot afford to play for amusement and we can see no reason why the principle which exists in almost every other sport should be considered detrimental to football. The sooner the Football Association opens its eyes to the fact that the recognition of professionalism is a certainty, the better it will be for the consolidation of the game.[398]

A partial rebuttal of the stance taken by the *Sporting Life* is contained in an article in *Church Monthly*[399] in 1897 by Rev J E C Welldon, then Headmaster of Harrow School. He was an Old Etonian and had played in the Cup Final of 1875/76 and before going on to marvel at the growth of the sport, began by addressing the question of whether cricket or football is the better game. It is, he says,

...as idle as the corresponding question of whether winter or summer is the better season of the year. Each derives a part of its charm from the contrast with the other.

When I used to play football for the Old Etonians there was only a thin ring of spectators lining the ground at the Kennington Oval during the final match for the Association Cup. Since then the number of spectators has risen to twenty or thirty thousand, and once it is said even to forty thousand. It has been established that the sum of five million pounds has been taken as gate-money in a single year from the spectators of football matches.

It is the easiest of games to learn. Everyone can play football; almost everyone does play it. The effort to force a ball through a definite space at one end or other of a field is a problem which everyone can understand, if it is not in the power of everyone to solve it...

It is pre-eminently the democratic game. Society cares little for it, fashionable mothers dislike and dread it; but it is dear to the heart of the people....

.... there is a danger that football, invaluable as it is, may be marred by certain evils of recent origin. Professionalism is invading football, as it has invaded other games. When I played football a professional player was hardly known; today most of the great players are professionals. Against professionals as men I do not say a word, but professionalism is the bane of athletic games.

He goes on to list three "evils" arising from professionalism: brutality, violence and playing for victory at all costs at the expense of skill; sharp practice and cheating in a game which demands a chivalrous and gentlemanly approach; and betting which taints it with an alien, illegitimate interest, sport ceasing to be sport when tainted with the love of money. More than a hundred years on, it is difficult to argue that he was entirely wrong. "May the honour of athletic games remain pure and bright," he concludes. It was a forlorn, Canute-type hope.

In football, professionalism was just beginning to emerge from the woodwork, having been around for some time. J C Clegg of Sheffield, later Sir Charles and President of the Football Association, who played in the first international in 1872, is reported to have said that none of the southern amateurs spoke to him, so he wouldn't play again.[400] He didn't and was, at least in the early stages of the dispute, a staunch opponent of professionalism, but it is significant that even at this early stage in the development of the game, there is an implied juxtaposition of "southern amateurs" and "northern professionals". J A H Catton, however, suggests that this was more of a north-south divide than a professional-amateur divide, that individualism was rampant and that Clegg was reluctantly forced to the conclusion that some members of the English eleven were awful snobs and not much troubled about a "mon fra' Sheffield". It is unlikely that his observations would have included Alcock or Kinnaird with whom he was later to be bracketed as one of the great organisers of association football.

The first stirrings of professionalism - or, at least, the first perceived - were the presence of James Love and Fergus Suter in the Darwen team that took Old Etonians to a second replay in the fourth ties of the 1879 Challenge Cup. It was the beginning of a six year battle. Alcock, not unexpectedly, was alive to the issue:

> The question of professionalism at football is too wide in its bearings to be treated with the care that it requires in a brief review such as this, but it will be well for those who have the interest of the game at heart to recognise the existence of a problem that will in all likelihood have to be mastered before long.[401]

He was absolutely right. What had been a small cloud on the horizon in the 1870s was now looming larger and could no longer be ignored. It featured in the correspondence columns of his newly-established *Football* at the beginning of the 1882-83 season. The Amateur Athletics Association had ruled that a professional cricketer could not compete as an amateur. Whether football should adopt the same stance was, said the Editor, a "knotty point" and one to be dealt with by the authorities before many seasons have departed. "The sooner the better" he judged would be the response of many of his readers.

Contrasting viewpoints were expressed. 'Midland Meanderings', a regular feature of the newspaper, derided the assumption that because a man was a professional cricketer he must be a professional footballer,[402] while 'Anti-Professional' of Bolton took the stance which was entirely predictable from his *nom de plume*:

> There are several clubs in the county of Lancashire who unblushingly admit to paying their first eleven so much every match if they win, and half if they lose, besides giving them a stated sum every time they turn up to practice. This is the bare, solid truth, and if it is contradicted by all the Lancashire clubs, then it will necessitate my giving names.

Suter, he added, who had defected from Darwen to Blackburn Rovers, had been paid £100 by the latter to prevent his former club from reclaiming him.[402]

A sub-committee and commission were established by the Association with a remit to collect evidence of professionalism. Representatives from Birmingham, Lancashire and Sheffield were included. By their very nature, payments in the form of the sovereign in the boot, cash payments from gate money with the balance being recorded as the gross receipts and notional employment in local industry were difficult to detect. By 1884, having carefully weighed the arguments on both sides, Alcock nailed his colours to the recognition of professionalism:

> The extraordinary development of football has brought with it a corresponding increase in the responsibilities of its administrators. The question of professionalism has already given rise to great discussion, but I am inclined to think that it will have to be met in a far broader spirit than has yet marked the action of the majority of footballers. The recognition of professionalism is, I am fully convinced, an event of the near future, and it seems to me a short-sighted policy to attempt to repress a system which would to my mind tend to remove many of the impurities which at present are seriously injuring the game. It is clearly right that the distinction between amateur and professional players should be clearly marked. An amateur ought to be one who receives no more than his bare expenses, and there is no reason why the Cup, if such is the wish of the general body of footballers, should not be confined to amateurs. At the same time professional football will have to be admitted sooner or later, and the sooner it is recognised and legalised under proper conditions, the better it will be for the game.[404]

There was, of course, no question of confining the Cup to amateurs. A separate amateur competition would be established in 1893 and there would be a temporary amateur breakaway from the Association between 1906 and 1914. In the early 1880s, however, it was the attraction of the Cup that was a catalyst of professionalism and saw first Blackburn Rovers, then Blackburn Olympic appear in the Final Tie, followed by a transfer of power from the amateur south to the professional north and the eventual acceptance of professionalism in Scotland, the source of the first professional players. "You might as well try to stop the flow of Niagara with a kitchen chair as endeavour to stem the tide of professionalism," said J H McLaughlin.

In 1884, matters were brought to a head when Accrington Stanley and Preston North End were excluded from the FA Cup for professionalism, in the case of the latter following a letter of protest from Upton Park after a 1-1 draw in the fourth round. Preston's response was effectively - Yes, we

PROFESSIONALISM

pay our players, so what? Major William Sudell, Preston's manager, preferred frankness and honesty to the deceit and hypocrisy of veiled professionalism. The cat was out of the bag: the Association could ignore the matter no more.

Alcock's viewpoint was shared by Lord Kinnaird, then Treasurer of the Association. It was a realistic and pragmatic stance, an acceptance of the inevitable, supported by Lancastrians R P Gregson and Dr E S Morley. Less wholehearted support came from Major Marindin, President of the Association and N L ('Pa') Jackson, founder of the Corinthians, and direct opposition came from the Sheffield and Birmingham Associations represented by J C Clegg, C Crump and J H Cofield.

It seemed strange, as the *Sporting Life* had hinted, that some of the main opposition to paid players came from areas where the practice was prevalent, but whereas Lancashire accepted the inevitability of the professional and Alcock and Kinnaird who had no vested interest were in a position to take an objective view, the Sheffield and Birmingham delegates were alive to a likely dilution of their power and influence. The two viewpoints were polarized at a meeting of the Association in March 1885. It was, said a delegate, degrading for respectable men to play with professionals. Alcock countered:

> I cannot be called a supporter of professionalism, for when I played football, it was only played by amateurs. But until professionalism is legalised the deadlock which now exists will continue. I consider that veiled professionalism is the evil to be repressed, and I am sure that it now exists in nearly every football district. Professionals are necessary to the growth of the game and I object to the idea that they are the utter outcasts some people represent them to be. Furthermore I object to the argument that it is immoral to work for a living, and I cannot see why men should not, with that object, labour at football as at cricket.[405]

At a special general meeting of the Association, held at Anderson's Hotel, Fleet Street, on 20 July 1885, professionalism was recognised and legalised, but only just (by 35 votes to 15 - the required two-thirds majority) and subject to the "proper conditions" which Alcock had seen as desirable. Sudell had set out his stall in the clearest possible terms:

> Gentlemen, Preston are professionals, but if you refuse to legalise them, then we will be amateurs, and you cannot prove us otherwise.

Additions to the rules for Cup competitions were required, among the most significant of which were:

> Professionals shall be allowed to compete in all Cups provided they are qualified as follows: In Cup matches by birth or residence for two years past within six miles of the ground or headquarters of the club for which they play.

> No professional shall be allowed to play for more than one club in any one season without the permission of the Committee of the Football Association.

> All professionals shall be annually registered in a book to be kept by the Committee of the Football Association, and no professional shall be allowed to play unless he has been so registered.

The birth and residential qualifications are an echo of the work Alcock had been doing in county cricket in 1873 and once again, his influence was instrumental in changing the direction of a game. The Football Association had started in 1863 as a small interest group with a common Agenda and while splinter groups had formed early, it remained possible for him to exert a considerable interest on the future of football. However, the changes he could make on the longer established game of cricket where the gentleman-player device with all its superficial convenience but deep-seated inequalities was already in place, were rather more cosmetic.

While Alcock could never be accused of smugness or resting on his laurels, there is in the 1885 *Football Annual* a certain amount of satisfaction with a job well done:

> A notice of association football without reference to the important changes which have just taken place in the relations of the players would obviously be incomplete. After much opposition the advocates of professionalism have carried their point and this coming season, will for the first time, see Association Football divided into two sections, amateurs and professionals. The necessity of such a step has for some time been apparent and it is singular that many of those who most strenuously opposed the recognition of professionalism when the movement first commenced, have since become thoroughly convinced of the advisability of its adoption. The institution of a clear and distinct line to define unpaid from paid players had become an absolute necessity, and personally, as one who has urged the expediency of

recognising professionalism, I have heard no real argument to show that it will be injurious to the game. On the contrary, under proper management, there is no reason why professionals should not tend to the development of football, as they have unmistakably conduced to the development of cricket over many years.

Jackson was understandably less enthusiastic, identifying quite correctly the inevitable link between professional football and football as a business: "it is a regrettable fact that the manner in which the affairs of the Association were administered was rapidly changing, mainly by reason of the large proportion of council members who made a business of the game and consequently could no longer treat it as a sport."[406]

The legalisation of professionalism and the increased administrative complexity resulting from the consequent rewriting of the rulebook put more pressure on the Association's administration and resulted in the conversion of the post of honorary secretary to a paid one in 1886. The Surrey committee was unanimous that Alcock be permitted to take the post "if the opportunity presented itself".[407]

By 1914, there were some 4800 professionals, mainly from the skilled working class earning about £3 per week, twice the pay of the average working man. The best players could command £10 per week. But the social distinctions remained. In 1880, the Sheffield FA had advertised for a new Secretary, seeking "a gentleman of good position with whom distant officials would not deem it derogatory to correspond" while professional players often spent their post-playing days running shops or public houses. Arthur Wharton, the first black professional footballer, who kept goal for a number of northern clubs from 1888 to 1902, died a penniless coal-miner and James Trainor, a former Preston goalkeeper, was reduced to begging from supporters.[408]

The legalisation of professionalism in football did not eliminate social differences. In a way it exacerbated them. 'Pa' Jackson, founder of the Corinthians, who was as commercially-minded as any one in squeezing the last penny of gate-money from his various hosts, wrote of the 1898 international against Scotland:

The aggressiveness of the professional element exerted itself in many ways. Not content with almost filling the international team with professionals, it did all in its power to reduce the one or two amateurs who did play to the level of professionals. All were taken to the same hotel, all were expected to travel and to feed together. Until this year the amateurs had resisted this last request but in Glasgow the two amateurs, rather than appear to be exclusive or run the chance of making themselves unpopular with the 'pros', consented to lunch with them on the day of the match.

The professionals knew their game, but did they know their place?[409]

C B Fry saw a marked distinction between the amateur approach and "the northern pro" and his willingness to trip opponents and con the referee. In the early 1900s, he objected to what he saw as the unnecessary introduction of the penalty area:

It is a standing insult to sportsmen to have to play under a rule which assumes that players intend to trip, hack and push their opponents, and to behave like cads of the most unscrupulous kidney. I say that the lines marking the penalty area are a disgrace to the playing field of a public school.[410]

Cricket

Professionalism had been around for some time in cricket from the days in the eighteenth century when the game was played largely for gambling purposes and the aristocracy hired their own professionals or gardeners and under-butlers with cricketing skill to represent them and improve their chances of taking a substantial purse. By the time Alcock came on the scene the Gentlemen-Players divide was well established, a reflection of Victorian class-structure. They had separate dressing rooms, separate entrances to the playing area, were generally civil to each other, but did not mix socially. The Players played for a living and received a wage, usually on a match-by-match basis; the Gentlemen had other sources of income and were entitled to receive expenses. The reality was murkier and more complex.

Many an "amateur", so termed, playing in county cricket, is more heavily remunerated than an accredited "professional" player. The distinction had once a valid foundation, based essentially upon differences of wealth and social station…the social chasm separating the MCC member from a professional is wide and real, based upon wealth, educational opportunities and advancement. "Gentlemen were gentlemen and players were players much in the same way as a nobleman and his head gamekeeper might be.'[411]

The social and regional divisiveness in cricket was of longer standing than that in football, but no less sharp and to an extent exacerbated by it. Despite the progressive emancipation and increased respectability of the professional sport, *The Country Life Library of Sport* in 1903 had no doubt about the social inferiority of those who played cricket for a living: "The professional...comes from the factory, from the pit and from the slum."

Those not good enough for appointment at first-class level, it went on, were engaged by Clubs in South Lancashire and the West Riding where they spent several hours a week bowling to club members in the nets. The results of matches were tabulated in the sporting papers published on Sundays. One of these clubs then becomes champion of the local league and cricket was carried on in much the same way as football in senior leagues, junior leagues and Pleasant Sunday Afternoon leagues. The game was of a distinctly inferior type and the umpires often had more than their proper share in determining the result of a match.[412] There is no attempt to conceal the interlinear sneers and an obvious parallel with C B Fry's comments on the northern professionals' footballing equivalents.

Professional sportsmen were a part of a rising artisan class who find their way into contemporary literature in the novels of Charles Dickens and Elizabeth Gaskell. Except for the top échelon, professional cricket was a haphazard and precarious existence where many "though heroes on their own village green prove themselves valueless" and where there was "no royal road to success as a young professional", and earnings from playing the game had to be supplemented with commercial activities. Every considerate gentleman cricketer who wanted a bat or bag or pads, said *Cricket*, obtained them from a professional. There was not the need to resort to the subterfuge of veiled professionalism, as there was in pre-1885 football, but professionals, while perhaps envied by the amateurs for their playing skills, particularly bowling, which, by the very nature of the job, they practised regularly, were generally regarded as a lower form of life:

If he is about with betting men and always playing cards on wet cricket days, and loafing at drinking-bars, there will be rumours about him which many people will believe.

The professional's lot at both cricket and football was not a happy one. A feature on the rôle of the professional cricketer in the *St James Gazette*, reproduced in *Cricket*[413] stated that a first rate professional whose book was full for the season could earn £10-12 a week out of which he paid his travelling and inn expenses. Many sought regular employment when the season was over and a benefit could bring in a nest-egg of a few hundred pounds. The article went on to say, however, that the difference between the gains of the few who were very successful and the majority who were only moderately so was just as great in cricket as in other professions.

Many professionals were compelled to live fairly frugally, as Sir Home Gordon was to relate some sixty years later:

Some idea of what the old-timers were like may be gathered from what was related to me about them by C W Alcock when secretary at the Oval. He declared that in the seventies the Surrey professionals wore one suit of flannels right through the summer, the shirt often being a coloured one or dotted with red spots. There was also the instance later of a subsequently prominent Notts player coming up for the first time to Lord's, merely with his pads and bat strapped together. When it was noticed he had no baggage, he explained that as the weather was fine he intended to sleep each night in some park in his cricket clothes.[414]

Cricket was at this time a major spectator sport, providing income for the professionals' employers, but while the game itself grew in affluence, it was an affluence not shared in the same proportions by the hired labourers:

Within the last five-and-twenty or thirty years - owing to railway facilities, shorter hours of work, Saturday half-holidays and other causes - people have had more opportunities of taking their pleasure; and in London and the great cities during the summer thousands of all classes assemble to witness the matches between county elevens.

PROFESSIONALISM

Not all amateurs had been treated as generously as Walter Read; then again, not all were of the same ability. At the beginning of the 1886 season, E J Diver made an application to transfer from amateur to professional status. Given the class distinctions of the time, it was a bold step.

April 19, 1886

Dear Mr Alcock

Being heartily sick of office work and extremely fond of cricket but not having private means to allow me to continue as an amateur may I ask you to allow me to play in the eleven if you think me good enough as a professional. My interest in Surrey County Cricket is very great and rather than stand aloof from the game I would be for entering the lists as a professional. I sincerely trust you will think over this and let me know at your earliest convenience.

Yours truly, (sgd) E J Diver

The Club's reply was not exactly glowing with warmth and enthusiasm:

I am desired by the Committee to acknowledge receipt of your letter of 19th inst. They are glad to accept your services on the conditions specified therein. It must, however, be understood that in the interest of cricket in the County and of cricket generally the committee do not pledge themselves to play you continuously should unfortunately your services be hereafter considered of not sufficient importance. The Committee desire to acknowledge the value of your past support to the County.[415]

Diver's father was less than impressed, writing to the Committee about his son's appearance as a professional. Not wishing to involve themselves in a family dispute, the Committee sent Diver senior a copy of his son's letter "with the intimation that no encouragement had been given to E J Diver to become a professional."[416]

Diver's first game in his new capacity had been against Gloucestershire, a match in which W R Gilbert also made his first appearance as a professional. The latter was to disgrace himself and his profession by rifling his colleagues' pockets in the dressing room. He was summarily dismissed, emigrated to Canada and never played first-class cricket again, and says Rae, it was probably as a result of the intervention of W G Grace, there was no further reference to him in *Cricket*. That is not quite true.[417] He does get a mention in the later "Chat" on Diver.[418]

Some amateurs were clearly better remunerated than others and some of those without private means found the expense of playing too much. Diver was to say later "the expense of playing as an amateur was too great for me, so that I decided to become a professional, and I have never found that amongst gentlemen, it ever made any difference to me from a social point of view."[419]

The fact that Diver had previously played as a an amateur was probably in his favour, as was the fact that he played cricket rather than football where the gentlemen-players mechanism was already well established. He left Surrey at the end of the season, remaining perhaps an amateur in spirit, though like Alcock, a supporter of professional rights. When he said being a professional never made any difference from a social point of view he was perhaps conveniently forgetting that in 1899 as Warwickshire's first professional captain, he caused Essex to lodge a complaint that he had led his players on to the field via the amateurs' gate at Leyton, or earlier in 1893, when the professionals were offered meat pies at side tables in contrast with the amateurs and Australian tourists who were served salmon, he led his fellow professionals out in disgust. To be allowed in the dining room had been a concession. The professionals were normally expected to eat with the spectators. It was one of several ways in which, admittedly no different from the rest of the nineteenth century working-class, they were treated as second-class or even third-class citizens. Others were separate dressing rooms and entrances, separate travel arrangements and separate hotels and lodging-houses.[420] The distinctions reflected those of Victorian society with all its snobbishness and hypocrisy, exemplified in the three-class railway system. A letter to the *Sportsman* in 1865, concerned about the apparent rise in significance of the professional cricketer, had suggested:

> Let gentlemen resolve that they will employ professionals only in their proper position - that of auxiliaries (as the Marylebone Club has ever done) - and we shall soon pay as little attention to these vicious bickerings as we should to a wordy war occurring amongst our household servants.

The parallelism with household servants is of significance. As members of the working class, they had to know their place. Alcock as a Gladstonian

Liberal respected them as individuals and clearly related to them, championing their cause in both cricket and football, but like other liberals and reform movements, was powerless to make any but the most superficial changes to the fabric of society. That would require a world war and a few more generations.

The Players' Strike

The power of organised labour was beginning to grow. 1888 had seen the Match Girls Strike, the establishment of the Miners' Federation of Great Britain and the start of mass trade unionism of unskilled workers. The London Dock Strike followed in 1889 and Gas workers won a reduction in the working day from twelve to eight hours.

Had the 'double pay' strike of 1896 had the backing of all eight professionals summoned to the Oval for the decisive Test in a three match series, the result may well have been very different, but only five adopted a 'militant' stance and the Surrey Club were able to adopt a 'divide and rule' approach.

At this stage the home authority was responsible for selecting the team for international matches, so the Surrey committee and its Secretary were facing the dilemma of conflicting amateur and professional ethos. Alcock had been there before, in football, when the different interests of the amateur and professional game had been successfully harmonised. The results this time were different. The immediate problem was pragmatically resolved, but the resentment lingered on and grudges continued to be borne over a number of years.

The thirteen, eight professionals and five amateurs, were announced and invitations issued a week ahead of the match, the professionals' fee for which was to be, in accordance with the prevailing practice, £10 for the three day match, plus travelling and accommodation expenses. The following letter was received at The Oval:

We the following players having been asked to represent England v Australia on August 10 and two following days do hereby take the liberty to ask for increased terms viz. twenty pounds. The importance of such a fixture entitles us to make this demand.

The letter bore the signatures of William Gunn of Nottinghamshire and the four Surrey professionals, Bobby Abel, Tom Hayward, George Lohmann and Tom Richardson. There had been previous unsuccessful attempts at a pay increase for the Lord's and Old Trafford Tests and the Committee had agreed earlier that players representing Surrey against the Australians be paid £10.

The action was catalysed by the fact that the "amateur" Australians had been quite open about the amount they were making from a financially successful tour, but more particularly that the amateurs Rt Hon F S Jackson, Prince Ranjitsinhji, A E Stoddart and Major E G Wynyard were to receive £25. Amateur and captain W G Grace was to receive £40, twice his Gloucestershire match fee and this on the back of a recent testimonial of £2,377 2s.6d.[421] Stoddart, also at the time the England rugby captain, withdrew on the eve of the match amid speculation that he was in sympathy with the professionals and that his own expenses claims were under investigation. He was replaced by Archie MacLaren. A further reason, not mentioned by the players themselves, but hinted at by the *Daily Telegraph*, was that the Surrey Club would benefit from the match by £1,000 or £1,500.[422]

The other professionals selected were Dick Lilley and Jack Hearne, both in their first series and Yorkshireman Bobby Peel, recalled after three years. They declined to associate themselves with the dispute, presumably on the grounds that their case was not as strong and from a reluctance to jeopardise their chances of future selection.

On Thursday 6 August, four days before the match was due a peremptory telegram was sent to Leyton where Surrey had a county fixture: "Fee for playing England v Australia £10 or you are out of the match." Gunn was simply told that his terms were not acceptable and, being a man with other financial means (his flourishing cricket bat firm having been established ten years earlier) immediately announced that he had withdrawn from the team.

The following Monday, the morning of the match, the four Surrey players were called before a special committee meeting after which a joint letter signed by Richardson, Hayward and Abel was made available to the press:"The Australians are making large sums of money by these fixtures and it seemed to us only reasonable we should beneficiate in a small way out of the large sum of money received. But after further consideration we desire to withdraw our refusal to play."

Lohmann declined to sign until he had spoken with William Gunn and was omitted from the side.

In the following year's edition, the now authoritative *Wisden* gave an essentially factual account, but tended towards the moral high ground:[423]

The third and conquering test match was preceded by a regrettable incident, which for a time caused intense excitement in the cricket world. The Surrey Committee, after much deliberation, chose nine cricketers as certainties for the England eleven and four others from amongst whom the last two places would be filled. Early in the week previous to the match, however - indeed almost as soon as the selection had been known - they received a letter signed by Lohmann, Gunn, Abel, Richardson and Hayward, in which the players demanded £20 each for their services in the match. Ten pounds per man had been paid to the professionals in the matches at Lord's and Manchester, and the Surrey committee, without going into the question of whether or not £20 was an excessive fee for an occasion of such importance, declined point blank to be dictated to. It is betraying no secrets to say that they felt greatly aggrieved, on the eve of the most important match of the season, at being placed in a difficulty by four of their own professionals. However, they did not hesitate for a moment as to the course to be pursued, at once taking steps to secure the best possible substitutes for the revolting players. For two or three days the position remained unchanged, and as soon as the facts became known to the general public, nothing else in the way of cricket was talked about. Friendly counsels, however, were soon at work and on the evening of Saturday, August 8th, a communication was received at The Oval from Abel, Hayward and Richardson, to the effect that they withdrew from the position they had taken up, and placed themselves without reserve in the hands of the Surrey committee. Much gratified at the turn which things had taken, the Surrey committee resolved on the Saturday evening to let the final selection of the England team stand over until the meeting of the match committee on Monday morning. At that meeting, Sir Richard Webster[424] presided and after a good deal of deliberation, it was determined that Abel, Richardson, and Hayward should play for England. Among leading cricketers' opinions were a good deal divided as to the wisdom of the policy, but in our judgment the match committee took a just as well as a popular course of action. Lohmann did not act with the other professionals, but at a subsequent period, he wrote a letter of apology, and made his peace with the Surrey Club. Even when the question of the professionals had been settled, however, the committee were by no means at the end of their difficulties. Statements in certain newspapers as to the allowance made for expenses to the amateurs caused great irritation, and for a time there was much uncertainty as to how the England eleven would be finally constituted. In the end matters were smoothed over, but not till a definite statement - which will be found in another part of this ALMANACK - had been made public as to the financial relations between Mr W G Grace and the Surrey Club.

The Committee had been forced into a corner, but Alcock's response on its behalf reflected both his diplomacy and his close friendship with W G Grace:

The Committee of the Surrey County Cricket Club have observed paragraphs in the Press respecting the amounts alleged to be paid or promised to Dr W G Grace for playing in the match England v Australia. The Committee desire to give the statements contained in the paragraphs the most unqualified contradiction. During many years, on the occasion of Dr W G Grace playing at The Oval, at the request of the Surrey County Committee, in the matches Gentlemen v Players and England v Australia, Dr Grace has received the sum of £10 a match to cover his expenses in coming to and remaining in London during the three days. Beyond this amount Dr Grace has not received, directly or indirectly, one farthing for playing in a match at The Oval.[425]

The attitude of *Wisden* Editor, Sydney Pardon, was not far from Alcock's own. In 'Some Current Topics', the precursor of 'Notes by the Editor', he expresses the view that the players were right in principle but wrong in their timing and approach. He recognised that in 1880, Surrey had ensured that England went into the match with Australia with the strongest available team by paying the professionals £20. England v Australia had become a huge attraction and the players should be rewarded accordingly. Surrey had led the way with winter pay and star contracts which guaranteed leading players a regular income over several seasons; Yorkshire had followed suit and benefit matches were much more lucrative than a few years ago and while the lot of the professionals was improving, there was still scope for better treatment. The issue of amateurs' expenses was neatly sidestepped on the ground that Pardon did not have sufficient information and the position of W G Grace was recognised as being anamolous, but justified on the grounds that "nice customs curtsy to great kings" and the work he had done in popularising the game outweighed every other consideration.[426]

Baily's was almost entirely unsympathetic. A monthly sports magazine, the main interests of which were of the horse racing, hunting, shooting and fishing kind, with a pronounced right-of-centre bias, saw the issue in fairly clear cut Capital v Labour terms and pontificated:

> They [the strikers] should remember that county clubs have been built up often by liberal contributions of private individuals, and by hard, wholly unpaid work of amateurs, and that in the bad times there did not exist - as far as I know - a single case when players have not received their full pay.

The reality was, of course, not quite so simple: the "wholly unpaid work of amateurs" is at least challengeable and whatever may have been the case in mid-century, by 1896, the leading county sides generated much of their revenue from 'gates' swollen by the skills of their professional players. Notwithstanding, the regular *Our Van* column resorted to high-minded patriotism:

> ...we may dismiss the matter with the expression of deepest regret that, at a time when the eyes of the world were focused upon English cricket, and at the hour when the heartiest co-operation was requisite to successfully engage the colonial team, English cricketers should have been caught discussing and haggling over the pounds, shillings and pence of a cricket match with its most sordid surroundings.

A piece of doggerel in *Cricket Rhymes* by "Century", an anonymous young lady according to the Preface, put the professionals' viewpoint in a light-hearted way, but a serious overtone is detectable:

> Now this is what the "pros" all say:
> "Why should we receive less pay
> Than those who just for pleasure pay?
>
> 'Tis we who draw the people here,
> 'Tis we who cause the crowd to cheer
> When we professionals appear.

THE FATHER OF MODERN SPORT

The Oval ground belongs to us,
And that is why we've made a fuss
That we may all these things discuss.

You say we've left it rather late,
We should have chosen an earlier date,
But we were forced some days to wait.

We do not wish to lose our fame
Nor cease to play our national game;
We wish to go on just the same.

As we have reason to believe
The so-called "Amateurs" receive
A deal more than for us they leave.

We're hinting at no special one
And hope we are offending none."

(Signed by Abel, Lohmann and Gunn.)

Play on the first day was curtailed by rain and the press had ample
opportunity to seek views from those willing to give them - and there was
no shortage. Most were sympathetic to the professionals; a member of the
public expressing the view that the committee and officials were "supreme
and uncontrolled", a professional pointed out that gates had increased
threefold, but pay had remained the same, while a Surrey member,
commenting on the generally amicable relationships between the
professionals and the committee, gravely opined:

...it will be an awful pity if cricket is to come down to the level of running,
cycling and boxing, and lots of other so-called 'pastimes', and became nothing
but a money-grabbing concern.

Alcock, dignified and diplomatic, as ever, summed up the situation for
the press in reasoned and measured tones:

PROFESSIONALISM

Mr C W Alcock, the popular secretary of the Surrey Club, by whom the decision of the Oval Committee not to grant the increase was communicated to the five men, put the case for his organisation in a nutshell when he remarked to the writer:

"It is a question of principle, not of money, that is involved. In refusing to accede to the demands of the professionals," he went on "the committee were not animated in the slightest degree by any personal feelings. The point really is whether the Surrey Club is to manage its own affairs or whether the professional players are to do so and dictate their own terms. The Committee had no desire to treat the men shabbily, and I don't think that any one could accuse it of such conduct...

It is just as though a businessman had, metaphorically, a pistol held to his head by one of his employees with a demand for increased pay. Supposing your Editor had a sudden demand from one of his subordinates for the doubling of his salary. I am perfectly certain of the course he would take. But if a man came to him and represented that the work upon which he was engaged involved increased labour and responsibility justifying enhanced pay, he would, at all events consider the matter. That is the position of the committee.

The professionals involved are all most estimable, sociable and pleasant fellows, and our relations with them have always been very agreeable...

One thing I can say, that, if the players see their mistake and make manly amends, our relations with them will not be influenced in the least in the future...

It would be a most unfortunate thing if our relations were to come down merely to a commercial level. It would be injurious both to cricket and all concerned in it.

Alcock's own background as a professional journalist clearly gave him an empathy with the press covering the case, leading the *Daily Telegraph* to comment:

One satisfactory feature of the whole lamentable business was to be found in the attitude of Mr C W Alcock and the committee which he represents. Not a word escaped those in authority which was derogatory to the players or which could be construed to be an expression of ill-feeling towards any of the professionals.

Alcock was complimented on the courtesy with which he had treated the press and their requests for information, but in general the press took the side of the strikers, saying that working men could not afford to play merely for honour any more than a doctor could serve his patients or a Government minister serve the nation free of charge.[427]

England won a low-scoring match by 66 runs, non-rebels Peel and Hearne, taking all of the eighteen Australian wickets that fell to bowlers and ironically, in an echo of the Players of England v Australians in 1878, being rewarded with an additional £5 each for their efforts. Richardson, who had bowled a total of 159 overs in the earlier Tests, taking 24 wickets in the process (He and Lohmann had bowled Australia out for 53 in 22.3 overs at Lord's) was allowed just six. Abel contributed 26 and 21, significant in the context of 145 and 84 all out; Hayward a more modest 0 and 13.

Lohmann was told he would not be selected for Surrey until the matter was resolved. Forced into a corner, he was compelled to apologise and agreed to the following letter being sent to the press:

August 12 1896

To the Committee of the Surrey Club.

Gentlemen -

I beg to express my sincere apologies for my refusal to sign the document placing myself unreservedly in the hands of the committee (in company with Abel, Hayward and Richardson) on Monday morning. At the same time my colleagues signed the withdrawal of the position taken up I expected William Gunn to be here, and having associated myself with him, merely desired to wait until his arrival before taking any action. I would add that when the original letter was drawn up my idea was that a request was being preferred instead of a demand being made, and that the expression "demand" which I now see to have been so unfortunate, was inserted against my wish and better judgement. Whilst tendering my apologies I wish to express my heartfelt gratitude to the Surrey Club for the many great kindnesses I have received at their hands, both in times of health and sickness.

My career as a cricketer has been so entirely bound up with the Surrey Club, that I should regret if any action of mine caused a rupture with the club with which my happiest days have been spent, and to which I am so much indebted.

I am, gentlemen, your obedient servant., Geo A Lohmann

Summoned before the committee and compelled to grovel, he took refuge in semantics by saying that the letter was intended as a "request", not a "demand". He had been an important part of Surrey's revival in the 1880s, but played no more cricket for Surrey or England after the end of the 1896 season. Bobby Abel played no more Test cricket, Richardson no more after the Australian tour of 1897/98. The younger Hayward was too valuable to discard and went on to play 35 more Tests. Gunn played one more - at Trent Bridge three years later, selected by his own Committee, exempt from Surrey's internal repercussions, and doubtless recalling an earlier difference of opinion with Surrey over the position of the seven Notts strikers in the earlier dispute of 1881.[428]

The issues on that occasion were the right to arrange fixtures and a greater measure of security for players. Jack Holden, the Notts Secretary and Chief Constable of the City of Nottingham, held firm against the strikers, notwithstanding the intervention of the local MP and the MCC. Holden had urged Alcock not to select any of the seven in the Players side to meet the Gentlemen at The Oval. However, having taken the advice of Henry Perkins, the MCC Secretary who had raised no objection, Alcock went ahead and chose them. There had been a long history of rivalry and acrimony between Surrey and Notts throughout the nineteenth century and this incident and the later decision to play Gunn in defiance of Surrey's 1896 decision form part of that saga.

There was no doubt that the professionals had a strong case. Comparators have an important role to play in pay negotiations and there can be no denying that the expenses of the 'amateurs' both English and Australian were valid ones in this case. Indeed, the pay of professionals for Test matches was increased to £20 only two years later. So it must be asked why Alcock with his history of sympathy towards professionalism in football and willingness to take a more tolerant line towards the Notts strikers, took such a harsh line towards the 'Oval Five' (or four plus one). The answer must in part lie in that the professionalism he supported was controlled professionalism, not haphazard militancy and as he says in *Surrey Cricket*, he responded as might be expected to a 'peremptory demand, not a request for consideration'.[429] Furthermore, there was an absence of solidarity, support for the Surrey strike was not unanimous, the eight professionals involved in the 1896 strike being split eventually into four camps, three who were not supportive, three who caved in on the day, one who declined to play on receipt of Alcock's telegram and one who held out on the day. It was perhaps more in sorrow than in anger that he was to write six years later:

> The subject even at this distance revives rather unpleasant memories, and one would like to ignore it. but the faithful chronicler has a duty to perform...The Surrey Club Committee very naturally felt that such an ultimatum ought not to have been hurled at them on the very eve of the match, and by their own men....Looking at the action of the Players from the most favourable point of view, the best that one could say is that they were badly advised...From a Surrey standpoint it certainly seemed ungrateful that the third and last of the three Test matches, and particularly that on their own county ground, should have been chosen as the occasion for presenting such an ultimatum.[430]

As a tangent of the players' strike, the Surrey committee had to deal with the case of Henry Wood who had cashed in on the topicality of players' pay and the treatment of professionals by giving an interview to the recently established *Daily Mail*. Tabloid journalism was in its infancy and the beginnings of a tendency to 'sensationalise' news rather than merely report it are detectable. Alongside a report that mixed bathing was becoming popular in some European resorts and a comment from the Chairman of the Beach Committee that it would never do at Brighton or any other English seaside town that he knew, the *Mail* ran a multi-headlined feature:

CRICKET REVOLT...PROFESSIONALS' EARNINGS
...WOOD'S BITTER WORDS

In a 'remarkable interview' it was stated that nobody could have any sympathy with the system of 'starvation wages' paid to the heroes of our cleanest sport. Leading jockeys were paid up to £20,000 a year; baseball players up to £1,000. The Australians had each received £500 gross for the tour. The average English professional was far worse off. During the course of a twelve-year career (he was now 42 and presumably judged he had not too much to lose by selling a story to the press), Wood had not managed to save a penny.

"If only I had been an amateur" says he, adding that the professional drifts into penury and the gentleman who plays for the love of the game

PROFESSIONALISM

makes LOTS OF MONEY at it. Professionals were paid £2 a week, £5 a match with an extra £1 if they were on the winning side. From this they had to pay railway fares, hotel bills and lunches, so the committee were giving £6 with one hand and taking away £4 with the other in compelling players to meet expenses. The Committee could well afford to pay, but had never done so. He had managed to obtain a job in the winter "turfing" at 26s per week and when he had been injured, had been obliged to meet the doctor's bill from his "scanty resources". £50 had gone to the occultist who diagnosed that his eyes were strained through watching the ball. When asked about a pension fund "Wood laughed" and "the flood tide of his indignation" was at its fullest. Maurice Read had left the Club dissatisfied with his conditions. Lohmann was paid £300 a year but that was exceptional. The average professional received no more than £150 a year. Amateurs received £20, £30 or £50 a match for expenses.

For balance, other opinions were sought: professionals said they were underpaid; amateurs said it was not appropriate to raise the matter at this time. Unsurprisingly, the Committee was not amused. At a time when they were dealing with the Players' strike and its aftermath and when a choleric Mr Read was about to challenge its decision, it was something they could do without. The figures given by Wood were selective but not incorrect. Players on star contracts could expect to earn more than twice as much as Wood and his fellow run-of-the-mill professionals, but it has to be said that star contracts were introduced, less as a result of the committee's benevolence than of a wish to ward off approaches by other counties which had occurred in the case of George Lohmann and Tom Richardson.[431] Nonetheless, Surrey were more generous than other counties, with Yorkshire not too far behind, the autocratic Lord Hawke, while ruling the county club with a rod of iron, having none the less a pay and rewards policy effective enough to ensure that his professionals were relatively well rewarded for their performances. Surrey too were tolerably generous in what may be termed 'welfare' payments, meeting, for example, the cost of Jupp's funeral and making a grant to his son and two sisters.

Like Lohmann, Wood was compelled to grovel, sending a letter to the committee saying that nine out of ten of the statements attributed to him were untrue. Representatives from the *Daily Mail* attended and suggested that if Wood had a grievance about being misreported, the proper course would be for him to resort to law. It was a suggestion that neither Wood nor the Committee was inclined to pursue. Wood was cautioned and the Committee moved on to Lohmann's letter.[432]

The real discrepancy, however, and the cause of the genuine and justifiable grievance of both Wood and the international strikers was the discrepancy between professionals' pay and amateurs' expenses. Walter Read received a regular annual bonus of £100. By contrast, Lohmann never received more than £50.

By the 1890s, the Club was becoming more professional off the field as well as on it. In 1889, the General Committee of twenty-four had divided itself into three sub-committees of eight each, Finance, Ground and Match,[433] divide and rule in practice, if not necessarily in intention, but the effect could only be to strengthen Alcock's arm as overall co-ordinator or *de facto* Chief Executive. In 1888, the Committee agreed that it was desirable that a Clerk be appointed for the cricket season.[434] Not until 1890, however, was a motion referred to and approved by the Finance Committee "that a respectable Clerk be appointed at a salary not exceeding £150 a year". The appointment of H Lowman Taylor at a salary of £2 per week was approved, but by early 1891, the Finance Committee had come to the conclusion that he did not measure up to the job.[435] So the recruitment process began again and this time "competent" was substituted for "respectable". Professionalism was beginning to hit the offices as well as the field of play.

Two years later, the Club decided to appoint a Cricket Instructor. The Match Committee recommended that the wording "(an amateur preferred)" be included, a proposal not accepted by the General Committee who substituted the words "(amateur or professional)", a perceptible shift of emphasis.[436]

It is naïve to assume that the difference between amateurs and professionals was that the latter were paid and the former were not. They were treated differently: when team photographs became part of the cricket scene, the amateurs were presented with a framed photograph, professionals with a photograph. Both were paid but in different ways and the amount depended not on whether the recipient were amateur or professional but on the economic law of supply and demand and on his value to the club. Thus the amateur Mr Read was paid more than the amateur Mr Diver and the professional Lohmann more than the professional Wood. It is all too easy with the benefit of hindsight to view these arrangements as dishonest and hypocritical. The defence of Alcock and his committee would be to point generally to the structure of society at the time, but more specifically to Surrey's prestige and position in the County Championship in the 1890s. In a *fin-de-siècle* feature in *Cricket* one of the advantages of the cricket of 1900 over that of fifty years earlier is listed as that of the "paid amateur". The amateur-professional divide was not one of money, but of social class. The pretence that it was otherwise continued until 1963.

Rugby Football

Professionalism in rugby became an issue a decade later than it was in the association game and was solved in a quite different way. While the 'dribbling game' managed to reach a measure of accommodation, albeit uneasy at times, rugby went in the opposite direction and divided into two separate governing bodies and two separate codes. Alcock was something of a catalyst in the formation of the Rugby Football Union in 1871, but apart from encouraging rugby union internationals and arranging for them to be hosted at The Oval was not directly involved. Had he been, the whole history of rugby football might have been different. As it was, the Rugby Football Union adhered firmly to the amateur ethic for a hundred years, living at times uncomfortably and antagonistically alongside its sister sports of association football and rugby league.

There was a clear link between competition and professionalism and the relative paucity of Challenge Cups in the rugby game meant that professionalism remained an avoidable issue until 1895. In his review of the 1881-82 football season, Alcock mentions the Yorkshire County Challenge Cup, the Welsh Union Cup and the Northumberland County Cup. It is a strong clue to the source of the challenge to the purely amateur game:

> The Rugby Union is not favoured, if favour it is, with so many Challenge Cups as the Association. To some players this may appear unfortunate, but others,

many of whom are men whose opinion should be highly respected, congratulate the devotees of the rugby game because there are so few of these cup competitions, which they consider to be a great injury to the game and give greater encouragement to the 'professional' element and to betting. [437]

In 1895, rugby faced the same issues which had confronted the association game a decade earlier. However, the battle-lines on this occasion were drawn up on a direct north-south split and the solution was quite the opposite. Direct and to the point, J A Millar and M Newsome, Yorkshire members of the RFU committee, proposed and seconded "that players be allowed compensation for *bona fide* lost time". W Cail and G Rowland Hill, respectively President and Honorary Secretary of the Union, countered with the following amendment:

That this Meeting, believing that the above principle is contrary to the true interest of the Game and its spirit, declines to sanction the same.

Two special trains were commissioned for the northern delegates, but some of their passengers, unused to London, managed to get themselves lost and failed to arrive at the meeting. Their southern counterparts, seemingly better organised, found proxies for 120 clubs unable to be represented. Additionally, some of the northerners alleged subsequently, the Colleges of Oxford and Cambridge Universities had a vote each, rather than one for each university. Whatever the reasons, the facts of the voting were uncontestable. 282 voted for the amendment; 136 against and the great schism was complete.

Although the original cause of the split was "broken time", it was perhaps inevitable that open professionalism would follow, however vigorously the newly-established Northern Union might deny it. *Smirk's Handbook of Northern Rugby Union Matches* saw the situation as follows:

CAUSE OF THE SPLIT

The reasons of the split with the Rugby Union are well known, but it may be mentioned that the principal cause was the desire to establish the legislation of payment for *bona fide* broken time. The proposal is a reasonable one for the majority of the Counties above named [438] are chiefly the artisan class, engaged on day wage, and who can ill afford to lose their work to follow football playing.

PROFESSIONALISM

THE QUESTION OF OPEN PROFESSIONALISM

It is of course hinted that the legalisation of payment for broken time practically means open professionalism, but this is certainly not the intention of those at the head of affairs and for some time at any rate it is not likely to come about...

There was, suggested the Handbook, no reason why the Northern League should not be to Rugby Football what the League has been to the Association Game and hoped that the Northern Rugby Union would prosper and revive interest in the handling game. Alas, though the Northern Union did come to flourish as the Rugby League, the hope for harmonious relations between the League and Union codes was a forlorn one as the rift widened. In the north unrestricted professionalism soon followed and in the south, professionalism became widely defined, so that even taking the field with or against a professional was sufficient for a player's amateur status to be forfeited. Rugby had no Alcock.

REFERENCES

375. *The Evolution of English Sport* p 45
376. *Cricketers' Companion 1880* pp 7-8
377. *Cricket* 29 June 1905
378. *Victoria History of the Counties of England - Surrey*
379. Surrey CCC minutes 14 March 1881
380. p clxxiv
381. Alverstone & Alcock *Surrey Cricket* p 335
382. Surrey CCC minutes 11 August 1881
383. Surrey CCC minutes 14 August 1882
384. Surrey CCC minutes 30 August 1882
385. Surrey CCC minutes 4 July and 18 August 1884
386. Surrey CCC minutes 12 September 1884
387. Surrey CCC minutes 27 August 1885
388. Surrey CCC minutes 20 June 1895
389. Surrey CCC minutes 18 October 1894
390. *Richmond and Twickenham Times* 17 August 1895   A letter concerning

Edwin Ash's resignation as Secretary to the Richmond Athletic Association begins: "I have been so very busy with Read's benefit..."

391. Surrey CCC minutes 21 November 1895

392. Surrey CCC minutes 3 September 1896

393. Sissons *The Players* p 159

394. Surrey CCC minutes 21 March 1889

395. Football Sub-Committee minutes 11 October 1894

396. Football Sub-Committee minutes 5 March 1895

397. Football Sub-Committee minutes 20 February 1895

398. 15 September 1884

399. p 45

400. Fowler *Barbarians, Gentlemen & Players: Association Football to 1914* in *Family History Monthly* September 2000

401. *Football Annual* 1881

402. *Football* 18 October 1882

403. *Football* 1 November 1882

404. *Football Annual* 1884

405. Green *History of the Football Association* p 61

406. Jackson *Sporting Days and Sporting Ways* p 101

407. Surrey CCC minutes 24 August 1886

408. Surrey CCC minutes 24 August 1886

409. Edworthy *England: The Official FA History* p 60

410. Wilton *C B Fry, an English Hero* p142

411. Knight *The Complete Cricketer* pp 297 & 306, quoting Fuller Pilch

412. p 198

413. 22 September 1887 p 426

414. Gordon *Background of Cricket* p 115

415. Surrey CCC minutes 19 April 1886

416. Surrey CCC minutes 6 May 1886

417. Rae *W G* p 303

418. *Cricket* 21 December 1899

419. *Cricket* 21 December 1899 p 469

420. Sissons *The Players* p 167

421. Keating in *The Guardian* 27 November 2000

422. 8 August 1896

423. p 247

424. later Lord Alverstone
425. p liv
426. pp lvii - lix
427. *Daily Telegraph* 10 and 11 August
428. Sissons *The Players* p 177
429. p 273
430. Alverstone & Alcock *Surrey Cricket* p 272-3
431. Alverstone & Alcock *Surrey Cricket* pp 105-113
432. Special Committee meeting 12 August 1896
433. Surrey CCC minutes 16 May 1889
434. Surrey CCC minutes 7 June 1888
435. Surrey CCC minutes 15 January 1891
436. Surrey CCC minutes 18 February 1892
437. *Football* 4 October 1882
438. The original Northern Union comprised eleven clubs from Yorkshire, nine from Lancashire and two from Cheshire.

CHAPTER 9

INTERNATIONAL SPORT

IT IS NOT EASY TO IDENTIFY with precision the first international sports fixture. Lions v Christians in Rome in the first century AD might be a strong contender, albeit with the proviso that participation was involuntary on both sides and there was never any suggestion of a return fixture or political unrest causing the match to be moved to a neutral venue. Even earlier than that, there is evidence that China might have played Japan at something which might have been football.[439]

Modern international sport, however, would appear to have its roots in the nineteenth century and be not unconnected with the rise of national consciousness and imperial aspirations. While it was doubtless competitive, it did not reach the internecine quasi-civil war dimensions of some South American contests of the twentieth century and the international vision of Baron de Coubertin translated into the first modern Olympic Games of 1896 was of competition between individuals rather than teams. National medal tables were for the future.

The first international cricket match, indeed possibly the first international sports fixture of any kind was not, as pub quiz pundits might have us believe, between England and Australia, but between the United States and Canada at the St George's cricket ground in Harlem, New York on 24 and 25 September 1844. Charles Alcock was under two years old at the time, so it can be said with confidence that this was one international fixture he did not organise. It is a fixture which, without being remotely near first-class status, has continued intermittently ever since.

Association Football

But it was to international football that Alcock first gave his attention, though the five pseudo-internationals played between 1870 and 1872 were of novelty value, rather than between two fully representative national sides. The first full rugby international was played in 1871, followed the next year by the first international under the association code. From that point there was no looking back.

The first pseudo-international was arranged and played a year before Alcock took up his appointment as Secretary to Surrey County Cricket Club, so even at this stage he was not without influence. As it happens, the match was not played on the scheduled day because of a heavy frost, but took place a fortnight later. However, the first tentative steps had been taken to establishing The Oval as possibly the nearest there has been to an English national sports centre before or since.

The matches were, Alcock says, "under the auspices, although not directly under the control of the Football Association", but they have never been regarded as official internationals as the soi-disant Scotland team comprised London-based players with Scottish connections, but, nevertheless the way had been paved for the first international proper, Scotland v England on St Andrew's Day, 30 November 1872.

The result of that first association football international, a goalless draw, was not reproduced in England-Scotland matches until 1970 at Wembley. The return was played twelve months later at The Oval, now recognised as the headquarters of football in London. This time England triumphed 4-2 and, although by the turn of the century football was beginning to overtake cricket as the major spectator attraction, Alcock is able to refer to the pardonable pride occasioned by the passage of 3,000 spectators through the turnstiles.

Matches were played in Scotland and England in alternate years, the Scotland ones in Glasgow and the England ones generally at The Oval, except in 1883 and 1887 when they were staged in Blackburn and Sheffield. Although football at The Oval continued until 1895, the last international was played in 1889 and after that the fixture meandered between Blackburn, Richmond, Goodison Park, Crystal Palace, Stamford Bridge and Birmingham before finally finding a home at Wembley in 1924.

The inaugural contest in 1872, however, led to the establishment of the Scottish Football Association as a separate body. Wales and Ireland followed suit and the Home International Championship, football's oldest international series, was launched in 1883/84. Wales joined the international scene in 1879 and Ireland in 1882. The latter began with a series of heavy defeats 13-0, 7-0 and 8-1 against England and 5-0, 8-2 and 7-2 to Scotland, but the Home International Championship was off the ground. Ireland was replaced by Northern Ireland in 1921, but war years apart, the format of the competition remained unchanged until 1983-84 when the combined forces of other international matches, domestic fixture congestion and hooliganism caused the series to be discontinued. Anglo-Scottish matches tottered on until 1989 and occur now only in the context of the World Cup or European Nations Championship.

There is no doubt that the Scottish connection opened England's eyes to the possibility of playing the game in ways other than dribbling and "backing up", as Scotland demonstrated the possibilities of the "combination" game, not as a one-off in a single fixture, but consistently over a period of two decades. The first result was something of a surprise, as the English intention was to provide a lesson to the Scots in the skills of the game and although England won the following year, they managed only one more victory (5-4 in 1879) before 1891. There was the occasional draw, but it was a period of Scottish dominance and the thirty goals they scored in six matches between 1878 and 1883 persuaded the English that further modifications were required to what started as a 1-1-8 dribbling game if they were to offer a serious challenge. So in 1884, the half-back line was increased by one at the expense of the forward line and the 2-3-5 system which was to survive well into the twentieth century was introduced. England still lost 1-0.

One of the objectives in 'Pa' Jackson's establishment of the Corinthians in 1882 was to challenge the supremacy of Scotland. The playing strength of the Club was such that the 1886 England side comprised nine Corinthians and two from Blackburn Rovers. In 1894, a side composed entirely of Corinthians met and defeated Wales 5-1 at Wrexham. The Corinthians continued to be a force in football, but as the professionals were able to devote time to fitness and training, so the balance of international sides began to change in favour of the professionals and by the early 1890s the pendulum in Anglo-Scottish football had begun to swing towards England. Tactical changes and the Corinthians had played their part, but so to an extent had Alcock. Although he had not himself played serious football since 1875, he was sufficiently astute tactically to recognise that a different approach was required.

As in cricket, overseas connections were developed: a team was selected for a tour of Australia.[440] There is, however, no record of its ever having taken place, the first tour to that part of the world being in 1925, though not with the team selected for the 1882 tour: the game was to be taught in Germany and Princeton v Yale on Thanksgiving Day was reported in *Football*.[441] Development in the United States and the Empire was, however, somewhat slower than in continental Europe. Denmark's Boldspil Union was established in 1889; other nations followed suit. In 1899, Alcock as Vice-President of the FA accompanied a side of amateurs and professionals to Berlin, Prague and Karlsruhe. Four matches were played, all won easily, 38 goals scored and four conceded. The Corinthians had toured South Africa in 1897 and the first stirrings of international football in Europe can be traced to a match between Austria and Hungary in 1902. The way was open for the Association to take the lead in establishing an international administrative body.

But the initiative came from elsewhere, specifically from Robert Guérin and the *Union des Sociétés Françaises des Sports Athlétiques*. England was invited to take the lead. In the form of Alcock's successor, Frederick Wall, they declined to do so and on 21 May 1904 FIFA was born, not in London as would have been logical, but in Paris. There were parallels with 1880 and establishment attitudes to Australia. So England, having been tardy in joining FIFA, then, along with the other British Associations seceding between 1927 and the Second World War over the issue of "broken time" payments in the Olympic Games, were twenty years late entering the World Cup. Having taught the world the game, the home nations have been overtaken and - with the sole exception of England's World Cup win at home in 1966 - been off the pace for much of the twentieth-century. Would it have been different if Alcock had remained in charge?

Nevertheless, the baby conceived from Alcock's seed in 1871 lived well into its second century and became the forerunner of similar international tournaments in Europe, South America, Oceania and in 1930, despite British insularity at the time, of the Jules Rimet Trophy, the World Cup.

THE FATHER OF MODERN SPORT

Cricket

Enthusiasm for cricket and for honing cricket skills had been in evidence in Australia before any tour was organised in either direction. There are reports of matches in Sydney in the 1830s and clubs in the early 1840s and matches in Queensland from 1844, sixteen years before its separation from New South Wales, include such fixtures as Smokers v Non-Smokers, Bewhiskereds v Clean-shavens and Married v Single. The first inter-colonial match was New South Wales v Victoria in the Sydney domain in January 1857. A letter to the *Field* in May 1861 from 'An Old Bushman' read:

> When I was in Melbourne, the young colonists were cricket mad, and it was a pleasing sight to see how assiduously they stuck to their practice. Always at it, I never went by the cricket-ground in the season without seeing play.[442]

Even earlier, the *Australian and New Zealand Gazette* had stated:

> Cricket is a game exceedingly popular in these colonies and under the able guidance of several gentlemen who formerly were well known at Lord's and the Universities, the eleven will find that their task will be more difficult than it was in America.[443]

Before regular tours by Australian teams there was much ignorance about Australia and its inhabitants and A G Steel mentioned that the "lower classes", perhaps conditioned by memories of the 1868 tour, expected to find Gregory's team of 1878 as black as the Aboriginals. Nor was it only the lower classes. Steel tells the story of his conversation with Rev Arthur Ward:

> One day in the pavilion at Lord's, the writer, who had been chosen to represent the Gentlemen of England against the visitors in a forthcoming match, was sitting beside Spofforth watching a game, in which neither was taking part. Mr Ward, coming up, accosted the writer, "Well, Mr Steel, so I hear you are going to play against the niggers on Monday?" His face was quite a picture when Spofforth was introduced to him as "the demon nigger bowler".[444]

218

INTERNATIONAL SPORT

Following the volte-face and eventual success of 1880, the Surrey Committee's attitude was totally different for the 1882 tour. The fact that planning had began much earlier and there was obviously more flexibility in the fixture list were not the only reasons that the suggestion from MCC that The Oval be made available for four matches, including one with the Gentlemen of England and one with England was this time accepted positively and with alacrity.[445]

Alcock had had a part in organising the 1878 tour and intervened in 1880. For 1882, he had played a fuller role in organising a tour of which all 38 fixtures were eleven-a-side and which was to have a dramatic finale. From then, until the establishment of the Board of Control of Test Matches at Home in 1898, he continued to organise the programmes for Australian touring sides as well as those for the Parsees, Philadelphians, South Africans and Gentlemen of Holland. Of the Parsees tour of 1886, Vasant Raji says that "C W Alcock, the secretary of the Surrey Cricket Club, was requested to be the agent of the team, a task which he performed very ably". There is every reason to suppose that similar comments could have been made on Alcock's work for other touring sides.

After a four match series in Australia in 1881/82, the mother country offered her 'colonials' just one Test in 1882, again at The Oval. Australia won by 7 runs. 'The Demon' Spofforth had 14 wickets for 90 runs. For Alcock and for all present, it was a memorable match:

> The most exciting finish I have ever seen - and I should not like to see such another - was in the match when the Australians beat England by seven runs. It is impossible to describe the state people were in just before the end of the game. Men who were noted for their coolness at critical moments were shaking like a leaf - some were shivering with cold - some even fainted. I was as excited and nervous as anybody. At times there was an awful silence. And all the while Blackham was standing up to Spofforth with the utmost calmness, taking him as easily and certainly as if he were bowling slow, instead of at a tremendous pace. A slight mistake might have lost his side the match, but he worked like a machine.[446]
>
> The scene when the game was over can hardly be described. The reaction after the severe tension of the last half-hour left the spectators almost paralysed. The effect in many ways was not without its comic side. In the high pressure of such a sensational finish, it is said that the reporters, whose duty

it was to telegraph to the evening papers, were so overcome as to forget to transmit the result. In some cases the excitement took a strange form. As I was going from the pavilion to the Press Box immediately after the match, I thought I recognised the form of an old habitué of the Oval on one of the seats in the stand. He was leaning over the seat, and touching him on the back, I asked if there was anything the matter with him. "Oh no," was his reply, "only I don't know whether to cry or be sick."[447]

'Pa' Jackson's version was more concerned with Alcock's own reaction:

I was in the office of the Surrey County Club at the finish and never shall I forget the outcome of the match had upon the members of the club committee and some of their friends, who chanced to be there. Charlie Alcock, the Secretary, sat down on the huge iron safe and buried his head in his hands, seemingly oblivious to everything.[448]

The historical significance of some matches, like the first FA Cup Final or the first international is sometimes only realised later. On this occasion, however, contemporary evidence suggests that the importance of this one was realised at the time. An England team, selected as such, had succumbed at home to "the colonials". Having been at one stage 66 for 4, requiring 85 to win, England managed to be bowled out for 77. Repercussions followed. Peate, being last out, was blamed, as no 11s and goalkeepers often are when their error is merely the last of several. W G, having made 32, allegedly blamed the others and the selection of the team and the captaincy of A N Hornby were criticised retrospectively. It was a blueprint with which English cricket followers were to become all too familiar over several generations.

Writing many years later in *The Cricketer*, Spofforth was to attribute Australia's victory to superior tactics, their acumen in the way of field placings and arranging matters so that he and Boyle were bowling at the batsmen they were most likely to dismiss - strategies probably not considered by their English equivalents at the time:

Four wickets were down, and only 32 runs were required; but I must confess I never thought they would be got. A Lyttelton and A P Lucas then came together and at one time Boyle bowled no less than nine overs for one run, and I ten overs for two runs. Then we agreed to let Lyttelton get a run, so as to change ends. Bannerman was to allow one to pass at mid-off which he did, and Lyttelton faced me, when I bowled him. That was the real turning point, as Lucas getting opposite to me again, turned the first ball into his wicket, and six wickets were down for 63, and we all felt we were on top…[449]

The Ashes were born when the now legendary mock obituary in the *Sporting Times* marked the end of an era and the beginning of another:

In affectionate Remembrance
of
ENGLISH CRICKET
which died at The Oval
on
29th August 1882
Deeply lamented by a large circle of
Sorrowing Friends and Acquaintances
NB. The body will be cremated and
the Ashes taken to Australia

The mythical Ashes became real ashes on Hon Ivo Bligh's 1882-83 tour of Australia when a stump, a bail or a veil (versions vary) was burnt and the resultant ashes placed in the famous urn which, despite occasional Australian protests, still has a permanent home in the Lord's Museum.

Despite what was seen as a national disaster in cricketing terms, the four matches in which the Australians had appeared at The Oval had made a significant difference to the Club's finances. Match receipts in 1881 had been £ 2,260. For 1882 they were £12,329. The Australians took 50% of the gate money for matches in which they had been involved, but an increase approaching 500% ensured that never again would there be hesitation on financial grounds about hosting an Australian touring side. Alcock's subsequent comments on 1880 and "the eternal fitness of things" were well justified.

Alcock was not slow to show his admiration for and analyse the reasons for the superiority of Australian cricket, attributing its success to condition, physique and the fact that, with particular reference to 1884, the tour "was purely a business one, their sole object being to play cricket and win matches". Unlike their Australian counterparts, players in England had limited time to go into strict training, the amateurs because of their social engagements and the professionals because of their related business commitments, such as selling cricket materials. The "colonials", conversely, benefited from the effects of a hard, healthy outdoor life, had more time to practice and could throw a cricket ball a hundred yards, while most Englishmen could not manage over fifty.

F R Spofforth, writing some years later in *Cricket* has a similar viewpoint, saying:

> Australians are much better than Englishmen in picking up and starting quickly after a ball. They not only start quicker but run faster after it and if you were to put the Australian team and an England team in line and let them run a sprint, about eight Australians would come in first.[450]

From 1884, three matches for the Ashes series became the norm and from 1899, five. Alcock was entrusted with the arrangements and the initial correspondence took the form of an exchange of telegrams with G Alexander of the Melbourne Club. The brisk efficiency contrasts sharply with the tortuous fixture arranging process of four years earlier. Alcock telegraphed: 'Condition you play same four matches Oval as eightytwo Surrey give ground and stands any match you like end August.' Alexander replied 'Accept your offer leave five vacant dates obtain the best terms you can with Counties three matches England if possible. Letter last mail.'[451]

However, matches other than Tests - now officially designated as such - continued to attract large attendances and, occasionally, disturbances. In days when the timings of lunch and tea intervals were more flexible than they were subsequently to become, it was decided in the Players v Australia match in 1884 that with 11 runs required to win and nine wickets standing, lunch would be taken. Murdoch was happy to continue, but the Club had an eye on catering profits. The crowd turned ugly. Alcock appealed to Australian all-rounder, George Giffen. "You seem to be all right with them Giffen. Perhaps they will listen to you." Giffen made himself scarce. A similar request was made to Ted Peate of Yorkshire, himself later to be dismissed by that county as part of Lord Hawke's purge of unruly elements. 'Naw, sir,' protested Peate. "Ah didn't cum here t'quell riot; Ah cum t'play cricket.'[452]

Always aware of the contribution made by Australians to English cricket, Alcock was also conscious of England's missionary role and its responsibility to spread the cricket gospel on a global scale. It has been less successful in doing that than it has in football, but Queen Victoria's Diamond Jubilee was an occasion for imperialism and for retrospection and, fully alive to the progress of the game nationally and internationally and to the concept of a cricket empire, he was able to say:

> That English cricket has benefited materially by the periodical appearances of Australian cricketers will be generally and ungrudgingly admitted. Besides Australians too, there have been Parsees, Americans, Canadians and South Africans, at one time or other over here, perfecting or at least improving their education in cricket.[453]

The professionals' strike of 1896 had the effect of improving the pay of those who played the game for a living, but it did more than that. It drew attention to the anomaly of a national side being selected by a local committee, at the time that of Surrey, MCC or Lancashire, leaving Yorkshire, not a Test match county at the time, out in the cold. Lord Hawke was less than impressed and used the occasion of the opening of a new pavilion in Bedale to say so. He suggested the responsibility for selection and payment of test teams should be undertaken by MCC. £10 with £5 travelling expenses had been mooted, but he proposed £20 and have done with it. Lord's should have one Test match, but there was no reason why the other two should be allocated to the Oval and Manchester. Yorkshire had a ground second to none and two or three grounds capable of accommodating 30,000. It was only fair that Yorkshire should be allocated a Test match. The county had allowed its players to take part year after year and had never had a Test match. If no change were made, then Yorkshire would take a strong stand and not allow players to take part in Test matches, unless they were organised by M C C. The ultimatum was greeted with applause (telling an audience what it wants to hear is a sure fire way of eliciting applause). The strength of the argument and of Lord Hawke's personality made the resistance difficult and neither Surrey, nor Alcock, attempted to do so. Had Alcock not wrested the initiative from MCC in 1880, international cricket in England would not have started - or at least would have been delayed. Those circumstances no longer applied, however, and it was now appropriate that the control of international cricket should be handed back to where it should logically have been in the first place. Consequently, the Board of Control of Test Matches at Home was established by MCC at the request of the counties in 1898 and Headingley became a Test venue in 1899, the year which saw the first five match series in England.

Rugby

To complete a hat-trick in international sports innovation, for a brief period in the 1870s, Alcock introduced rugby union to The Oval. It was at the time a game of twenty-a-side and prolonged scrummages with the result determined by goals (converted tries), but in the four England-Scotland and three England-Ireland matches played between 1872 and 1879, we have the seeds of Five and Six Nations Championship.

An unquestioning belief in the value of sport in general and international sport in particular did not, however, go unchallenged and a hard-hitting article in the *National Review* was reproduced in *Cricket*.[454] The writer, 'Old Harrovian', quite possibly reacting against the compulsory games ethos, suggested that the composition of the Australian Eleven was critically discussed by those who had not the vaguest idea of the constitution of the Australian Commonwealth.

...even if the battle of Waterloo was won on the playing fields of Eton, no one will seriously deny that far more is required from both officers and men in modern warfare than can ever be learned at games....

If only a tenth part of the thousands who spend their time at Old Trafford or The Oval could be induced to join the Volunteers, to form shooting clubs or to take any kind of exercise, how much better it would be for the national physique and also for the country's safety!...

There is, however, little chance of any such wholesome revival in public taste unless the lead is given by the rich. In social matters, as in politics, the signal for reform must come from the upper classes. It is for the boys in the great public schools, by displaying more keenness in their work, by encouraging the volunteer movement and - last, but not least - by remembering that every form of sport is a recreation, and not a business, to set an example which cannot fail to have the most excellent effect throughout the country.

It was not a point of view with which Charles Alcock could be expected to agree wholeheartedly - or at all. Wearing his rational recreation, *mens sana in corpore sano* hat, he refutes the allegations, stating that in France boys are being encouraged to play games, the Germans have concluded that the gymnasium[455] is not all that is required to improve the race and cricket, football and lawn tennis are increasing in popularity in Holland. "All work and no play makes Jack a dull boy" and it is far better that he should play games in his few leisure hours than discuss the constitution in a beer garden.

Baily's was somewhat sceptical about the value of overseas tours to countries where the prospect of a reasonable contest was remote, for instance, Canada and the United States:

> it is…humiliating to think that the richest country in the world cannot send out eleven gentlemen without making a comparatively poor dependency pay for their expenses. As for the cricket, it is of course the poorest excuse for getting a cheap holiday and unbounded hospitality.[456]

It is beyond question that international sport would have happened anyway and there can be very few sports that are peculiar to one nation. Australian Rules Football has its adherents outside the Antipodes and games once peculiar to the United States - baseball, basketball and American football - are enjoyed elsewhere. Satellite television and the speed of communication have resulted in the much-vaunted global village becoming a reality. Even the World Series, once confined to the United States (although its title was borrowed by Kerry Packer for cricket purposes) now has a following which more accurately reflects its title, even though participation may not be global.

British insularity has meant that the development has perhaps been slower than would otherwise have been the case, as witness the initial reluctance to embrace international cricket with Australia and to become involved with FIFA. The global village has made sporting evangelism much easier. In the nineteenth century it needed its visionaries. Charles Alcock was one of them.

REFERENCES

439. About 50 BC according to a text in the Munich Ethnological Museum - *Purcell's Encyclopedia of Association Football*.
440. *Football* 22 November 1882
441. *Football* 20 December 1882
442. *Field* 11 May 1861
443. quoted in *The Field* 28 April 1860
444. Steel & Lyttelton *The Badminton Library: Cricket* p 315
445. Surrey CCC minutes 27 October 1871
446. Bettesworth *Chats on the Cricket Field* p 23
447. Alverstone & Alcock *Surrey Cricket* p 250
448. Jackson *Sporting Days and Sporting Ways* p 42
449. *Cricketer* 28 May 1921
450. *Cricket* 29 January 1903
451. Surrey CCC minutes 6 November 1883
452. Standing *Anglo-Australian Cricket 1862-1926* p 53 - quoting Giffen *With Bat and Ball*
453. *Cricket under Queen Victoria*
454. 21 September 1905
455. school
456. October 1872

CHAPTER 10

THE ELDER STATESMAN

Football

THE RESPECT WITH WHICH ALCOCK continued to be held by his colleagues at the Football Association can be gauged by the attempts (ultimately successful) to retain him when his resignation from the post of Secretary in 1886 became a real possibility. There were two attempts to resign for two separate reasons. Firstly and most obviously, pressure of work at The Oval and the *Cricket* office at 17 Paternoster Square, as well as at the conveniently adjacent no 28 where after eighteen years of peripatetic existence, the Association had established its first regular office in September 1881; and secondly, his changed position on the Committee after the legalisation of professionalism and the subsequent *coup d'état* by the northern clubs.

Antagonism between the north and south of England is not confined to the sports field, still less to football, but it was at its sharpest in 1886, a year after the legalisation of professionalism when Dr Morley of Blackburn sent the following telegram to Major Marindin:

> We protest against the studied discourtesies and lack of consideration shown towards the northern members of the Committee and decline to assist in the selection of the England team.[457]

Increased administrative work mainly caused by the advent of professionalism had led to the position of Honorary Secretary being converted to a salaried post. It was partly a case of "If you can't beat 'em, join 'em", but largely a recognition that the nature of the job had changed beyond all recognition since the creation of the Association more than two decades earlier. Compared with his pay at The Oval, now £400, the stipend of £200 was modest, especially as the expense of a paid Clerk had to be met from that sum. The published records of the FA do not reveal that the Clerk was Alcock's own son, William Edward Forster, who sadly died of epilepsy[458] the following March.

On 21 March he was buried alongside his infant brother, Charles Ernest, in West Norwood cemetery. There was a Surrey committee meeting the day after William's death. It was one of the very few that Alcock missed before his long-term illness in 1903 and also one of the rare occasions that the Assistant Secretaryship held by W W Read was anything more than a sinecure. The Committee formally recorded its condolences:

> It was resolved that the following expression of regret be sent to the Secretary...That this meeting of the General Committee of the Surrey County CC beg to offer to Mr and Mrs Alcock their extreme regret and deep sympathy in the great loss they have sustained in the death of their only son.[459]

So, of two sons and six daughters, Charles and Eliza had lost the former. In days before the suffragette movement and female emancipation when the position of women was generally one of subservience, that must have been quite a blow. Five years later a proposal to the Committee that lady members be admitted was peremptorily dismissed.[460]

Around the same time a proposal that the Oval be used for women's football was "not entertained". The organiser of the British Ladies' Football Club, in an interview with a sporting newspaper which would not look out of place had it emanated from an activist in the women's movements of the following century, fumed:

> Aren't women as good as men? We ladies have too long borne the degradation of presumed inferiority to the other sex. If men can play football, so can women.

The sporting newspaper's response would now be regarded as overtly sexist and ensure the correspondence columns were filled for several issues to come.

> We do not feel disposed to deny this, nor do we doubt that Miss Honeyball and her companions will look very attractive in blue serge knickers on the divided skirt pattern and cardinal and pale blue blouses respectively, but we doubt whether the public will come for such a show; and ungallant as Mr Alcock and his Committee are suggested to have been in refusing the use of the Oval for such a purpose, there are other committees who will have serious

doubts in the same direction. We are not prudes, either on the prowl or on the growl, but there is a good deal of difference between a lot of schoolgirls romping after a ball in their own field in their own way, and a promiscuously selected set trying to make money out of that which would be just as interesting as if a troupe of males attempted to exhibit themselves as champions at skipping rope.[461]

A good deal of water, Jackson conceded, had flowed under the bridge since that paragraph was penned. And more still since Jackson's comment in 1932.

But life at Surrey County Cricket Club and the Football Association went on and the modest remuneration offered by the latter had been sufficient to retain the "great and experienced services of Mr Alcock". One administrative detail was to be finalised. As a paid official, appointed, rather than elected, he no longer had a seat on the committee; but a proposal that the Secretary be automatically elected to the Committee was carried.

The southern delegates, having monopolised the Association since its inception, had become complacent and lax about attendance at meetings. Matters came to a head at the 1886 Annual General Meeting when all the members of the nominated committee were deposed. Some distinguished servants of the early game lost their seats, among them N L Jackson, John Smith, A T B Dunn, R A Lunnon, A H Hunter and M P Betts. Deprived of his power base and unwilling to act without a voice on the Committee, Alcock tendered his resignation for the second time and was supported in his action by Major Marindin who threatened to withdraw from the Presidency.

The heated discussion which ensued included expressions of regret at the attitude of two such honoured and valued officers and such was Alcock's standing that the newly elected W H Jope of Walsall offered to resign his place in his favour. The whole question was left over for further discussion. The 'northern caucus' - essentially Lancastrian, the Sheffield and Birmingham contingents having opposed professionalism the previous year - was magnanimous in victory, initiating behind the scenes discussions with the defeated members, as a result of which the previous position was re-established whereby Alcock, as long as he remained Secretary, would have a vote on the Committee and the Committee was authorised to fill any vacancies that might occur. Messrs Jope and D

Haigh retired from the committee and after a further ballot, involving southern representatives only, P M Walters of Old Carthusians and 'Pa' Jackson were elected to replace them, though Jackson did not continue as Assistant Secretary.

But football and society were changing and the old boy network was no longer appropriate for the government of a game which was now more democratic and socially inclusive. Consequently a committee comprising a President, three Vice-Presidents, a Treasurer and a Secretary yielded to a Council comprising the six officers plus ten divisional representatives elected by the clubs and nominees of affiliated associations. Kinnaird and Alcock were men able to adjust to the demands of a widening democracy, but others, of the opinion that the true spirit of football was being stifled, continued to view the situation through the myopic rose-coloured spectacles of pure amateurism.

Jackson summed up the situation in the following terms:

> Previously the members were mostly gentlemen who gave their time and ability to the management of the Association solely on account of their love of sport. There were one or two of the Committee who, by reason of their connexion with the Press, probably obtained some slight emoluments for writing about the game, but their emoluments were not obtained because the writers happened to be members of the Committee. Under the new régime, however, there gradually crept in a class of men who followed football as a business quite as much as professional footballers themselves. Many of these had ostensibly other occupations, but it was in connexion with football that they chiefly made their living.[462]

On his retirement from the post of Secretary in 1895, Alcock was appointed Vice-President and continued to be active in the Association's administration. With Lord Kinnaird and his predecessor as President, Major (later Sir Francis) Marindin, Alcock had formed part of what Geoffrey Green has called "the original great triumvirate".[463] Supported by men such as Charles Crump, who, like Marindin and Alcock had refereed early Cup Finals, J C (later Sir Charles) Clegg, Chairman of the Council, and Alcock's successor as Secretary, Frederick Wall, they took the game from its raw amateur - and often amateurish - beginnings to the professional and sophisticated administration of the new century. Alcock continued to serve on the Finance Committee and with Clegg and Crump was part of the three-man Emergency Committee.

One of the last things Alcock did was to serve on a Commission which investigated a West Ham United v Millwall match on 17 September 1906 which was "not contested in a friendly spirit, the play on the whole was far too vigorous, and there were too many fouls which were unchecked" and the match was not properly controlled by the referee. One player was suspended for fourteen days, the referee for the remainder of the season, the players of both teams were censured and both Clubs severely censured for not having reported matters to the Football Association. Hands-on and involved to the end.

Cricket

The workload at the Oval, as at the FA, was increasing. Indeed, there were times when there were potential conflicts of interest and Alcock was writing to himself, as for example when the FA asked for the use of the Oval for an international football match against Scotland and the Committee declined on the grounds that April 19 was too late in the year.[464] On reconsideration, however, the decision was reversed, but it was decided that in future, no football be permitted after the end of March.

His management style at the Oval remained literally "hands-on". Fred Boyington, the Surrey scorer, in a "Chat" in *Cricket* relates a story of how Alcock dealt with a spot of crowd trouble at a Surrey-Notts Bank Holiday fixture with over 20,000 in the ground. Some of the spectators were throwing turf. Alcock asked them to stop. Most were obliging, but one failed to do so and threw a large piece of turf at another man. Prefacing his punch-line by "he had been a famous athlete in his younger days", Boyington tells how "Mr Alcock grasped hold of him, lifted him off his feet and threw him right among the spectators" and afterwards confessed that he was never sure that he had correctly identified the offender.[465]

In a parallel gesture to that of the Football Association seventeen years earlier, in 1898 the Committee announced that Alcock's testimonial had raised £470 and that it had been decided to present him with a silver bowl and a purse of money to commemorate his long service. The Committee had contributed 100 guineas. The total haul was well over a year's pay and was doubtless a welcome bonus.

In 1887, the "cricket parliament" advocated by the *Sporting Life* in 1864 became a reality, though not in the terms originally envisaged. The earlier concept had been for a body to challenge and usurp the MCC, but the body now established was intentionally under its auspices. It was short-lived, its dissolution being reported to the Committee on 18 December 1890. It was a forerunner in fact of the ECB's First Class Forum and its passing was regretted by Lord Harris, who, though now Governor of Bombay and no longer directly involved, wrote to Ivo Bligh that the Council had been and remained necessary. The annual meeting of secretaries to fix the dates of matches was no longer manageable. Without the Council behind it, the position of MCC was weaker.

A comment in *Cricket*, probably by Alcock, regrets the "undignified downfall of a body which ought to have able to conduct its affairs in an orderly way".[466] There was no shortage of Agenda items, for instance, standards of umpiring, qualifications and classification of counties. The Laws and management of the game remained firmly within the province of MCC to which Lord Harris and Alcock saw the Council as complementary. In 1904 the Council was resurrected in the form of the Advisory County Cricket Committee which, under the auspices of MCC ran parallel to the Board of Control until merged into the Test and County Cricket Board in 1969.

Civic Service

In resigning the honorary secretaryship of what was popularly known as the Richmond Athletic Association, Edwin Ash addressed his letter formally and correctly to "Councillor C W Alcock JP, Chairman of the Richmond Town Cricket and Athletic Association". The form of address neatly summarised the three new strings Alcock added to his bow when the family moved from Streatham to Richmond in 1891. It was part of Charles Alcock's nature that not content with an outstanding career as a journalist, administrator of cricket and football and pioneer of international sport, he would wish to use part of his self-apparently very limited spare time to devote himself to public service, albeit in a capacity that enhanced the social status to which his generation was sensitive. It was now "forty years on" from his Harrow days, but the child being father of the man, the ethos of fortititude, self-rule and public spirit was still in evidence.

The family lived at a house called Heathlands on Kew Road, almost immediately opposite the pagoda in Kew Gardens. It no longer exists, but the fact that one of its neighbours, Thorneycroft, has been replaced by a sizeable block of flats called Thorneycroft Court suggest it was a large house capable of accommodating a large reasonably affluent large late-Victorian family. It was occupied by a retired ship furnisher, his wife and two servants. The Alcock's domestic staff had increased by one since the previous Census. They now had a cook and two housemaids.

He was about to enter his sixth decade at a time when the age profile of the population was different and people over 50 were regarded euphemistically as elderly or, in plainer terms, just old. Logic dictated that he should be easing off a bit and winding down to retirement. But Alcock chose to disregard the dictates of logic. He stood down from the Secretaryship of the Football Association in 1895, but was made a Vice-President and continued to play an active part in the administration. Additionally, he also took a major part in constituent associations, being the first Vice-President of the Surrey County FA, Vice-President of the London FA and President of the Sussex County FA.[467]

Before that, however, on his move to Richmond, he began to play his part in the life of the town. On 24 March 1892 at a by-election, he was elected unopposed for the North Ward to a vacancy on the Town Council. Although party political allegiance in local politics was less significant then than it has since become, it is no surprise that he stood as a Liberal. His lifestyle reflected a Gladstonian liberalism with its cult of the individual and he was a member of the executive of the local Liberal Association. He was appointed to the Finance, Health, Tradesmen's Accounts and School Attendance committees[468] and his administrative and commercial experience doubtless enabled him to make a significant contribution to all of them. Richmond was then staunchly Conservative, but receptive to new ideas. Newspaper editorials commented on, and within limits, welcomed trade unionism[469] and a public lecture by Keir Hardie, elected as the first Labour MP two years earlier and Chairman of the Independent Labour Party, attracted a capacity audience at the Radical Club in 1893.

At an election on 1 November 1893, Alcock came third in a contest for two seats, polling 279 votes to 365 for Montague Claude Cook and 348 for Robert Base Smith. The *Richmond and Twickenham Times* reported that the name of the unsuccessful candidate was given first and that when it was discovered that he was not elected, some expressions of regret were to be heard. There is a slight hint that there had been some internal antagonism, but the newspaper does not elaborate:

> And yet, probably because of some little feeling of pique arising out of his refusal to accept a nomination tendered under circumstances which must have made it distasteful to him..[470]

It is more likely that the real reason had been an increase in the rates of about 20% to cover the cost not of freebies by councillors, but eminently worthwhile projects such as the laying of new sewers, the purchase of a new cemetery, the construction of a footbridge and lock and the erection of the Town Hall. The electorate, however, then as now, were desirous of having their cake and eating it, and were more influenced by the effect on their pockets rather than improved civic amenities. Of nine councillors standing for re-election only five retained their seats.

The *Richmond and Twickenham Times* was sympathetic and complimentary:

> Richmond has lost the service of one who served her well and who deserved honour rather than the indignity of rejection. Looking at the matter broadly and with an eye to the welfare of the whole borough, rather to the feeling existing in any particular ward, it is impossible not to regret that Mr ALCOCK is no longer a member of the Council. He is a man of independent views, conspicuously fair in his judgment, most conscientious in his performance of public duty and possessing that ability which, united with good judgment and sterling integrity, goes far to make an ideal public man...his defeat is an unfortunate incident.[471]

Within just over six months, however, he was back, again elected unopposed at a by-election on 23 May 1894. This time he was appointed to serve on the Richmond Free Library Committee, and was involved in the licensing sessions of the borough, making decisions on the granting and renewal of licenses to Richmond's public houses. Two months earlier, as a member of the executive of the Richmond District Liberal Association, he was appointed a delegate to the National Liberal Federation. In October, however, he announced that he would not stand at the forthcoming Council elections.[472]

In 1892 Richmond was granted its own Commission of the Peace, having previously had a hybrid system somewhere between a county bench and a borough bench. Charles Alcock, following in the footsteps of his father in Chingford, was one of its first JPs, being commissioned on 6 February 1893. At his busiest, he seemed to average about one day a week and this on top of his commitment to Surrey, the FA and *Cricket*. Although part of a "bench" and never acting alone, the Alcock ability for judgment, to weigh up pros and cons is in evidence, generally flavoured with humanity and compassion. Cases of obstructing the footway, stealing poultry or a hundredweight of coal, acting as a driver without showing a badge, giving short weight, failing to display Factory Act notices, being drunk in charge of a horse and cart and riding a bicycle in a manner dangerous to the public were met with a notional fine or discharge under the First Offenders Act, but cases of cruelty to animals and assault usually attracted a prison sentence accompanied by hard labour. The latter sentence was handed out to one found drunk and begging. The fact that he was "most abusive and used the filthiest language" did not help his case. A thirteen year old errand boy, sentenced to receive six strokes with the birch rod for stealing pigeons "howled dismally" when hearing the verdict.[473] His reaction to the application of the sentence is not recorded.

Alcock was also JP for Surrey in the Richmond Petty Sessional Division. He was to move house twice more. He had left Heathlands by 1897-98; there was a brief period for which his contact address was the Oval,[474] then he moved to York Mansions, Battersea Park[475] before returning to Richmond, to Hazelwood in Ennerdale Road which remained in the family's possession until his widow's death in 1937. The 1901 Census of Population shows Charles and Eliza living there with Florence, Helen and Violet. Under "Profession or Occupation", Charles is shown as JP for Surrey and a Journalist. There is no mention of the Secretaryship of Surrey County Cricket Club, nor any entry in that column for his wife or Florence or Helen. Elizabeth, Charlotte and Marion are not recorded. Violet, the youngest daughter, now aged 22, is shown as a Journalist. It is entirely possible that she was providing some assistance to her father who, as well as churning out regular editions of *Cricket*, was at this time heavily involved in *Surrey Cricket: its History and Associations* and *Cricket Stories, Wise and Otherwise*. The household was completed by a Cook and a Housemaid.

On top of all this, he was Chairman of the Richmond Cricket and Athletic Association, no tin-pot local sports club organising paperchases and "hare and hounds", but a company with shareholders, a Board of Directors and a Company Secretary who had been the first Honorary Secretary of the Rugby Union. It was an overarching body for a number of subsidiary clubs, including Richmond Rugby Club and the Mid-Surrey Golf Club, recently established in Old Deer Park. Alcock was a Vice-President. In addition to its athletic activities, it hosted horse shows and the Royal Horticultural Society[476] and gave generously to charity when handsome profits were made from events such as the North v South rugby match.[477] Despite his civic activities, he still found time is 1893 to organise a match between C W Alcock's XI and Richmond Town CC for the benefit of Tate the "ground man".

His Obituary in a local newspaper recorded that:

For many years Mr Alcock resided in Richmond, and took a good deal of interest in local affairs. He was chairman of the Richmond Athletic Association and a justice of the peace for the borough, receiving the commission on February 6th 1893. He was also a member of the Richmond Town Council at one time, for the North Ward. He was elected to that body unopposed at a bye-election [sic] on March 24th, 1892. On November 1st, 1893, on seeking re-election, he was defeated by Messrs Cook and Smith, but on May 23rd 1894, he was again returned unopposed at a bye-election [sic]. A short time later, however, he retired from the public life of the borough.[478]

His status in the Borough also merited an obituary notice in the *Richmond and Twickenham Times* which euphemistically records that "another old acquaintance has also just passed beyond the veil."[479]

For much of 1903, Alcock was seriously ill as the bronchitis which had afflicted him two years earlier became more serious and caused him to give up work for about six months. *Cricket* continued well enough without him, but the administration at The Oval was weakened by his absence and the Club was obliged to appoint C A Stein as Honorary Secretary during his absence.

It was a source of much concern that the health of Mr Alcock completely broke down early in the season. He was ordered away for six months' complete rest and change and the committee are happy to say that he is now back at his post restored to health.[480]

The same year Charles and Eliza moved to Brighton, almost certainly because of Charles' health, but possibly with a view to spending their retirement years by the sea. He had a monumental capacity for work and it seems unlikely that he faced the prospect with enthusiasm. His nature was such that he revelled in indulging in several activities simultaneously and would find it difficult to reconcile himself to the idea of doing nothing. Basil Easterbrook suggested as much in his feature on Alcock in the 1980 edition of *Wisden*:[481]

In *The Way of All Flesh*, Samuel Butler wrote "Youth is like Spring, an overpraised season". I am old enough to understand that this can apply to many of us, but never, I suspect, to Charles Alcock. He could never have led a lotus-eating existence in an age when someone of his background was not expected to work; but after playing two great team games with no little distinction he devoted the whole of his life to promoting their growth so that they could be enjoyed by an ever-widening circle of people. As an English gentleman of a certain period he practised reticence in his opinions and actions. It had not become fashionable to give free rein to displays of emotionalism embracing everything from bedroom athletics to racism. There is, however, some evidence that he dreaded the thought of approaching retirement, for he once remarked to Ashley Cooper: "I cannot visualise myself just sitting in the chimney corner." I could be wrong, but I believe that at the end of the winter, with what in all probability would have been his last season as part of the pulse of cricket ahead of him, he quietly turned his face to the wall.

The Alcocks lived in 7 Arundel Road on the eastern fringe of Regency Brighton in Kemptown (or Kemp Town, as it was then styled). The house still stands, now a little run down and divided into student flats, but then a large Victorian semi-detached, a few yards from the sea and round the corner from the highly fashionable Corinthian-columned Arundel Terrace which at the time of the Alcocks brief period in Brighton housed *inter alia* a Lieutenant Colonel, the Misses and a Barrister-at-Law. Arundel Terrace today is a Grade 1 listed building, whose apartments appear in estate agents' windows in Brighton with no price tags, falling into the "If you have to ask the price, you can't afford it" category. By contrast, the Bush Public House at nos 1-3 Arundel Road offers holidaymakers and locals a choice of steak and kidney pie, special Chinese rice and rump steak and chips to accompany their lunchtime pints.

The Family

It is fashionable in days of increased leisure to talk of the work-life balance. The phraseology would be foreign to Victorians and Edwardians, but the concept would be recognisable. Work and family life were compartmentalised, the former providing the means to sustain the latter. Charles Handy's concept of a portfolio career where the individual determined the balance between employment, self-employment, charity work and leisure was for the future. For those obliged to earn their living, working time was scheduled by the factory or the office and the few hours left over were for football, cricket or spending time with the family. Charles Alcock defied these conventions having what Handy would recognise as a portfolio career of administration, writing and public service. The one thing that seems to be missing is leisure and family life. It is difficult to imagine what time he might have had for it.

There are few references to family life in his writing, newspaper reports or committee minutes. Conventional condolences were expressed by the committee on the death of his son, there is a reference to Alcock showing the locket given to him by Southerton to his wife and correspondence between the committee and Eliza during Alcock's illness and after his death. This is not in itself surprising as it was relatively rare though far from unknown for women to be prominent in public life and in a world dominated by male politicians, inventors, business and entrepreneurs, the names of Elizabeth Fry, Florence Nightingale and Elizabeth Garrett Anderson are exceptional. Likewise, whole biographies and autobiographies were written without reference to Mrs Hirst, Mrs Rhodes and Mrs Strudwick. *Don't Tell Kath* is of more recent vintage.

Nonetheless, one might expect the occasional reference in local newspapers to the families of eminent local burgesses. The wives of other dignitaries are mentioned in connection with church bazaars, charity work and flower shows, but the Alcock family do not seem to appear.[482] Both his sons had died, one in infancy and one aged 21. Of his six daughters, it is known that five died unmarried.[483] It is difficult to avoid the conclusion that he was not particularly close to his family. His multifarious activities would not have left him much time. Certainly, once he had moved to London, all contact with Sunderland seems to have been severed, a fact bewailed by north-easterners Arthur Appleton and Alisdair Wilson.

He may have retained contact with his parents who spent their later years in Chingford, but he seems to have lost touch with his elder brother who settled in Northchurch, Hertfordshire and made a significant contribution to the life of the parish. A number of dignitaries were present at Charles' funeral, but no family members are mentioned in press reports. Not conclusive in itself, but by contrast, John's funeral (he died three years later on 13 March 1910) was attended by his three sisters Anne, Ada and Edith. None of Charles' family are mentioned as being present.

John was a pillar of his local community in Berkhamsted and Northchurch, presiding over the Parish Council and contesting unsuccessfully a seat on the Hertfordshire County Council. He was a sidesman at the Parish Church and a member of the Church of England Missionary Society. Unlike his brother, he was an ardent Unionist. a trustee of the Berkhamsted and Northchurch Conservative Club and a successful exhibitor of orchids, a classic example of what some historians have called "gentlemanly capitalism". He left a widow, two sons and a daughter.[484]

Death and Funeral

Whether Charles Alcock would have thrown himself into the civic life of Brighton or - unlikely - lapsed into inertia in retirement we shall never know. The grim reaper did not give him the option and on 26 February 1907 a combination of a dilated heart, chronic bronchitis, glycosuria and albuminuria,[485] the latter two conditions associated with diabetes and kidney disease, brought an end to one of the most active and influential lives of the previous century. He had, according to the local newspaper, been unwell for months past,[486] and doubtless overwork and what would later in the century have been diagnosed as stress were contributory factors. Eliza was at his bedside.

On the following Saturday, 2 March, the *Brighton Gazette*, ironically, alongside an advertisement for Markham's Cherry Cough Cure, effective *inter alia* for bronchitis (but, alas, not in this case), carried a simple death announcement:

> ALCOCK - On February 26th at 7 Arundel Road, Brighton, Charles W Alcock, J.P. aged 64 years.

His companions in the Deaths column were aged 61, 82, 42 and 91 - a tribute to the longevity of the residents of this south coast resort.

He was buried the following Saturday, at West Norwood Cemetery, in the grave first used for his infant son, Charles, in 1874 and subsequently his eldest son, William, who had followed seven years later aged only 21. Marion was to join them in 1922 and finally Eliza in 1937, having outlived her husband by 30 years - another generation.[487] Both Charles and his father had outlived two of their sons, a fact commemorated on the tombstone of each of them. The grave lay neglected for many years, but thanks to the efforts of the Friends of West Norwood Cemetery and financial assistance from the Football Association, Surrey County Cricket Club and English Heritage, it was rededicated on 28 July 1999. There are no known surviving relatives to maintain the grave, but arrangements have been made to include it on the Cemetery Superintendent's maintenance schedule.

Alcock's was not the only loss suffered by the cricket world in 1907. Walter Read had died in January, as had Alfred Shaw who played in the 1880 Test Match. Edward Pooley, whose name Alcock had been obliged to include in Surrey's minutes on more occasions than he would have wished, died in Lambeth Workhouse in July and Henry Boyle who had toured England on six occasions, including one as Player-Manager in 1890, died in Bendigo, Victoria in November. It was in many ways the end of an era.

THE ELDER STATESMAN

The funeral was well attended, not least by dignitaries from the world of football and cricket. The *Brighton Gazette*, mistakenly giving his last address as Arundel Terrace, rather than Arundel Road (An error he would not have minded!) reported as follows:

> The funeral of the late Mr C W Alcock of Arundel Terrace, Brighton took place on Saturday at Norwood Cemetery and was largely attended. Among the many people present well known in connection with sport were Lord Kinnaird (President of the Football Association), Messrs John Shuter, F E Lacey, A J Webbe, C E Horner, Denzil Onslow, D L A Jephson, H D G Leveson-Gower, GS Sherrington, C Crump, F J Wall, Robert Abel, T Hayward, E G Hayes, H Wood and Walter Lees.
>
> Lord Alverstone, president of the Surrey Club has received the following letter from Sir Arthur Briggs, the private secretary of the Prince of Wales:
>
> The Prince of Wales was grieved to hear of the death of Mr Alcock, secretary of the Surrey Club and Ground, as his Royal Highness had the pleasure of meeting him on several occasions. The Prince would be much obliged to you if you would be kind enough to convey to Mr Alcock's family the expression of his sympathy and condolence in their sorrow, and say that his Royal Highness fully realises what a great loss the Surrey Club has sustained by his death.
>
> The funeral arrangements were carried out by Mr T Willmer of Eastern Road, Brighton.

He shares his final resting place with some distinguished people - sugar magnate and philanthropist, Sir Henry Tate, Mrs Beeton of cookery book fame, prize fighter Tom King, and from the world of cricket, William Clarke, Lord Hawke, William Mortlock and Edward Barratt.

For a man of business so well organised, it seems extraordinary that he did not leave a will. Maybe it was a question of the cobbler's children being the worst shod. Hairdressers are often bald, dentists frequently have rotten teeth and the personal financial position of Financial Advisers has often much scope for improvement. Be that as it may, there seems to have been little problem about the granting of probate to "Eliza Caroline Alcock of 7 Arundel Road aforesaid the lawful widow and relict". The gross value of the estate was £3186.15s.2d, the net value £2309.8s.11d, not a huge sum and in today's terms little more than £150,000 or so.

Alcock, the Man
Posthumous and Contemporary Tributes

F S Ashley-Cooper, in his Obituary of Alcock in *Cricket*[488] paid tribute to his seemingly limitless industry. "I have seen him writing a letter, carrying on a conversation with several people and watching a match out of the corner of his eye simultaneously." It was, said Ashley-Cooper, quite the exception to find him unoccupied in any way and there could be no more appropriate epitaph than "He was a worker".

> even during the past week, when he must have known that he would most probably not live to see the present number, he wrote making arrangements for its contents. To all those who know how splendid a worker he was, the act will be recognised as very characteristic of him.

Indeed, the Protestant work ethic seems to have impregnated Alcock's whole existence, but quantity of work need not be synonymous with quality of work. In Alcock's case, however, it is fair to say that it was. He used time management techniques yet to be codified by the gurus and consultants of later generations and in his own, which was not without its entrepreneurs and where the concept of empire-building had not yet acquired derogatory overtones, he was seen as a nineteenth century equivalent of Renaissance man, according to a current American cynic, a term used nowadays for anyone that can walk and chew gum simultaneously, but then applied to those who were in the jargon of a subsequent age, multi-skilled.

There is no doubt that he filled Kipling's unforgiving minute with at least sixty seconds' worth of distance running. Kipling was the "poet of Empire", being awarded the Nobel prize for literature in the year of Alcock's death, and Alcock, the Father of Modern Sport, was still a child of his time. *If* might have been written for him; certainly, his tributes from the Prince of Wales and K S Ranjitsinhji, a Prince in his own right, who refers to Alcock as "Surrey's most popular secretary",[489] might be bracketed with his dealings with large attendances in the couplet:

> If you can talk with crowds and keep your virtue,
> Or walk with Kings - nor lose the common touch

and the aim to be "a Man, my Son" would have seemed to him to be a suitable aspiration for schoolboy and mill-worker, amateur and professional and the customers appearing before him in Richmond Magistrates Court. The Club's Yearbook paid tribute in suitably reverential term:

> The members will have heard with deep regret of the death of Mr C W Alcock who has for 35 years held the post of Secretary to the Club. It is quite impossible to overestimate the value of Mr Alcock's services to the Club, or to speak too highly of the great part he took in the rehabilitation of Surrey Cricket and the furtherance of Football, and all other manly sports. His loss to the Club will be severely felt, and the Committee have ventured on behalf of the members to express to his widow and family their deep sympathy in this great affliction.[490]

The following year, *Wisden* had a rather more in-depth appreciation:

> When he went to the Oval, Surrey's fortunes were at their lowest ebb, and for fully ten years those responsible for the management had an uphill task. It was Mr Alcock's good fortune, while he was still in his full vigour to see Surrey under John Shuter's captaincy win back the first place among the counties and hold it with little variation for many seasons. He was not by any means a demonstrative man, but no one felt a keener satisfaction than he did when at last success came back to the Oval. He was a loyal servant to the Club, and possessed the sovereign merit of a calm and well-balanced judgment. Whatever question arose he could see it from every side.[491]

The Council of the Football Association passed the following vote of condolence at its Council meeting on 11 March 1907:

> That this meeting of The Football Association desires to place on record the expression of deep regret on account of the death of Mr C W Alcock, which occurred on February 26th last, and to tender sincere condolence and heartfelt sympathy to Mrs Alcock and the members of the sorrowing family in their great bereavement. The formation and success of The Football Association are very largely due to the enthusiasm and true sportsmanlike instincts of Mr Alcock, and it would be difficult adequately to estimate the value of the services he has rendered to the Association and to the game generally during

the long period of more than 40 years to which his connection with this particular branch of sport extended. It is sufficient to say that he was particularly fitted to deal with the requirements and conditions of the game at a time when he took part in its management, and that he will always be remembered as an earnest, trusted and highly esteemed officer of the Association and a firm and valued friend and colleague. He was a good man in the broadest sense of the term, and his removal is mourned by his colleagues and the Football World at large.

Eliza replied : "It is not necessary for me to add that his love for football was the love of a lifetime and almost as long was his association with many of his footballing friends and colleagues." Is she perhaps implying that she might have appreciated a little more of his love and association for herself?

Tributes were world wide. From Budapest came the following:

Dear Sir

The Hungarian Football Association has learned of the heavy loss to the English Football Association by the death of Mr C W Alcock, whose working has also roused great appreciation beyond England's frontiers. We, therefore, ask you to accept the sympathy of the entire Hungarian football sport, and of the Hungarian Football Association, and remain, dear Sir.

Yours truly, R MALECKI (Secretary)

The Editor of *Baily's Magazine* paid tribute to his management skills, in particular his "tactful diplomacy" and commented on how his "manly straightforwardness" was able to "carry him through situations which might have baffled the entire Surrey committee", in particular strengthening the team by recruiting from outside the county and keeping the lid on potential discontent in a second eleven that was a match for most county first elevens.

W G Grace referred to him as "one of my oldest friends" and said that he proved to be "the right man in the right place":[492]

During his régime the Surrey Club has enjoyed unbroken prosperity, and has held a prominent, at time a pre-eminent place among the counties. Moreover, improvements have repeatedly been effected at Kennington Oval, the latest of course being the erection of a magnificent pavilion...

Under 'Some of my Contemporaries', he wrote:

Mr C W ALCOCK before he entered on his secretarial duties in 1872 had distinguished himself in the football field. His knowledge of cricket and cricketers is profound and comprehensive. He is a cricket encyclopædia, full of reliable information and is always ready to serve cricket by any means in his power. The service he has rendered to visiting teams from Australia and America, have won him friends in far-distant lands while his geniality, courtesy and ability as Secretary of the Surrey Club have made him deservedly popular amongst frequenters of the Oval. Surrey has had its ups and downs during his Secretaryship, but the club was never more prosperous than it is today.[493]

Bryon Butler described Alcock the Administrator as "liberal, catholic, a perceptive judge of character, a calm man who used words sparingly yet tellingly, but could also be caustic and stubborn". Using words sparingly as an administrator was in direct contrast to his approach to journalism, but that apart, the description is probably equally applicable to Alcock, the man who, according to David Lemmon "was a man of calm, quiet intelligence, immense energy and great vision. No man before or since has done more to further the cause of Surrey cricket. So much that is good and is now taken for granted was brought about by his administration."[494]

He was, said Sir Home Gordon, "popular and able"[495] - a rare combination, but a judgment borne out by a number of his contemporaries of all social classes who commented on his geniality and sense of humour and enthusiasm for anecdotes. He was a worker, a man for all seasons, a patrician who had understood plebeians and sympathised with their cause.

Geoffrey Green in his *History of the Football Association* reproduces the following tribute from one of Alcock's contemporaries:

When the flashing meteors have come and gone, when the league tables are full and complete, and when the present fades into the past, the name of C W Alcock will stand out all the more prominently like a rugged rock in a sea of bubbles. Like a thread of gold his career runs through the weaving of the story of Association football, and his tall and dignified form strides the river of the game from its source. When needed, he can deliver a telling speech with the best, and it will contain as much truth and fact and information to the square inch as most. His face still mirrors the moving joy of the tough conflict which he loves to watch from the Grand Stand; his censure of evil practices that sometimes disgrace the game he loves is as caustic as ever; his advice is much sought after and his opinion as highly esteemed. He is as good a judge of a player's form and abilities now as when he himself took part in the rough and tumble of earlier days, just as he is keen to note a weak point in an argument or a loophole in a rule as the most astute football lawyer. Still a jovial comrade with a wealth of football anecdote; still as determined to probe the bottom of anything that reflects upon the game, but with a blend of good nature that declines to press too hard upon a luckless defender, he is the Grand Old Man of the Association, loved and respected by everybody.[496]

Green added his own tribute: "If ever there was leadership, here it was, he strode like some benevolent genius across the sporting fields".

It is not easy to find anything uncomplimentary written about Alcock. *Baily's Magazine* was once critical of his interpretation of cricket law, the local paper refers to a spot of petulance and J A H Catton refers to "those who complained about him as a letter writer",[497] but does not clarify whether the complaints are that he resorted to writing letters rather than taking action or that his letters were of poor quality. In neither case would the evidence support the complaint. Catton, in any case, is quick to defend Alcock, saying he was never given sufficient credit by the clubs and public for "the noble work he did". He does suggest that the game might have outgrown him and that no one else could have undertaken the job. Those few instances apart, however, everything written about him has been entirely complimentary verging at times on eulogy. Given the conflicting currents which he faced in cricket, football, journalism and public life and the opposition which some of his activities was bound to raise, that is a remarkable achievement. Perhaps in the less democratic nineteenth century, there was more respect for autocracy and entrepreneurial success than in our own more egalitarian age when the tendency is to find something to criticise in our managers and national leaders. It is not only a question of *de mortuis nil nisi bonum*. Compliments abounded in his lifetime:

THE ELDER STATESMAN

To what has been written above by that greatest authority on Surrey, Mr C W Alcock little need be added; but the history of county cricket would be very incomplete without reference to the magnificent work done by Mr Alcock. When Lord Alverstone presented him with a large silver bowl, for which many friends subscribed, even his warm praise fell short of the dues on the most energetic secretary that any county ever possessed.[498]

Richard Daft tells a story which demonstrates Alcock's kindness and humanity. William Walker, groundsman at Trent Bridge from 1877 to 1893, visited London in 1891 intending to spend some time at Lord's on his way to the Oval to watch the Notts County-Blackburn Rovers Cup Final. Delayed at Lord's, he sped by hansom cab across the capital arriving late at the Oval. He was found a "snug seat in an excellent position, through the kindness of Mr Alcock or one of the committee". It was more likely to be Mr Alcock. The Committee had voted themselves complimentary tickets and were doubtless well installed by the time Walker arrived. The only fly in the ointment for the well-treated guest was that County lost 3-1.[499]

He was clearly a genial man, known as "Charlie" to his friends, physically imposing, good company and possessing a wealth of anecdotes. 'Pa' Jackson mentions that Alcock was particularly kind to him when he became the first FA committee member who was not a committee nominee.[500] He was, said Ashley-Cooper a "capital raconteur".[501] W G Grace relates:

> Mr Alcock is fond of telling two stories against me.[502] In our younger days he often came down to Downend to stay with my father and mother. On one occasion he and my brother Fred and my brother-in-law, John Dann, were following the Duke of Beaufort's hounds, and to save climbing a hill, cut along a valley. Alcock says he looked up and saw me and the grey horse I was riding go head over heels. They all three saw me tumble and I got chaffed for a good many years about my horsemanship.

Catton, in his *Wickets and Goals*, published in 1926, relates a number of Alcock stories, one of which is perhaps inevitably about W G Grace. It was in 1878, during the Billy Midwinter controversy. Midwinter, the only cricketer to represent Australia in England and England in Australia, was on tour with the Australian side and allegedly 'kidnapped' by W G Grace to represent Gloucestershire for which the tourist had a birth qualification:

He spoke to me of his first chat with Midwinter who was generally regarded as an Australian. Mr Alcock was in his office at The Oval, and he asked Midwinter where he was born, no doubt with the idea of qualifying him for Surrey. But W G Grace walked into the room, and as Midwinter answered, "I was born in Gloucestershire", Grace promptly said, "Then, you're the man for me," and, added Mr Alcock, "at that moment I knew that I had no chance."

The other concerns John Beaumont, a Yorkshire-born fast bowler who played for Surrey in the late 1880s:

He went to the secretary of the Surrey County Cricket Club and asked permission to go to Yorkshire for the week-end. Mr Alcock desired to know his reason, and Beaumont said that a brother-in-law had been irritating his wife and he just wanted to see him for a little conversation.

"Well," said Mr Alcock, "I'll give you leave to run down to Halifax, but you must be here on Monday before noon, as we have a very important match commencing that day, and we want your help. Don't have any bother with him. Remember that - no bother."

Beaumont went home and was back at Kennington Oval by eleven o'clock in the morning. He reported his return to Mr Alcock who immediately said:

"I hope you did not have any bother with him"

"Oh, no, Mester Alcock," said he, "I'd no trouble with him. I just picked him up and dropped him o'er th'bannisters to th'floor below. That's all. I'd no bother with him."

It was a macho, 'manly', approach to life of which Alcock would have approved. Other Alcock stories told by Catton are of an occasion on which, despite its banning by the FA, Alcock and Arthur (later Lord) Kinnaird agreed to play a 'hacking' game, though Jackson's version is that Alcock declined to do so,[503] because Kinnaird was the better hacker, a judgment borne out on another occasion when Kinnaird's mother expressed her concern that Arthur might one day return from football with a broken leg, Alcock assured her that if he did, it would not be his own.

Leveson-Gower in *Country House Cricket*, attributes to "my old friend Mr C W Alcock" a monologue which he suspected might have been overheard on a tram:

No, Bill didn't get much out of his day's cricket. He had to pay eight bob for his railway fare, and lost 'is day's screw, and was fined a shilling for being late, and 'e didn't get no wickets, and 'e missed four ketches, and 'e got a couple of beautiful blobs. He felt sold, he did.

Despite the eulogies of previous hagiographers, there is not much to suggest that he was an original thinker or generator of ideas. He was not a revolutionary, nor even a reformer; a liberal not a socialist, accepting the structure of sport and society and changing it from within, rather than attacking it from without. Sports journalism and writing, knock-out and league competitions, professional and international sport were all in place when he began his journalistic and administrative duties. Like Montaigne he could perhaps say *J'ai fait ici un amas de fleurs étrangères, n'ayant fourni du mien que le filet à les lier* - I have made a bouquet of other men's flowers and nothing but the thread which binds them is my own. But what strength was in that thread - the strength was to see the potential of an idea and develop it to its maximum extent whether it was creating specialised magazines, writing definitive histories, or applying the ethos of both public school and industry to the rapidly expanding business of organised sport. At a time of enterprise and empire building, he was a pioneer.

By the early part of the twentieth century, in the spectator appeal stakes, football, in which Alcock had been involved from the outset, was overtaking cricket which was well established before he joined it and *Cricket* was reporting attendances of 100,000 at three league matches in the north compared with a few thousand at the Headingley Test Match.

Post Mortem

The appointment of William Findlay to succeed Alcock was something of a surprise. He is not in the short-list of candidates included in the minutes, but pencilled in later as an afterthought, as though to fudge the issue and make it appear that he was. "Not one person in a thousand anticipated that the honour of succeeding Mr Alcock would fall to Mr Findlay".[504]

The influence of Lord Harris is clear. Writing almost half a century later, Sir Henry Leveson-Gower, who was a member of the Surrey committee, after paying appropriate tribute to Alcock, recalls His Lordship's recommendation:

> No county has ever had a more far-seeing Secretary than Charles Alcock, and when he had retired beyond recall, a great successor was at hand. I well remember the late Lord Harris saying to me.
>
> "Your County will be very lucky if a great friend of mine and yours, William Findlay, could be induced to take Alcock's place. He is one in a thousand. Don't forget I told you!"[505]

Liverpudlian by birth, he was, like Lord Harris, educated at Eton and Oxford. Leveson-Gower had been at Winchester and Oxford. So, despite the short-list in the minutes, the 'old school tie' method of secretarial appointments was used, as it had been thirty-five years before. Again, the absence of the democratic process did not mean a bad appointment.

One of Findlay's early dilemmas was the dispute between Leveson-Gower and J N Crawford in 1909 over the selection of the Surrey team to play the Australians, resulting in the status-conscious Crawford complaining that he was being treated like a young professional and Leveson-Gower's ultimatum that "Either you or I must give up playing for Surrey". Crawford was dismissed and in acknowledging the Committee's resolution suggested that it might have been accompanied by thanks for his past services. He played for Surrey no more, at least not until after the First World War. The bulk of the correspondence was undertaken by the President, Lord Alverstone. It is tempting to speculate that had Alcock still been alive and in post, his diplomacy and pragmatism might have produced a solution which would have enabled the county to retain the services of one of its most talented all-rounders.

Findlay did, however, go on to have a successful administrative career, subsequently becoming Assistant Secretary, then Secretary of MCC. In 1937, the year of Eliza Alcock's death, he headed the Commission which looked into the problems of county cricket and inter alia proposed some streamlining The recommendations were ignored. *Plus ça change…*

In October 1907, the Committee agreed a grant of £200 to Mrs Alcock and an annuity of £20 "during the pleasure of the Committee". After correspondence, however, it was decided to increase this to £100, also "during the pleasure of the Committee". The amount was approved by the Annual General Meeting in 1908. At 25% of her deceased husband's salary, it was an amount which would compare favourably with provisions for a widow's pension in most present day pension schemes. It continued to her death.

Eliza retained Hazelwood and continued to reside there with her unmarried daughters for some years after Alcock's death. All were still there in 1930, though by 1932, Florence and Violet had moved to Worthing, leaving Eliza, Elizabeth and Helen.[506] Eliza died at the age of 96, following a fall while getting out of bed while on a visit to her youngest daughter in Worthing. A verdict of "misadventure" was returned at the inquest.[507] Her remaining four unmarried daughters benefited from the £1065.12s.9d she left in her will. Helen took Marion's share of Hazelwood as well as clothes and jewellery.

Elizabeth died in Lambeth in 1937, Florence in Worthing in 1938 and Helen in Chichester in 1946. The youngest daughter, Violet, died peacefully in her sleep at her home in Worthing on 20 February 1952,[508] two weeks into the reign of Queen Elizabeth II. She was the holder of an MBE. No relatives are mentioned in her will. Her estate was just under £5,000. A number of legacies for friends and acquaintances are listed with the residue destined for her doctor and a minister of religion. It was the end of the line.

REFERENCES

457. Green *History of the Football Association* p 117
458. William Edward's death certificate which also gives his occupation as 'Clerk to Football Association'
459. Surrey CCC minutes 17 March 1887
460. Surrey CCC minutes 7 July 1892
461. Jackson *Sporting Days and Sporting Ways* p 135
462. Green *History of the Football Association* p 124
463. *Association Football I* p 59
464. Surrey CCC minutes 20 December 1888
465. *Cricket* 18 December 1902

466. *Cricket* 26 March 1891

467. *Football* 4 October 1882

468. *Richmond and Twickenham Times* 12 May 1892

469. *Richmond and Twickenham Times* 3 September 1892

470. *Richmond and Twickenham Times* 4 November 1893

471. *Richmond and Twickenham Times* 4 November 1893

472. *Richmond and Twickenham Times* 13 October 1894

473. *Richmond and Twickenham Times* Various dates

474. Kelly's Directory 1898-99

475. Kelly's Directory 1899-1900

476. *Richmond and Twickenham Times* 24 November 1892

477. *Richmond and Twickenham Times* 9 September 1893

478. Thames Valley Times 27 Feb 1907

479. 2 Mar 1907

480. Surrey CCC Annual Report 1904 *Cricket* 28 April 1904

481. p 112

482. It is virtually impossible to be categorical, as trawling through several years of unindexed local newpapers is not a practical proposition, but those looked at for references to Alcock's civic activities do not contain any obvious references. The family continued to live in Richmond for thirty years after Charles' death, but there does not appear to be any mention in parish magazines of any activity in, for example, social organisations or charity work.

483. No marriage or death certificate has been traced for the third daughter, Charlotte Mabel (born 1872). It is possible that marriage, death or both occurred outside England and is therefore not indexed at the Family Records Centre. She is not mentioned at the family residence in the 1901 Census of Population, nor in her mother's will (1929) and is not in the family grave at West Norwood.

484. *Berkhamsted Gazette* 19 March 1910

485. Death certificate

486. *Thames Valley Times* 27 Feb 1907

487. Bob Flanagan *West Norwood Cemetery's Sportsmen* p 25

488. 28 February 1907

489. *The Jubilee Book of Cricket* p 424

490. *Surrey CCC Yearbook 1907* p 50

491. *Wisden* 1908 p 105
492. *'WG' Cricketing Reminiscences and Personal Recollections* p 124
493. *'WG' Cricketing Reminiscences and Personal Recollections* p 320
494. Lemmon *History of Surrey County Cricket Club* p 123
495. Gordon *Background of Cricket* p 28
496. p 159
497. Catton *Wickets and Goals* p 171
498. *Victoria History of the Counties of England - Surrey* p 533
499. Daft *A Cricketer's Yarns* p 89
500. Jackson *Sporting Days and Sporting Ways* p 48
501. *Cricket* 28 February 1907
502. The other one is about the footballing incident on Clapham Common - see Chapter 3
503. Jackson *Sporting Days and Sporting Ways* p 5
504. *Cricket* 11 April 1907
505. Leveson-Gower *Off and On the Field* p 88
506. Richmond Electoral Rolls 1930 to 1935
507. *Worthing Herald* 6 February 1937
508. *Worthing Herald* 22 February 1952

CHAPTER 11

THE ALCOCK LEGACY

The Debt of the 21st Century to the 19th

ON THE TOP FLOOR OF The Oval pavilion, adjacent to the Library is the C W Alcock Room, dedicated to the memory of the man who was Secretary of Surrey County Cricket Club for more than half his lifetime and who contributed more to the Club and to national and international sport than his predecessors and successors combined. Do Surrey members passing that way pause and consider Surrey's and sport's debt to him? Probably no more so than those who fortuitously find themselves on Sir Matt Busby Way or in the foyer of the Olivier Theatre are alive to the legacy they owe to those whose names are honoured there.

At a simple graveside ceremony in West Norwood Cemetery on 28 July 1999 tributes were paid by representatives of the interested bodies. Geoff Thompson, Chairman of the Football Association, placed Alcock in his historical and geographical context:

> We are thankful for him and for his vision and imagination. We share that gratitude with the many thousands of players who have participated in the FA Cup down the years and with the hundreds of millions of spectators who are able, thanks to television, to watch the spectacle all round the world. It is a sobering and humbling experience for us, in the midst of another era of great change in football, to recall and cherish the game's founding fathers.
>
> Gathered here remembering Charles Alcock and the origins and traditions of the game, we realise a number of things. The first is how little the basic game of football has changed since its codification by Alcock and his contemporaries. The aim is still to put the ball into the goal. The fundamentals of the game are just the same, however different the environment - matches can be played on a dirt strip in Africa or in a magnificent futuristic stadium in a Western European city.
>
> The second thing to consider is how much we need today men and women like Charles Alcock in the leadership of football, nationally and internationally.

THE ALCOCK LEGACY

We need individuals who have the imagination to think forward 50 or 100 years to see their ideas about the future of the game come to life and flourish. Visionaries like Charles Alcock...

However, I believe he leaves us a greater legacy. It is frequently said that football matches between international teams are today's peaceful re-enactments of the battles which used to be fought between armies. If Charles Alcock's ideas have led to nations contesting football matches instead of going to war, then the World's debt to him is great indeed.

The cliché that if you want something doing properly, then you give it to a busy man has already been mentioned and can be inferred from Alcock's multifarious activities. In general, clichés become clichés because they are true and this particular one is perhaps nowhere better exemplified. At times consecutively, at others simultaneously, he was a writer, editor, active sportsman, JP, chief administrator of two major organisations with lesser roles in other ones and fingers in numerous pies. For most of us, to have filled any one of these roles successfully would have been cause for satisfaction, but Alcock successfully managed to juggle the lot and at the same time make a major impact on the way sport was organised both during his lifetime and for what seems likely to be a hundred years at least after his death. Some administrators have vision, skills in assessing the broad picture and influencing events; others have an eye for detail and ensuring none of the minutiae are overlooked. Alcock had both and a century down the road, despite advances in technology, can still serve as a role model.

His Obituary in *Cricket*, the magazine he founded and edited for a quarter of a century, refers to his uncanny ability to keep a number of balls in the air simultaneously and suggests he could often be found writing a letter, watching cricket and holding several conversations all at the same time. What Alcock did in the way of organising sports competitions, grafting professionalism on to an amateur framework and pioneering international sport could and perhaps would in time have been done by others. There were after all contemporary, but independent arguments in the United States about baseball's organisation into leagues and similar amateur-professional conflicts. What is remarkable about Alcock, however, is the simultaneous range and depth of his contribution. He has been called 'the father of modern sport' and without disregarding his peripheral and minor achievements, his principal offspring are fourfold - sports journalism, the establishment of the competitive device, the pioneering of international sport and the codification of professionalism..

Sports Journalism

Much of what Alcock pioneered is still in evidence today. Of the magazines and newpapers with which he was associated, the *Sportsman* ceased publication in 1928 and only the *Field* has survived to the present day. It has no football now though it still concentrates on hunting, shooting, fishing and racing, supplemented by cars, property, fine arts, food and antiques. Other publications have their roots in Alcock's pioneering activities. The *Cricketer International* can trace its ancestry to *Cricket*. The *News of the World Football Annual* claims to be football's oldest annual and bears the name of the publication which owed its fame to Alcock though its direct antecedents are the *Athletic News Football Supplement and Club Directory*, the *Sunday Chronicle Annual* and the *Empire News*. His *Cricket Calendar* was a forerunner of similar twentieth-century publications by *The Times*, MCC, ECB and its predecessors and most counties. Numerous fanzines, Yearbooks, multi-coloured programmes and fixture cards, have their origins in Alcock's passion for compiling lists and categorising information.

In many ways Alcock was a child of his time, but he did have the capacity to see beyond it. The format he established for both cricket and football publications survived him. His opinions on football were clearly influential, those on cricket perhaps less so; but in football he formed the establishment and was part of it; in cricket, he often had to work against it. But he was nevertheless among the first to recognise that Australians had a contribution to make to the game and a hundred years and more on, English cricket has grudgingly conceded that there are lessons to be learned from the structure of the Australian game and value to be gained from a national cricket academy. Conversely, Australians take the view that England has done nothing for the game apart from invent it.

Radio, television and internet coverage have reduced the immediacy of the newspaper report. By the time a match report appears in print, details have been analysed and dissected *ad nauseam* by pundits and analysts, so that the immediacy has gone and newspapers are left to concentrate on personality cults, increasingly sophisticated sports photography and the private lives of sportsmen. It would have been unrecognisable to Alcock, concerned as he was with factual accuracy and balanced opinion. The near-immediacy of the Saturday evening sports paper has gone, tabloids of sundry colours have been replaced by the immediacy of the Saturday afternoon television report and the posting of the information on the internet has provided the week-end fix for those not able to take advantage of instant reporting.

Having produced and featured in reports which required careful reading to discover the score, he would doubtless have been bemused by the plethora of computer-generated tabulations on possession, blocked shots, corners, fouls, completed passes, throw-ins, corner kicks, off sides, yellow cards, red cards, matches since scoring, even the bizarrely ambiguous "games between clean sheets".

The Competitive Device

Until Alcock's time, each sporting fixture had been an end in itself. No one had felt any need to make it part of a larger competition. His FA Cup, based on the Cock House Trophy competition at Harrow, has a claim to be the oldest national knock-out competition and remains perhaps the best known in the world. Part of the attraction is the tradition and romance, the giant-killing opportunities, the regular pattern of the rounds. The Final, usually in May, remains a huge sporting and social occasion. It is out of reach of all but a handful of the 600 teams who now enter the competition. For some of these interest in the trophy ceases with the Extra Preliminary Round before the end of August. It is a far cry from those fifteen pioneering sides of 1872. Recent changes such as Manchester United's failure to defend the Trophy in 1999-2000 because of their involvement in the World Club Championship, penalty shoot-outs in place of multiple replays, the retiming of the replays themselves and, horror of horrors, the rescheduling of the Third Round from the first week of January to December - albeit for one year only - have all had their detractors. Add to that the counter-attraction of the Premiership and European competitions and managers' and players' attitudes that the League is the main competition and the Cup an irritating diversion and Alcock's legacy may seem a little less significant. Certainly, continental attitudes are to attach more importance to League and European competitions with the national knock-out a poor third.

Furthermore, the competition is now effectively run by the media. It is the old story of the piper and the tune. Uniform kick-off times are a thing of the past. In the quarter-finals of 2002, not one of the quarter-finals kicked off at the once traditional time of 3 pm on Saturday. To maximise television coverage, one match was played on Saturday evening, the others spread through Sunday. For some time, both semi-finals have been played on Sunday.

But the Cup still retains a huge popular appeal and when a lower division side come within fifteen minutes of a Cardiff final, then even without the romantic resonance of Wembley, supporters of Wycombe Wanderers *et al* have cause to be grateful to Charles Alcock and his pioneering idea.

The knock-out system with its sudden death drama has survived intact albeit with various embellishments, such as league and cup competitions combined. Promotion in the Nationwide Football League is determined primarily by league positions but with the final place decided by a mini knock-out among the next four best-placed clubs, thus resurrecting a system similar to the "test matches" which operated in the late nineteenth century. Baseball, Australian Rules Football and Rugby League operate primarily on a league basis, then resort to the World series or play-offs to determine the eventual Champions. The European Champions' League starts with a few eliminators to reduce the field to manageable proportions, then has a series of mini-leagues which produce quarter-finalists and a reversion to the knock-out format. There are variations on this theme in domestic and international cricket competitions and a complex scheme has recently been introduced in Davis Cup tennis where until not very long ago a straight replica of the Cock House Cup competition was in force where there was a knock-out which conferred the right to play the previous winners in the Challenge Round. Golf has its cut-off, Grand Slam Tennis operates on the knock-out system. The ramifications of an internal school competition have been world wide.

Cricket - at least at county level - was not unexpectedly tardy in adopting the knock-out device. After its one unsuccessful attempt in 1873, the idea was mooted on several occasions, not least in 1957 as a response to falling attendances and part of the campaign for "brighter cricket". It was shelved by the Advisory County Committee:

> Reasons given for shelving yet again a cricket cup were that no satisfactory solution had been found for rain-ruined and other drawn matches and that difficulties abounded in fitting such a competition into the present framework of the County Championship. Doubts also existed as to whether a knock-out cup would be a financial success.[509]

What had been proposed was a two-day, two-innings competition. The idea of playing a 65-overs a side match on one day owed much to the initiative of Mike Turner, Leicestershire's long-serving secretary. In 1962, an experimental Midlands Knock-Out Competition was played. Only four counties participated, but the tournament paved the way for the Gillette Cup, launched the following year.

The non-competitive "fancy hat", cricket which Alcock played rather than organised has continued into the twenty-first century, of less significance in the total cricket firmament than it used to be but still strong enough to organise a recent wandering club's festival at Oxford and exemplified by MCC, the Forty Club, the Cricket Society, Free Foresters and various county-based clubs with strange suffixes like Hogs, Dumplings, even "Gentlemen". The Incogniti continue to exist as do the Butterflies and the oldest of the wandering sides, I Zingari, celebrated its 150th anniversary in 1995. In an article in *Wisden* of that year, John Woodcock looks nostalgically back to a time when, without the benefit of "given men", they were able to compete in first-class fixtures with Yorkshire, the Australians and the Gentlemen of England. Professionalism and more league and cup competitions, extending even to the clubs of the south of England by the 1960s, have reduced the number of players available and friendly cricket now attracts fewer players. It would all doubtless have happened without Alcock, but the quality of amateur sport is inevitably a casualty of the growth of professionalism and international sport.

When the FA Cup was first established, Challenge Cups and amateurism were not seen as mutually exclusive, but once challenge cups began attracting the professionals, amateur sport began to see them as something to be avoided. There were, of course, amateur leagues and amateur cups and the FA Amateur Cup, established in 1893, symbolises an amateur spirit determined not to be submerged by the professionalism which had begun to dominate the game. But rugby union for a long time set its face against any form of competitive device at club level. Not until 1971/72, a hundred years after its equivalent in the association game, was a national knock-out competition introduced and when the Allied Dunbar Premiership arrived, the terminology of 'merit table' was preferred to avoid any possible confusion with rugby league. It was only with the final acceptance of professionalism that the term 'League' was given official recognition by the union game.

International Sport

International sport would almost certainly have developed without Alcock and the increased sophistication of communications and the speed of world-wide travel makes a France v New Zealand rugby match easier to arrange than an inter-village cricket match a hundred years ago. The development of the railways certainly made travelling within the UK much more straightforward than it had been, but inter-continental travel was still by ship and those early cricket tours were not the kind of whistle-stop efforts we have today where replacement players can be flown out within a few hours, but long and arduous affairs of six months or more, a tribute to the perseverance and stamina of those who took part in them.

But those one-off Test Matches tagged on to the end of the 1880 and 1882 seasons were the start of a feature of Anglo-Australian sporting relations which was to remain significant throughout the twentieth century, so much so that in 1932/33, the very fabric of the British Empire was under threat and whatever the ICC might do about ten nation rolling Test match ratings, the Ashes will hold a special place in the affections and hostilities of players and spectators alike. International cricket is now of course far more than a post-season afterthought. Without it the professional game would not survive for it is international cricket rather than domestic contests which attracts spectators and more significantly, corporate hospitality and the financial interests of cable and satellite television companies. At the end of the nineteenth century, England and Australia were touring each other's countries every couple of years or so and South Africa had just come on the scene. Between September 1999 and August 2000, there were nineteen separate Test series involving between one and five Test matches and that number has increased since. Test playing countries can now expect to play two to three series a "season" and the notion of a season has virtually disappeared. The concepts of our winter game and our summer game no longer have any meaning. The major sports run alongside one another for twelve months at a time and then start again.

A triangular tournament involving what were then the only three Test playing nations was held in England in 1912. Cricket's World Cup played every three or four years involves the ten full members of the ICC with two or three associate members thrown in for good measure. There are still parts of the world where cricket is unknown, but it is developing. The European Cricket Council continues to expand; *Wisden* in its *Cricket Round the World* section lists a couple of dozen or so countries not normally associated with the game from Argentina to Vanuatu, taking in Estonia, Iceland and Panama on the way and despite recent political upheavals, Afghanistan now has a national team. In football, globalisation is virtually complete. At the last count, membership of FIFA was 204, progress indeed from those tentative Anglo-Scottish internationals of the 1870s and all part of Charles Alcock's rich legacy.

Professionalism

Finally, and perhaps most significantly, Alcock was among the first to give serious recognition to professional sport and to sport as a business rather than a pastime. Although a product of the public school system with its emphasis on the cult of the gentleman amateur, Alcock's family background had perhaps given him a hard northern edge which made it easier for him to reconcile the conflicting approaches of the amateur and the professional. Professional cricket in the nineteenth century was a rough, tough business, fraught with confrontation and controversy, both within the professional ranks and between the professionals and the establishment. The gentleman-player relationship was not always straightforward either in cricket or in football.

In the former, debates on broken time payments were still going in 1957, long after the issues had been settled, albeit in different ways, in rugby and association football. A Special Committee appointed by MCC rejected any solution based on the abolition of the distinction between amateurs and professionals and, with a not unexpected complacency and reliance on tradition, took the view that it had nothing to learn from other sports because:

(a) In no other sport had amateurs and professionals been so long, so continuously, so widely, and so closely associated.
(b) No other sport made such great and continuous demands on the players' time.

The question of the Assistant Secretary à la Walter Read was effectively fudged and put into the 'too difficult' tray:

...the Committee considered the problem of the pseudo Assistant Secretary, who might, in fact, be paid for playing cricket under the umbrella of his nominal secretarial duties. They felt that it was impossible to legislate for these cases under any general formula and that they must be examined individually under machinery created for the purpose: see para 7(ii).

The paragraph to which reference is made reads, indecisively:

The Committee were agreed that a satisfactory solution of the problems of Amateur Status could only be reached with the goodwill and co-operation of County Committees: they were confident that this would be forthcoming.

All was solved, at least notionally, in 1963 when the distinction between amateur and professional was discontinued and all became 'cricketers'.

Meanwhile, in what was at the time still "our winter game", although the FA Cup started as an amateur competition and the FA Amateur Cup was to become a competition in its own right from 1894 onwards, the northern professional clubs were absorbed into the competition more easily than was the case in rugby where the Northern Union broke away in 1895 to establish its own code of what subsequently became professional rugby league.

The professional-amateur-shamateur debate rumbled on through the twentieth century, as various sports which had not benefited from Alcock's diplomacy and foresight, including athletics, tennis and finally rugby union grappled with the conflict between maintaining the amateur ethos and competing successfully at international level. Investigative journalism with an intensity unknown in the preceding century provided examples of sportsmen and sportswomen incurring the same costs and receiving widely differing expenses. The merging of the worlds of amateur and professional tennis took place in the 1960s - athletics followed suit in the 1980s.

In 1972, the centenary year of the FA Cup and a hundred years almost to the day since the first association football international, the Football Association bowed to reality and abolished the word "amateur", describing all who took part in the game as "players" whether paid or not. *The Times* approved, but was critical of the delay:

Bearing in mind modern society, its climate and conditions, this is a step that ought logically to have been taken a decade or more ago. For too long have certain voices of authority clung blindly to the ideas and values of another age. The point even was reached somewhere in the mid-Sixties when amateur clubs and their players were required to sign affidavits declaring their true blue amateurism where money was not supposed to enter to corrupt the individual. Some did so: others refused to perjure themselves. it was a charade; a farce.

For years now, even before the war, certain so-called amateur clubs were only too keen to acquire the best players with the lure of financial rewards. I know of one who was offered the purchase of a house, freehold, if he would join a club that existed like a wolf in sheep's clothing. Charlton Athletic once could not even afford to sign an amateur centre forward as a professional because the rules of the day did not permit them to pay a man in question more than he was already receiving from a club in the Athenian League.

Hypocrisy has at last been swept away. We no longer live in the days and aura of the Corinthians, the Casuals, Pegasus and Dulwich Hamlet, It is sad but inevitable.[510]

The rigid class structure that characterised the society which Alcock knew and understood has gone. True, institutions like the House of Lords and its ancillaries are still extant, but their role is now diminished. The MCC is a private cricket club which happens to have a Test match ground. No longer can it be regarded as the establishment at play. "We of the sinking middle class...may sink without further struggles into the working class where we belong," said George Orwell in *The Road to Wigan Pier*. That may be slightly exaggerated, but no longer would Alcock, as he did when confronting emerging professionalism, be compelled to defend the dignity of working for a living. Gradually, pragmatism seeped through and the last real bastion fell in 1995 when, a hundred years after "the great schism", rugby union finally bowed to the inevitable and accepted professionalism. Within a few years they had learned the power of the strike weapon, having followed in the steps of association football in England (1909 and 1961) and Italy (1996) and American football (1987), baseball and ice hockey (1994). With all due respect to curling, croquet and a few others, there are no major sports where professionalism and its less savoury appendages of greed, commercialism and exploitation have not infiltrated.

The odd vestige of former days still lingered in club cricket and when in 1995, the National Cricket Association, since merged into the England and Wales Cricket Board, changed its eligibility rules to allow professionals to take part in its competitions, a number of southern clubs withdrew in protest and/or under threat of expulsion from the Club Cricket Conference (Object 2(a): To foster amateur cricket). The secession did not last long. The advent of the ECB in 1997 and its implementation of the recommendation in the MacLaurin Report *Raising the Standard* that a network of Premier Leagues be established, introduced unrestricted professionalism to areas where it had been hitherto unknown - at least, officially.

The style and tactics of the football of Alcock's time would be unrecognisable today. Formations have become far more defensive and the last links with the dribbling game and wing play were probably Sir Stanley Matthews and Sir Thomas Finney. "Combination" football has become the norm and modern tactical roots can be traced to Hungary and Brazil rather than Kennington Oval and Battersea Park. The genealogical line from the Alcock brothers' Forest Club can be traced through the Wanderers and the Corinthians to the 1939 merger with the Casuals to the present Corinthian-Casuals Club. Across the border, Wanderers' great rivals, Queen's Park are still in existence, but a resurrection of the clash between these great clubs of the 1870s would now be a match between Clubs in the Scottish League Division 3 and the same Division of the Ryman League. Major contributors to professional nineteenth century football have enjoyed varying fortunes. Preston North End and Blackburn Rovers have had their ups and downs over 120 years or so and the latter with a fine sense of history became in February 2002 the first Premiership or Football League side to win cups in three centuries.

Football now has a realistic claim to be the nearest mankind has come to a global religion. Rapid air transport and satellite television have made the global village a reality and given it advantages not enjoyed by its potential competitors of Islam, Christianity and Communism. Pop music and the film industry may be in the same league, but even they come nowhere near the vast television audiences attracted by the World Cup. It has been estimated that the total turnover of world football is somewhere round £250 billion. Media rights contracts are now measured in billions rather than millions and the turnover of the world's richest club, Manchester United, is over £100 million - even allowing for inflation, vastly different sums from those the Surrey committee and the Corinthians used to squabble over in the late nineteenth century and from the £442 generated by the 1885 FA Cup Final between Blackburn Rovers and Queen's Park. The £1,000 transfer fee paid by Middlesbrough to Sunderland for Alf Common in 1905 caused the FA to start drafting legislation. Early twenty-first century transfers of Marc Overmars, Nicolas Anelka and Juan Sebastian Veron for over £22 million each, and of Rio Ferdinand from Leeds to Manchester United for an alleged £30million, were accepted as part of football life's rich pattern.

Comparing wages, expenses, admission charges etc with their present day equivalents is not a straightforward exercise - and ultimately fairly meaningless, except for those who make a special study of hyperinflation. Prices and wages throughout Alcock's life were relatively stable. The current Consumer Prices Index (formerly the Retail Price Index) is now between 40 and 50 times what it was in 1915. So, if a rough rule of thumb would be to multiply 19th century figures by about 50 to arrive at their early 21st century equivalents, then even allowing for inflation, admission charges have increased by a factor of about 5, wages by 150 and transfer fees by 500.

The game has also generated a parallel universe in the form of the football pools. That their popularity has more to do with gambling than sport is evidenced by the sharp decline in business since the launch of the

National Lottery in 1994. They are nevertheless still significant enough to persuade punters to place their stakes not only on the actual results of matches, but also on what a panel of experts say the results of abandoned matches would have been if they had been played.

Alcock's own administrative style was nothing if not professional. Most county cricket clubs have now restyled their Secretaries as Chief Executives. In some cases this reflects a more executive role with county clubs being more executive led and less committee led. In others it is merely a change of title. But whatever the realities of twenty-first century nomenclature, Charles Alcock, administrator extraordinaire, pioneer and visionary without ever relinquishing the title of Secretary has a strong claim to being the first Chief Executive.

He would doubtless have foreseen the explosion of commercialism, along with the growth of professional sport, but would not perhaps have approved of the lack of dignity epitomised in replica kits etc, but then again a decline in formality is only one of many ways in which society has changed between the nineteenth century and the twenty-first.

If by some miracle Charles Alcock were able to return today and look out from what was his office (now the President's Room), what would his reaction be? The gasometers he would recognise and the adjacent terrace houses, then respectable family dwellings, now boarded up and epitomising the inner city blight which surrounds a Kennington Oval which since Alcock's time has been reincarnated as first The Oval, then the Foster's Oval, and now the AMP Oval. The perimeter advertising, but not the advertising itself, would be novel to him, an extension of the commercialism he introduced over a hundred years earlier. On his desk would be not the *Sportsman* or the *Sporting Life* (still extant, but now, as a website devoted to racing), but one or more of the sports supplements, issued daily with the broadsheets, or a *Champions' League Handbook*, all part of the legacy of sports journalism which he pioneered.

Would he have approved? Doubtless he would be proud of the fact that the solitary Test Match of 1880 had now developed into seven Test matches and ten one-day internationals per annum in England alone and many times that throughout the world played by the ten full members of the International Cricket Council. In between there are four senior domestic competitions, including two divisions with promotion and relegated and a knock-out competition, concepts both rejected in the nineteenth century. No football at The Oval now, but impossible to escape its influence. By the time of Alcock's death the game that was once subject to the whims of obnoxious park-keepers had already expanded into a world game. The extent of football's popularity nationally is demonstrated by the BBC Sports Personality of the Year award for 2001. It went to David Beckham, his last minute goal against Greece which sealed England's place in the 2002 World Cup Finals was still fresh in the public mind. Ellen MacArthur's arguably superior feat of sailing a yacht round the world single-handed was not a serious competitor.

The rise and rise of association football he would doubtless have observed with satisfaction, acknowledging that trends in sport follow trends in society and that football, having been the people's game in its Shrove Tuesday form, adopted by the public schools as part of its rational recreation ethic, then taken over again by an expanding working class has now followed the upward social mobility of that working class to a world of hospitality boxes in all-seater stadia. UEFA now employs over 140 staff at its new headquarters on the shores of Lake Geneva and has recently made senior legal appointments in Commercial Legal Services and Intellectual Property. It all seems a little different from well-intentioned amateurs grappling with the laws of the game in gaslit London taverns.

No longer is football 'our winter game', but everybody's all-the-year round game. The concept of a close season has become meaningless. In June 2001, the gap between the last match of 2000-01 (England's World Cup Qualifier against Greece) and the first of 2001-02 (Intertoto Cup matches in Scotland, Wales and Ireland) was just ten days. Rugby League Football is now at senior level a summer sport and the World Cup held in the Northern hemisphere summer of 2002 held billions enthralled. There were no refreshment breaks mid-way through each half when football was played in winter in Battersea Park, although one suspects that those planned for the World Cup had more to with television commercial breaks than the ambient summer temperatures of Korea and Japan.

However, the professionalism which he pragmatically recognised has perhaps spiralled beyond recognition. He was an advocate of controlled professionalism, but the abolition of the maximum wage in 1961 and the Bosman ruling by the European Court of Justice in 1995 that clubs have no right to transfer fees for out-of-contract players have led to a players' market and to unfettered professionalism. It was inevitable that once professionalism was recognised, it would spill over into commercialism and at its highest levels, sport would become a business, not a pastime, and spawn highly paid superstars, megastores, replica kits at exorbitant prices, multi-million media contracts and a huge world-wide betting industry. It is not a great step from that scenario to dishonesty, sleaze, match-fixing and other questionable activities that the nineteenth century would not have regarded as "manly". A hundred years after the foundation of the Football Association, ten players were jailed and banned for life for taking bribes. There have been other, not dissimilar, cases. Might Alcock have had just a slight reservation about the series of Pandora's boxes he had opened and consider whether sport in general and football in particular have not perhaps become victims of their own success?

REFERENCES

509. *Wisden* 1958 p 1004
510. *Times* 28 November 1972

APPENDIX

CHRONOLOGY

1791	Great grandfather, tenant of the Cannon Inn, dies in Newcastle
1820	Grandfather moves from Newcastle to Sunderland and establishes family upholstery business
1830	Father establishes Alcock Shipyard with his brother John Thomas
1842	**Born at 10 Norfolk Street, Sunderland**
1845	Surrey County Cricket Club established
1846	Cambridge Rules for football drawn up
1847	Family moves to 10 Fawcett Street, Sunderland
1849	Surrey Football Club established
1851	Family moves to 17 John Street, Sunderland
	Brother Horatio dies, aged six months.
	Great Exhibition
1855	Family move to 'Sunnyside', King's Head Hill, Chingford
	Enrolled at Harrow School
	Sheffield Foot Ball Club founded
1858	Brother William dies, aged 11; buried at Chingford Parish Church
1859	**Leaves Harrow School and joins father's marine insurance business**
	Establishes Forest Football Club
1861	Charles Alcock and Co, Ship and Insurance Brokers established in City
	Abolition of tax on newsprint
	First England tour to Australia under H H Stephenson
1862	Plays for MCC at Lord's. Rules for "the simplest game"
	Dingley Dell Rules in use
1863	Proposal for "Cricket Parliament" in *Sporting Life*
	Football Association established: brother John founder member
	Blackheath secede
1864	First Geneva Conventions
	Wisden launched
	Forest becomes The Wanderers : captain and secretary
	Marries Eliza Caroline Ovenden in Islington
1865	**Replaces brother John on FA Committee**
	Living at 33 Sherborne Street, Islington
	Eldest son, William, born

Butterflies cricket tour to Paris. *Sportsman* launched
1866 **First representative association football match: London v Sheffield**
1867 Second Reform Act. Queenberry Rules for boxing
Athletics, football and cricket sub-editor of the *Field* and the *Sportsman*
First association football county match: Middlesex v Surrey and Kent
1868 *Football Annual* launched. Aborigine tour of England
1869 The Oval becomes Wanderers' home ground
Eldest daughter, Elizabeth, born
1870 Education Act
Elected Honorary Secretary to FA
First North v South association football match
First of England-Scotland pseudo-internationals
Living at Grassendale, Rosendale Road, Dulwich
Daughter Florence born
1871 **Proposes FA Challenge Cup competition**
Rugby Football Union established
First rugby union international: Scotland v England in Edinburgh
Professional baseball league established in USA
1872 First rugby union international at the Oval: Scotland v England
Captains Wanderers to victory in first FA Cup Final
Becomes editor of *James Lillywhite's Cricketers' Annual*
First paid Secretary of Surrey County Cricket Club
First association football international: Scotland v England at
Partick: umpires
Daughter Charlotte born
1873 **Regulations on county qualifications in cricket established**
MCC County Cup
Moves to Jersey Lodge, Norwood Lane
Son Charles born
1874 Son Charles dies; buried at West Norwood
MCC regional competition
Baseball played at Lord's
Daughter Helen born
Football, Our Winter Game
1875 Referees FA Cup Final and replay
Plays only full international: England v Scotland at The Oval
Retires from active football after Wanderers v Queen's Park
Daughter Marion born
MCC establishes Tennis Committee
Lacrosse at The Oval

1876	Amalgamation of London and Sheffield codes of Laws
1877	First Test Match played in Melbourne
1878	Moves to 90 Lordship Park, Stoke Newington
	Wanderers win FA Cup for fifth time in seven years
	Daughter Violet born
	First 'white' Australian tour of England: beat MCC at Lord's
1878-79	Lord Harris's team tours Australia
1879	Referees FA Cup Final
	Calcutta Cup
	Last international rugby match at The Oval
1880	Moves to 36 Somerleyton Road, Brixton
	First Test Match in England: England v Australia at The Oval
1881	Father dies in Chingford
1882	Old Etonians last amateur side to win FA Cup
	Cricket and *Football* launched
	Australia beat England for the first time in England at The Oval.
	Mock obituary in *Sporting Times* leads to creation of Ashes.
	Corinthians founded by N L (Pa) Jackson
1883	Blackburn Olympic become first team from outside London to win FA Cup
	Football discontinued
1884	Accrington Stanley and Preston North End expelled from FA Cup for professionalism
1885	**Professionalism legalised in association football**
1886	**Becomes paid Secretary of FA**
	Tour of Parsee cricketers
1887	Living at 16 Stanthorpe Road, Streatham
	County Cricket Council established
	Son William dies; buried at West Norwood
1888	Baseball played at The Oval
	FA Cup competition reorganised
	Football League established
1889	Lord Kinnaird succeeds Major Marindin as President of FA
	Last association football international played at The Oval
1890	*Football: The Association Game*
	Last London v Sheffield match
	Mother dies in Chingford
	County Championship established
	County Cricket Council dissolved
1891	Moves to Heathlands, Kew Road, Richmond

	Last rugby match at The Oval
1892	Last FA Cup Final at The Oval
	Elected to Richmond Town Council
	Chairman, Richmond Cricket and Athletic Association
	Vice-President, Mid-Surrey Golf Club
1893	Interview with W A Bettesworth
	JP for Richmond
	FA Amateur Cup established
1894	Retires from Town Council
1895	Football discontinued at The Oval

The "great schism" in rugby: Northern Union formed by professional clubs

Retires as FA Secretary; appointed Vice-President

Famous Cricketers and Cricket Grounds

Famous Footballers and Athletes

Relinquishes Secretaryship of FA: succeeded by Frederick Wall

Appointed Vice-President of FA

1896	Professional cricketers' strike
	First Modern Olympic Games
1897	Corinthians tour South Africa
	Move to York Mansions, Battersea Park
	JP for Surrey
1898	Board of Control of Test Matches at Home established
	Oval pavilion completed
1899	FA tour to Berlin, Prague and Karlsruhe
	First five Test series in England
1900	*Lillywhite* discontinued
1901	Moves back to Richmond - Hazelwood, Ennerdale Road
	Cricket Stories: Wise and Otherwise
1902	Austria v Hungary
	Surrey Cricket: Its History and Associations
	Brother Arthur dies
1903	Acquires second residence at 7 Arundel Road, Brighton
	Absent from work most of year with chronic bronchitis
1904	FIFA established in Paris
	Advisory County Cricket Committee
1906	Serves on FA Disciplinary Commission and Emergency Committee
1907	**Dies at 7 Arundel Road, Brighton**
	William Findlay appointed Secretary to Surrey CCC
1908	Surrey agrees pension for Alcock's widow

1910 Brother John dies in Northchurch, Herts
1922 Marion dies; buried at West Norwood
1937 Eliza dies in Worthing
     Elizabeth dies in Lambeth
1938 Florence dies in Worthing
1946 Helen dies in Chichester
1952 Violet dies in Worthing
1999 Grave rededicated

BIBLIOGRAPHY

BOOKS, ANNUALS, PERIODICALS

Abel, Robert *Life and Reminiscences of Robert Abel in the Cricket Field* (told by
himself and edited by H V Dorey),
Cricket and Sports Publishers Ltd, 1910

Alcock, C W *Football, Our Winter Game*,
The Field, 1874

Alcock C W *Cricket Stories: Wise and Otherwise*
Arrowsmith, 1901

Alcock C W (Ed) *James Lillywhite's Cricketers' Annual* 1872-1900

Alverstone, Lord and Alcock, C W *Surrey Cricket: Its History and Associations*,
Longmans, Green and Co, 1902

Bailey, Philip, Thorn, Philip & Wynne-Thomas, Peter *Who's Who of Cricketers*, Guild
Publishing 1984

Bailey, Steve *Sporting Heritage No 1*
Association of Sports Historians [undated]

Bardsley, C W *A Dictionary of English and Welsh Surnames*
Heraldry Today, 1901

Bettesworth, W A *Chats on the Cricket Field*
Merritt & Hatcher, 1910

Barrett, Norman *Purcell's Encyclopedia of Association Football*
Purnell, 1972

Barrett, Norman (Ed) *The Daily Telegraph Football Chronicle*
Ebury Press, 1996

Birley, Sir Robert *Sport and the Making of Britain*
Manchester University Press, 1993

*The Book of Football: A Complete History and Record
of the Association and Rugby Games*
Amalgamated Press 1906

Booth, John Bennion *Old Pink 'Un Days*
Grant Richards, 1924

Bowen, Rowland *Cricket: A History of its Growth and Development
throughout the World*
Eyre and Spottiswood, 1970

Brooke, Robert *A History of the County Cricket Championship*
Guinness Publishing, 1991

Butler, Bryon *The Official History of the Football Association*
Queen Anne Press 1991

Butler, Bryon *The Official Illustrated History of the FA Cup*
Headline 1996

THE FATHER OF MODERN SPORT

Brooke, Robert *A History of the County Cricket Championship*
Guinness Publishing, 1991

Cardus, Neville *Cricket*
Longmans, Green and Co, 1930

Catton, J A H *Wickets and Goals*
Chapman & Hall, 1926

Commemorating the 100th Anniversary (of Corinthian FC and Casuals FC) 1982

Cottle, Basil *The Penguin Dictionary of Surnames*
Penguin, 1967

Daft, Richard *A Cricketer's Yarns*
Chapman and Hall, 1926

Dunning, Eric *Something of a Curate's Egg: Comments on Adrian Harvey's 'An Epoch in the Annals of National Sport'*
International Journal of the History of Sport Issue 18.4

Edworthy, Niall *England: The Official F A History*
Virgin, 1997

Fabian, A H & Green, Geoffrey *Association Football*
Caxton Publishing Company, 1960

Farror, Morley and Lamming, Douglas *A Century of English International Football 1872-1972*
Robert Hale and Co 1972

Flanagan, Bob *West Norwood Cemetery's Sportsmen*
Local History Publications, 1995

Gannaway, Norman *Association Football in Hampshire until 1914*
Hampshire County Council, 1996

Gibson, Alfred & Pickford, William *Association Football and the Men Who Made it* Caxton Publishing Company, 1904

Goulstone, John *Football's Secret History*
3-2 Books, 2001

Gordon, Sir Home *Background of Cricket*
Arthur Barker Ltd, 1939

Grace, W G *'WG' Cricketing Reminiscences and Personal Recollections*
James Bowden,1899

Grayson, Edward *Corinthians and Cricketers and towards a New Sporting Era*
Yore Publications, 1996

Green, Geoffrey *History of the Football Association*
Naldrett Press, 1953

Hammond, Dave *The Club: Life and Times of Blackheath Football Club*
MacAitch, 1999

Harvey, Adrian *'An Epoch in the Annals of National Sport': Football in Sheffield and the Creation of Modern Soccer and Rugby International*
Journal of the History of Sport Issue 18.4

Hawke, Lord, Harris, Lord and Gordon, Sir Home

THE FATHER OF MODERN SPORT

The Memorial Biography of W G Grace
Constable and Co, 1919
Heads, Ian & Lester, Gary *200 Years of Australian Sport*
Lester Townsend Publishing, 1988
Horton, Ed *Moving the Goalposts: Football's Exploitation*
Mainstream, 1997
Howson, E W & Warner, G T *Harrow School*
Arnold, 1898
Hughes, Thomas *Tom Brown's School Days*
Dent, 1975
Jackson, N L *Association Football*
George Newnes Ltd, 1900
Jackson, N L *Sporting Days and Sporting Ways*
Hurst & Blackett Ltd, 1932
James, Brian *England v Scotland*
Pelham Books, 1969
Knight, Albert E *The Complete Cricketer*
Methuen, 1906
Laborde, E D *Harrow School: Yesterday and Today*
Winchester Publications, 1948
Lemmon, David *The History of Surrey County Cricket Club*
Christopher Helm, 1989
Leveson-Gower, Sir Henry *Off and On the Field*
Stanley Paul and Co, 1953
Lillywhite, James *Cricketers' Annual 1872-1900*
Lillywhite, John, John and James, *Cricketers' Companion 1865-1885*
Low, Robert *W G: A Life of W G Grace*
Richard Cohen Books, 1997
Lyttelton, R H; Page, Arthur and Noel, Evan B *Fifty Years of School Sport: Eton, Harrow and Winchester*
Southwood, 1922
Marylebone Cricket Club Scores
Longmans and Co, 1882
Midwinter, Eric *The Illustrated History of County Cricket*
Kingswood Press, 1992
Montgomery H H *Old Cricket and Cricketers*
Stacey, Gold, Wright & Co, 1890
News of the World Football Annual
Pawson, Tony *100 Years of the FA Cup*
Heinemann, 1972
Phythian, Graham *Olympic FC, the Forgotten Giantkillers*
New Millennium, 1998
Powell, W R (ed) *History of the County of Essex Vol VI*
Oxford University Press, 1973

Radnedge, Keir *The Ultimate Encyclopedia of Soccer*
Carlton/Hodder & Stoughton, 1997
Rae, Simon *W G Grace: A Life*
Faber and Faber, 1998
Ranjitsinhji, K S *The Jubilee Book of Cricket*
Blackwood, 1897
Reyburn, Wallace *The Men in White: The Story of English Rugby*
Pelham Books, 1975
Read, W W *Annals of Cricket*
Sampson, Low, Marston & Co, 1896
School of Architecture and Interior Design, Brighton Polytechnic
A Guide to the Buildings of Brighton
McMillan Martin Ltd [undated - c late 1980s]
Scores and Biographies of Famous Cricketers
Seddon, Peter J A *Comprehensive Guide to the Literature of Association Football*
British Library, 1995
Simpson, David *The Millennium History of North-East England*
Northern Echo, 1999
Sissons, Ric *The Players: A Social History of the Professional Cricketer*
Kingswood Press, 1988
Smirk's Handbook of Northern Rugby-Union Matches
Smirk, Wigan, 1895/96
Standing, Percy Cross *Anglo-Australian Cricket 1862-1926*
Faber & Gwyer, 1926
Steven, Andrew *Unique Styles of Football at Three English Public Schools*
(in Sportimonium)
Leuven, Belgium, 1993
Stogdon, J H (ed) *Harrow School Register*
Longman, 1925
Strutt, Joseph *The Sports and Pastimes of the People of England*
Thomas Tegg, 1831
Sunderland Poll Books and Commercial Directories:
(Pigott's, Barnett's, Williams's, White's, Ward's, Christies)
Titley U A & McWhirter, Ross *Centenary History of the Rugby Football Union*
RFU, 1970
Tyerman, Christopher *A History of Harrow School 1324-1991*
Oxford University Press, 2000
Walvin, James *The People's Game: The History of Football Revisited*
Mainstream, 1994
West, G Derek *Guide to James Lillywhite's Cricketers' Annual*
North Moreton Press, 1993
West, G Derek *And Blaming it on You*
Journal of the Cricket Society, Autumn 1999

THE FATHER OF MODERN SPORT

Wigglesworth, Neil *The Evolution of English Sport*
Frank Cass, 1996
Wilson, Alisdair R *Football under the Skin: A Historical Glimpse at Soccer
in Tyne and Wear 1879-1988*
Tyne and Wear Museums Service 1988
Wilton, Iain *C B Fry, An English Hero*
Richard Cohen Books, 1999
Wisden Cricketers' Almanack 1864 onwards
Woolgar, Jason *England: The Official R F U History*
Virgin, 1999
Yapp, Nick *A History of the Foster's Oval*
Pelham Books, 1990
Young, Percy M *A History of British Football*
Arrow, 1973

ARTICLES

Alcock, C W *Cricket under Queen Victoria*
Diamond Jubilee Number of the Illustrated Sporting and Dramatic News 1897
Andrew, Christopher *1883 Cup Final: 'Patricians v Plebeians'*
Appleton, Arthur *Occupant at no 10*
Sunderland Echo 30 April 1984
Bailey, J F A *Forgotten Precursor of Limited Overs Cricket*
Journal of the Cricket Society Spring 2000
Brown, Richard *Fragments of History: A Practical Guide to Chingford Old Church 1990*
Butler, Bryon *FA pay homage to forgotten father of English Sport*
Daily Telegraph 30 November 1992
Butler, Bryon *Alcock, the forgotten inventor of the FA Cup*
Daily Telegraph 24 August 1999
Easterbrook, Basil *The Man who made All Seasons: Charles William Alcock*
Wisden 1980
Flanagan, Bob *Rededication of the Memorial to Charles Alcock*
Friends of West Norwood Cemetery Newsletter September 1999
Guérin, Robert *La Création de la FIFA et l'Erreur de l'Angleterre*
FIFA 1929
Keating, Frank *England's strikers who took the liberty and paid the penalty*
Guardian 27 November 2000
Midwinter, Eric *Charles Alcock: The Inventor of Modern Sport*
Cricket Lore May 1992
Mr J N Crawford and the Surrey County CC - The Full Correspondence
Journal of the Cricket Society Spring 1980
Myrone, Martin *Prudery, Pornography and the Victorian Nude*
(in Exposed: The Victorian Nude Tate Publishing 2001)

THE FATHER OF MODERN SPORT

The first born international player of all times
FIFA News May 1993
Perrin, F W *Recollections of Woodford 70 Years Ago*
Woodford Historical Society Transactions 1986
Raiji, Vasant *The First Parsee Team in England 1886*
Journal of the Cricket Society Spring 1986
Reynolds, Adrienne *Forest School and the FA Cup*
Forest School Magazine 1998
Rosenwater, Irving *Cricket Literature of the 1870s*
Journal of the Cricket Society Autumn 1979
Sissons, Ric *George Lohmann - The Beau Ideal*
Journal of the Cricket Society Spring 1990
Wynne-Thomas, Peter *The Honourable Thing: The Hon Secs Who Created County Cricket*
Cricket Lore June 2001

NEWSPAPERS AND PERIODICALS

Baily's Magazine of Sports and Pastimes
Baily's Monthly Magazine of Sports and Pastimes
Bell's Life in London
Bell's Life in Victoria
Berkhamsted Gazette
Church Monthly
Cricket
Cricket Lore
Cricket Quarterly
Cricketer International
Daily Mail
Daily Telegraph
Eton College Chronicle
Field
Football
Football Annual
Forest School Magazine
Glasgow Herald
The Harrovian
International Journal of the History of Sport
Journal of the Cricket Society
Richmond Express
Richmond and Twickenham Times
Sporting Life
Sporting Times
Sportsman

Sunderland and Durham County Herald
Sunderland Echo
Times
Times Literary Supplement
The Triumvirate
The Tyro
Worthing Herald

OTHER SOURCES

Alcock, P W *The Alcock Family of Sunderland*
(unpublished manuscript in Sunderland Local studies department)
Censuses of Population 1841 - 1901
Register of Births, Marriages and Deaths
International Genealogical Index
Electoral Rolls
Commercial Directories for Brighton (*Towner's, Pike's*) Chingford (*Kelly's*), Hertfordshire
(*Kelly's*), Richmond (*Kelly's*), Sunderland (*Pigott's, Barnett's, Williams's, White's, Ward's,
Christies*) and Surrey (*Kelly's*)
Post Office London and London Suburban Directories
Surrey County Cricket Club minutes (Surrey History Centre)

INDEX